- KPSV -

OKANAGAN COLLEGE LIBRARY

03554474

P9-DUJ-771

The Future of Environmental Criticism

Blackwell Manifestos

In this new series major critics make timely interventions to address important concepts and subjects, including topics as diverse as, for example: Culture, Race, Religion, History, Society, Geography, Literature, Literary Theory, Shakespeare, Cinema, and Modernism. Written accessibly and with verve and spirit, these books follow no uniform prescription but set out to engage and challenge the broadest range of readers, from undergraduates to postgraduates, university teachers and general readers – all those, in short, interested in ongoing debates and controversies in the humanities and social sciences.

OKANAGAN COLLEGE
LIBRARY
BRITISH COLUMBIA

The Future of Environmental Criticism:

Environmental Crisis and Literary Imagination

Lawrence Buell

Blackwell
Publishing

© 2005 by Lawrence Buell

BLACKWELL PUBLISHING
350 Main Street, Malden, MA 02148-5020, USA
9600 Garsington Road, Oxford OX4 2DQ, UK
550 Swanston Street, Carlton, Victoria 3053, Australia

The right of Lawrence Buell to be identified as the Author of this Work has been asserted in accordance with the UK Copyright, Designs, and Patents Act 1988.

All rights reserved. No part of this publication may be reproduced, stored in a retrieval system, or transmitted, in any form or by any means, electronic, mechanical, photocopying, recording or otherwise, except as permitted by the UK Copyright, Designs, and Patents Act 1988, without the prior permission of the publisher.

First published 2005 by Blackwell Publishing Ltd

1 2005

Library of Congress Cataloging-in-Publication Data

Buell, Lawrence.
  The future of environmental criticism : environmental crisis and literary imagination / Lawrence Buell.
    p. cm.—(Blackwell manifestos)
  Includes bibliographical references and index.
  ISBN-13: 978-1-4051-2475-1 (hardcover : acid-free paper)
  ISBN-10: 1-4051-2475-X (hardcover : acid-free paper)
  ISBN-13: 978-1-4051-2476-8 (pbk. : acid-free paper)
  ISBN-10: 1-4051-2476-8 (pbk. : acid-free paper)
    1. American literature—History and criticism—Theory, etc. 2. Environmental protection in literature. 3. English literature—History and criticism—Theory, etc. 4. Criticism—English-speaking countries. 5. Environmental policy in literature. 6. Nature conservation in literature. 7. Landscape in literature. 8. Ecology in literature. 9. Nature in literature. I. Title. II. Series.

  PS169.E25B837 2005
  809′.933556—dc22
                                                          2005000465

A catalogue record for this title is available from the British Library.

Set in 11.5 on 13.5 pt Bembo
by SNP Best-set Typesetter Ltd, Hong Kong
Printed and bound in Great Britain
by TJ International Ltd, Padstow, Cornwall

The publisher's policy is to use permanent paper from mills that operate a sustainable forestry policy, and which has been manufactured from pulp processed using acid-free and elementary chlorine-free practices. Furthermore, the publisher ensures that the text paper and cover board used have met acceptable environmental accreditation standards.

For further information on
Blackwell Publishing, visit our website:
www.blackwellpublishing.com

Contents

Preface

This book is written for all who have the time and will to think strenuously about the implications of the endangered state and uncertain fate of life on earth for literary and cultural studies – and vice versa. W. E. B. Du Bois predicted that the great public issue of the twentieth century would be the problem of the color line. In the century just begun, that problem shows no sign of abating. But ultimately a still more pressing question may prove to be whether planetary life will remain viable for most of the earth's inhabitants without major changes in the way we live now. Like racism, environmental crisis is a broadly cultural issue, not the property of a single discipline. All thinking persons have a stake in it. For science, engineering, and public policy that is most obviously so. These are the bases on which university programs in environmental studies have generally built. But no less intrinsically important are the environmental humanities – history, philosophy, religion, cultural geography, literature, and the other arts. For technological breakthroughs, legislative reforms, and paper covenants about environmental welfare to take effect, or even to be generated in the first place, requires a climate of transformed environmental values, perception, and will. To that end, the power of story, image, and artistic performance and the resources of aesthetics, ethics, and cultural theory are crucial.

The Future of Environmental Criticism focuses especially on what literature and criticism and theory relevant to it have to say about these matters. This book is the third in a trilogy of books including also *The Environmental Imagination* (1995) and *Writing for an Endangered World* (2001), which expanded and complicated the earlier work's framework while attempting to maintain the best virtues of the original. The present work is meant to double as a statement of my more considered judgments and as a concise, accessible road map of trends, emphases, and controversies within green literary studies more generally.

To speak of "judgments" does not mean wanting to impute fixed doctrinal positions to creative or critical work except insofar as it bends that way itself. Any serious reader knows that the kind of art, the kind of criticism, which takes the form of a waywardly insinuating thought experiment can be more instructive than the overtly polemical kind which "has a palpable design on us," as John Keats dismissively put it.[1] The scattershot *aperçu* of Theodor Adorno's *Minima Moralia* may prove a better guide than the more systematic polemics of Horkheimer and Adorno in *The Dialectic of Enlightenment*. The meanderingly proliferate catalogue in Walt Whitman's "Song of Myself" that begins "The pure contralto sings in the organ loft" discloses more about environmental being in the antebellum United States than the programmatic "I hear America singing." But the two modes also need each other, even as they pull against each other. The reason that Rachel Carson's *Silent Spring* (1962) became one of those few works of environmental writing to have an immediate and significant impact on public policy, while several other well-researched contemporary books on the same topic did not, was that this was an author also capable of writing *A Sense of Wonder*. And reciprocally: had celebration of nature's beauty been Carson's sole concern, her voice would have been lost to history.

This book, too, tries to be both sententious and exploratory. As an attempt to take stock of a fast-expanding inquiry it cannot be more than an interim statement — forcefully expressed I hope, yet designedly essayistic rather than "definitive." As literary ecodiscourse becomes more widely practiced, more globally networked, more interdisciplinary, and thus even more pluriform, the participants must become increasingly aware of speaking from some position within or around the movement rather than "for" it, like a Rousseauvian lawgiver. Readers of this book will quickly recognize its author as one whose particular base of operations is US literary and cultural history of the past two centuries, trying to extend his non-omniscient gaze as best he can.

Those already somewhat conversant with the environmental turn in literary and cultural studies will rightly sense that "environmental criticism" is a strategic ambiguity. I'll say more about terminology later on. But here briefly is why I make a point of not using "ecocriticism" in my main title even though it is the umbrella term by which literary-environmental studies is best known, even though I myself rely on it in many contexts below, and even though I expect it to be used as the term of primary reference for this book in notices and reviews. First, "ecocriticism" still invokes in some quarters the cartoon image of a club of intellectually shallow nature worshipers, an image slapped on the movement during its salad days that is no longer applicable today, if indeed it ever really was. Second and more important, I believe that "environmental" approximates better than "eco" the hybridity of the subject at issue – all "environments" in practice involving fusions of "natural" and "constructed" elements – as well as the movement's increasingly heterogeneous foci, especially its increasing engagements with metropolitan and/or toxified landscapes and with issues of environmental equity that challenge early ecocriticism's concentration on the literatures of nature and preservationist environmentalism. Third, "environmental criticism" somewhat better captures the interdisciplinary mix of literature-and-environment studies, which has always drawn on the human as well as the natural sciences and in recent years cross-pollinated more with cultural studies than with the sciences.

The four main sections of this book discuss, in turn, contemporary environmental criticism's emergence (chapter 1) and three of its most distinctive concerns: its investment in issues of environmental imaging and representation (chapter 2), its interest in reconception of place as a fundamental dimension of both art and lived experience (chapter 3), and its strong ethical and/or political commitment (chapter 4). In none of these domains has environmental criticism been monolithic. All are arenas of controversy, and in all of them the centers of gravity have been shifting. In short, environmental criticism is a project in motion and likely to remain so for a long time to come.

Acknowledgments

I can't begin to name all those whose wisdom and example have inspired me over the years to the point of feeling moved to undertake this book. So I limit myself to just four groups. For the opportunity to try out some of the ideas gathered here I am grateful to the Portuguese Association of English and American Studies, the English Department of Beijing University, the Tanner Center of the University of Utah, the Lilly Foundation-funded seminar in Religion and American Culture directed by Roger Lundin, the National Humanities Center, and the English Department of the University of North Carolina. For their intellectual vitality and reverse mentoring (whether they realize it or not), my deep thanks to those among my present and former graduate students who have taken an interest in humanistic environmental studies: Lan Bui, Rebecca Gould, Scott Hess, Steve Holmes, Stephanie LeMenager, Nathaniel Lewis, Suleiman Osman, Tovis Page, William Pannapacker, Judith Richardson, and Michael Ziser. For thoughtful and much-appreciated advice on specific points, my thanks to Joni Adamson, John Elder, Richard Forman, Wayne Franklin, George Handley, Eric Higgs, John Mitchell, Scott Slovic, and Louise Westling. Finally, I can't imagine having been able to complete this book without the research assistance of Emma Beavers, Jared Hickman, and Gretchen Hults. Its faults, of course, are mine alone.

1

The Emergence of Environmental Criticism

Until the end of the twentieth century, such a book as this could not have been written. The environmental turn in literary and cultural studies emerged as a self-conscious movement little more than a dozen years ago. Since then it has burgeoned, however. A telltale index is the growth within the last decade of the Association for the Study of Literature and Environment (ASLE) from a localized North American ferment into a thousand-member organization with chapters worldwide from the UK to Japan and Korea to Australia–New Zealand. The "Who's listening?" question which nagged me when I first entered the arena of environmental criticism has given way to "How can I keep pace with all this new work?"

To burgeon is not necessarily to mature or to prevail. "Ecocriticism," the commonest omnibus term for an increasingly heterogeneous movement, has not yet achieved the standing accorded (say) to gender or postcolonial or critical race studies. Eventually I believe it will; but it is still finding its path, a path bestrewn by obstacles both external and self-imposed.

At first sight, the belatedness and liminality of the recent environmental turn in literary-critical studies seems strange. For creative art and critical reflection have always taken a keen interest in how the material world is engaged, absorbed, and reshaped by theory, imagination, and *techne*. Humankind's earliest stories are of earth's creation, of its transformation by gods or by human ingenuity's "second nature," as Cicero first called it – tales that frame environmental ethics in varied ways. In at least one case they may have significantly influenced the course of world history. The opening chapters of Genesis, the first book in Hebrew and Christian scripture, have been blamed as the root cause of western technodominationism: God's mandate to man to take "dominion" over the creatures of the sea and earth and "subdue" them. Others retort that this thesis misreads both history and the biblical text: that "cultivate" is the more crucial term, implying pious stewardship rather than transformation.[1] My point in mentioning this debate is not to arbitrate it but merely to call attention to the antiquity and durability of environmental discourse – and its variety both within individual thought traditions and worldwide. By contrast to either reading of Judaeo-Christian thought, for example, Mayan mythography represents the gods as fashioning human beings after several false starts from corn gathered with the help of already-created animals, thereby symbolizing "the collective survival that must exist between humans, plants, and animals," whereas in Mäori cosmology, creation is an ongoing process: "humanity and all things of the natural world are always emerging, always unfolding."[2]

All this goes to show that if environmental criticism today is still an emergent discourse it is one with very ancient roots. In one form or another the "idea of nature" has been a dominant or at least residual concern for literary scholars and intellectual historians ever since these fields came into being.[3] That legacy calls into question just how marked a break from previous practice the contemporary movement is. What can be really new and different, much less "radical," about an area of inquiry that for more than a century has been an eminently safe and reputable pursuit? For one who knows the history of the permutations of critical thought about Romantic poetry, on the face of it early ecocriticism's insistence – in the face of then-fashionable poststructuralist and new historicist approaches – that Wordsworth was a poet of nature after all has a suspiciously retro, neo-Victorian ring, even when the argument is recast to emphasize not just love of nature but proto-ecological knowledge and environmentalist commitment. This is a specter that has bedeviled ecocriticism from its birth: the suspicion that it might not boil down to much more than old-fashioned enthusiasms dressed up in new clothes.

Yet the marked increase and sophistication of environmentality as an issue within literary and cultural studies since the 1980s is a countervailing fact, despite the wrangling over what it means and what should be done about it that will surely continue for some time to come. It testifies to the need to correct somehow against the marginalization of environmental issues in most versions of critical theory that dominated literary and cultural studies through the 1980s – even as "the environment" was becoming an increasingly salient public concern and a major topic of research in science, economics, law, and public policy – and certain humanities fields as well, notably history and ethics. In the book on Wordsworth that inaugurated British ecocriticism, Jonathan Bate framed the problem with the pardonable zeal of the insurgent: Geoffrey "Hartman threw out nature to bring us the transcendent imagination; [Jerome] McGann throws out the transcendent imagination to bring us history and society," after which Alan Liu categorically denies that there is such a thing as nature in Wordsworth except as "'constituted by acts of political definition'" (Bate 1991: 8, 18). Those prior imbalances, notwithstanding the brilliance with which they were argued, invited correction. Since then, indeed, British Romanticism has proven to be as fertile and varied ground for ecocritical revisionism as it was for previous critical revolutions from phenomenology through new historicism (e.g., Kroeber 1994; McKusick 2000; Morton 1994, 2000; Oerlemans 2002; Fletcher 2004; Hess 2004).

The imbalance to which Bate objected actually predated the late twentieth-century revolution in critical theory that began with Hartman's generation. My own literary education bears witness to this. As a schoolchild in the northeastern United States, I imbibed a commonly taught, watered-down version of Aristotelian poetic theory that defined "setting" as one of literature's four basic building blocks other than language itself – "plot," "character," and

3

"theme" being the others. But the term was vaguely defined and required nothing more in practice than a few perfunctory sentences about the locale of the work in question. In such rare cases as Thomas Hardy's *The Return of the Native*, we were given to understand that a nonhuman entity like Egdon Heath might be a book's main "character" or agential force. Otherwise, "setting" was mere backdrop for the human drama that really counted, even in texts like Wordsworth's "Tintern Abbey" or Thoreau's *Walden*. Although I first read them at roughly the same time as the controversy provoked by the serialization of Rachel Carson's *Silent Spring* in *The New Yorker*, and although my late father was fighting Carson-like battles as a member of our local planning commission, I doubt that any of this would have much affected my early *literary* training even if my instructors had taken notice of it. One of them assigned us a section of her previous bestseller *The Sea Around Us* (1950) as an example of mastery of the art of descriptive language. A description of trying on a suit of new clothes or of beholding oneself in a mirror would have served equally well.

Symptomatic of the mentality I assimilated was US writer Eudora Welty's demure apology at the start of her luminous essay on "Place in Fiction" for place as "one of the lesser angels that watch over the racing hand of fiction" relative to "character, plot, symbolic meaning," and especially "feeling, who in my eyes carries the crown, soars highest of them all and rightly relegates place into the shade" (Welty 1970: 125).

Why do the discourses of environment seem more crucial today than they did to Welty in the 1940s? The most obvious answer is that during the last third of the twentieth century "the environment" became front-page news. As the prospect of a sooner-or-later apocalypse by unintended environmental disaster came to seem likelier than apocalypse by deliberate nuclear *machismo*, public concern about the state and fate of "the environment" took increasing hold, initially in the West but now worldwide. The award of the 2004 Nobel Peace Prize to Kenyan environmental activist Wangari Maathai is, at this moment of writing, the latest sign of an advanc-

4

ing level of concern, which the "war against terror" since September 11, 2001 has upstaged but by no means suppressed. Underlying the advance has been a growing malaise about modern industrial society's inability to manage its unintended environmental consequences that Ulrich Beck, the Rachel Carson of contemporary social theory, calls "reflexive modernization," meaning in particular the fear that even the privileged classes of the world inhabit a global "risk society" whose hazards cannot be anticipated, calculated, and controlled, much less escaped (Beck, Giddens, and Lash 1994: 6; cf. Beck 1986; Willms 2004).

Environmental issues, in turn, have become an increasing provocation both for artists and for academics, giving rise within colleges and universities to cross-disciplinary environmental studies programs often galvanized by student demand as much as by faculty research agendas. Though natural and social scientists have so far been the major players in such programs, considerable numbers of humanists have also been drawn in, many of them bringing preexisting commitments of a citizenly kind to bear in environmentally directed teaching and scholarship. Indeed, many nonhumanists would agree – often more readily than doubt-prone humanists do – that issues of vision, value, culture, and imagination are keys to today's environmental crises at least as fundamental as scientific research, technological know-how, and legislative regulation. If we feel tokenized as players in environmental dialogue, both within the university and without, that may be more because of our own internal disputes and uncertainties about role, method, and voice than because of any stigma attached to the "impracticality" of the humanities either within academe or the wider world.

Fin-de-siècle Ferment: A Snapshot

Literature scholars who took the environmental turn in the 1980s and 1990s found themselves entering a mind-expanding though also vertiginous array of cross-disciplinary conversations – with life scientists, climatologists, public policy specialists, geographers, cultural anthropologists, landscape architects, environmental lawyers, even applied mathematicians and environmental engineers – conversations that tended to produce or reinforce disenchantment with the protocols of their home discipline. Two opposite reactions arising from this state of ferment that look more antipodal than they may actually have been were resistance to prevalent models of critical theory and the quest for theory.

A number of early ecocritics looked to the movement chiefly as a way of "rescuing" literature from the distantiations of reader from text and text from world that had been ushered in by the structuralist revolution in critical theory. These ecocritical dissenters sought to reconnect the work of (environmental) writing and criticism with environmental experience – meaning in particular the *natural* world.[4] I recall an intense exchange at the first international conference of the still-new ASLE in Fort Collins, Colorado, over the question of whether nature writing could be properly taught without some sort of outdoor *practicum* component, preferably *in situ*. Environmental literacy was seen as indispensable to such a pedagogy.[5] No less striking was the alliance at that gathering – an alliance that continues – between critics, writer-practitioners, and environmental activists. (These can be overlapping categories, of course.) The ecocritical movement's primary publications, the American *ISLE* (International Studies in Literature and Environment) and its younger British counterpart *Green Letters*, are remarkable among scholarly association journals for their mixture of scholarly, pedagogical, creative, and environmentalist contributions.

The conception of ecocriticism as an alliance of academic critics, artists, environmental educators, and green activists reinforced the penchant within the movement for decrying "the metropolitan tendency in literary studies towards high theory and abstraction," as one Australian ecocritic put it.[6] This undertone of complaint, in turn, fed mainstream academic critics' suspicions that ecocriticism was more an amateur enthusiasm than a legitimate new "field." Another ground of skepticism might have been the movement's provenance as an offshoot of an association of second-level prestige whose principal support base lay mostly outside the most prominent American university literature departments. For the Western American Literature Association to presume to instigate a revolution in literary studies seemed to some observers the equivalent of a new school of criticism in China being fomented from some outpost in that country's own "far west," Sinjiang.

But cross-disciplinary and extra-academic alliances also have had the positive and permanent advantages of stretching the new movement's horizons beyond the academy and of provoking a self-examination of premises that has intensified as the movement has evolved beyond an initial concentration on nature-oriented literature and on traditional forms of environmental education to take into account urban as well as rural loci and environmental justice concerns as well as nature preservation. From the start, calls "to reconnect the study of literature with the living earth" have focused participants' attention on the connection between academic work and public citizenship and advocacy.[7] The symbiosis between artistic accomplishment and environmentalist commitment in such writers as the American poets Gary Snyder and A. R. Ammons – to name but two among the scores of writers worldwide of whom the same might be said – has enriched the movement conceptually as well as aesthetically.[8]

Up to a point early ecocriticism's appeal to the authority of experiential immersion and the efficacy of practice over against the authority of "theory" reprised first-wave race, feminism, and sexuality studies ("Speaking as a woman/an African American/a gay white male, I . . ."). But an obvious difference between ecocriticism and emergent discourses on behalf of silenced or disempowered social groups was in the kind of identitarian claims that could plausibly be made in that context. One can speak as an environmentalist, one can "speak a word for Nature, for absolute freedom and wildness," as Thoreau did,[9] but self-evidently no human can speak *as* the environment, *as* nature, *as* a nonhuman animal. How do we know what it is like to be a bat, philosopher Thomas Nagel asks rhetorically, in a celebrated article.[10] Well, we don't. At most we can attempt to speak from the standpoint of understanding humans to be part of what Aldo Leopold called "the biotic community" – attempt, that is, to speak in cognizance of human being as ecologically or environmentally embedded. Although there is something potentially noble about human attempts to speak ecocentrically against human dominationism, unless one proceeds very cautiously there soon becomes something quixotic and presumptuous about it too. All too often, arguments about curbing species self-interest boil down to setting limits you mostly want to see other people observe.

This is where the distanced abstractions of the kind of theory ecocriticism initially reacted against can show to advantage. Take, for example, Michel Foucault's conception of "biopolitics" – the endeavor "to rationalize the problems presented to governmental practice by the phenomena characteristic of a group of living human beings constituted as a population: health, sanitation, birthrate, longevity, race" (Foucault 1994: 73). Early ecocriticism would have been likely to bristle at this lumping together of such heterogeneous categories under the sign of political practice; but one also needs an inner voice like Foucault's as reminder that the "who" that engages in ecocritical work is neither as individuated nor as extricated from social institutions as one might wish to think. One of the main differences between what I shall be calling first-wave and second-wave environmental criticism is that the revisionists have absorbed this sociocentric perspective to a greater degree.[11]

Given that it is self-evidently more problematic for an ecocritic to presume to speak for "nature" than for (say) a black critic to speak for black experience, one might suppose that early ecocriticism would have been driven quickly to pass through the appeal-to-experience stage into a discourse of theoretical reflection. Yet if your ultimate interest is the remediation of humankind's alienation from the natural world, you may well decide on principle to resist the abstractifications of theoretical analysis, indeed to resist standard modes of formal argument altogether in favor of a discourse where critical reflection is embedded within narratives of encounter with nature. A number of ecocritics have preferred this alternative path of "narrative scholarship," as Scott Slovic (1994) has called it.[12] A prominent example is pioneer ecocritic and recent ASLE president John Elder. Elder's first book (1985) was a largely analytical study of nature poetry and the conception of nature–culture relations more generally in the light of Whiteheadian process philosophy. But he cast his next in the form of a series of semi-autobiographical narratives of place, which are put in conversation with Robert Frost's "Directive," a poem of imagined return to a decayed farmstead in the same upper New England region (Elder 1998). We find a similar approach to the enlistment of environmental psychology in former ASLE president Ian Marshall's (2003) stirring book of mountaineering narratives and the conceptualization of islanded solitude in ecophilosopher Kathleen Dean Moore's (2004) narrative of an Alaskan summer.

Of course, there is nothing inherently untheoretical about rejecting standard modes of critical argument – Nietzsche and Derrida did that too – or in narrative scholarship as such. It can yield a higher degree of critical self-consciousness than otherwise, as the narrative-reflexive turn in cultural anthropology demonstrates. Anna Lowenhaupt Tsing's *In the Realm of the Diamond Queen* (1993), for instance, offers an account of the endangered Meratus peoples of Kalimantan (Indonesia) in which the author's portrayal of her halting acquisition of native environmental literacy plays a crucial part, as she skillfully weaves back and forth between her outsider's position in relation to her informants and the marginality of the Meratus themselves contending with the dominant cultures of their island, their nation, and transnational capitalism. The best ecocritical work of this kind is as insightful as Tsing's environmental ethnography. Besides, it would be a great mistake to interpret resistance to dominant strains of theory as proof of resistance to theory *tout court*.

On the contrary, literature-and-environment studies have striven almost from the start to define their position on the critical map analytically as well as through narrative practice. One strategy has been to build selectively on poststructuralist theory while resisting

9

the totalizing implications of its linguistic turn and its aftermaths, such that the word–world gets decoupled from the material world to the point of making it impossible to conceive of literary discourse as other than tropology or linguistic play or ideological formation. From this standpoint, "theory and ecology" might be seen as a fruitful, energizing collaboration to the end of calling into "question the concepts on which the old hierarchies are built" (meaning for this writer androcentrism specifically and anthropocentrism more generally), even as one resists an exclusive focus on "textuality, as networks of signifying systems of all kinds" that would privilege "networks of language and culture" to the eclipse of culture's imbrication in "the networks of the land" (Campbell 1989: 128, 133, 136). In a similar spirit, Verena Conley plumbs the archive of French critical theory over the past half-century, hoping to confirm the hypothesis "that the driving force of poststructural thought is indissolubly linked to ecology" (Conley 1997: 7), and succeeding in a number of instances (most notably Felix Guattari, Michel Serres, and Luce Irigiray), though she admits to not being able to do much with Derrida or Baudrillard. British ecocritic Dominic Head suggests a ground for dialogue between "the broader Green movement" and postmodern theory with respect to a comparable "deprivileging of the human subject" (Head 1998a: 28). Dana Phillips commends anthropologist of science Bruno Latour's canny reflections on the inextricable hybridization of nature and culture as a corrective against ecocriticism's incautious attempts to distinguish cleanly between the two (Phillips 2003: esp. 30–4).

Altogether, the story of literary ecotheory's relation to critical models has been unfolding less as a story of dogged recalcitrance – though there has been some of that – than as a quest *for* adequate models of inquiry from the plethora of possible alternatives that offer themselves from whatever disciplinary quarter. Cybernetics, evolutionary biology, landscape ecology, risk theory, phenomenology, environmental ethics, feminist theory, ecotheology, anthropology, psychology, science studies, critical race studies, postcolonial theory, environmental history – all these and more, each fraught with its own internal wranglings – have presented themselves as correctives or enhancements to literary theory's preexisting toolkit. The menu of approaches continues to expand, and the combinatorics have become ever more proliferate and complex.

The environmental turn in literary studies is best understood, then, less as a monolith than as a concourse of discrepant practices. In her introduction to the first significant critical collection, Cheryll Glotfelty was being candid rather than evasive in defining ecocriticism in extremely sweeping terms, as "the study of the relationship between literature and the physical environment," in whatever way these terms be defined (Glotfelty and Fromm 1996: xviii). It is not a revolution in the name of a dominant methodology in the sense that Russian and new critical formalism, phenomenology, deconstruction, and new historicism have been. It lacks the kind of paradigm-defining statement that, for example, Edward Said's *Orientalism* (1978) supplied for colonial discourse studies.[13] More like (say) feminism in this respect, ecocriticism gathers itself around a commitment to environmentality from whatever critical vantage point. A map of feminism must recognize fault lines dividing historical from poststructuralist feminisms, western traditions of women's studies from "womanist" approaches to the study of disprivileged women of color; and must recognize how these differences interact with other critical genealogies, such as postcolonial theory in the case of womanist revisionism. Broadly speaking, this is the kind of direction in which literary ecotheory has been evolving, toward increasing acknowledgment of ecocultural complexity after an initial concentration now increasingly (though by no means universally) thought to have been too narrowly focused. One of the catalysts, indeed, has been ecofeminism, itself an evolving congeries, on which more below.

That the environmental turn in literary studies has been more issue-driven than method or paradigm-driven is one reason why the catchy but totalizing rubric of "ecocriticism" is less indicative than "environmental criticism" or "literary-environmental studies." Being less cumbersome and (so far) much more widely used,

11

"ecocriticism" may well be here to stay. I have found it a convenient shorthand I cannot do without. But the term implies a nonexistent methodological holism. It overstates the degree to which the environmental turn in literary studies was ever a coordinated project.[14] The stigma of critical amateurism attached by skeptics at the start of the ecocritical insurgency, for which the media is as responsible as the movement,[15] has itself created internal disaffection with the rubric, a bit like the way a number of the so-called American Transcendentalists tended to shy away from that lumping label, which had been slapped on the movement by conservative detractors as a synonym for "German nonsense." Today, a number of younger scholars, in whose hands the future of environmental criticism lies, often seem to prefer not to self-identify as "ecocritics." On the other hand, the same was true in the 1980s for many putative new historicists who are now looked back upon as exemplars of that movement.[16]

A more substantive reason for belaboring the terminological issue is the implicit narrowness of the "eco," insofar as it connotes the "natural" *rather than* the "built" environment and, still more specifically, the field of ecology. "Ecocriticism is a name that implies more ecological literacy than its advocates now possess," pithily observes one who hopes to see more (Howarth 1996: 69). Although attempted reformation of literary studies via *rapprochement* with life sciences has been *one* of the movement's distinctive projects, it is only one such project – and a minority endeavor at that. From the start, and increasingly, the "eco" of practicing so-called ecocritics has been more aesthetic, ethical, and sociopolitical than scientist. The looser rubric of ASLE's flagship journal *ISLE* (Interdisciplinary Studies in Literature and Environment) better fits the actual mix, and all the more so now that environmental criticism's working conception of "environment" has broadened in recent years from "natural" to include also the urban, the interweave of "built" and "natural" dimensions in every locale, and the interpenetration of the local by the global.

On the other hand, "ecocriticism" suffices if – like poet-critic Gary Snyder – one is careful to use the term in mindfulness of its etymology and of its metaphorical stretch. "Ecology" derives etymologically from the Greek *oikos*, household, and in modern usage refers both to "the study of biological interrelationships and the flow of energy through organisms and inorganic matter." Metaphorically, furthermore, "ecology" can be stretched to cover "energy-exchange and interconnection" in "other realms" too: from technology-based communication systems to the "ecology" of thinking or composition (Snyder 2004: 5, 9). Indeed, "the ecology movement," particularly outside the United States, sometimes serves as a synonym for environmentalism. Looked at this way, a perfectly plausible case can be made for speaking of environmentally valenced work in literature studies as "ecocriticism."

From "Nature" in Literature X to the Beginnings of Ecocriticism

The term "ecocriticism" was coined in the late 1970s (Rueckert 1996), but its antecedents stretch back much further. The quest for an inception point can trap one in an infinite regress. For US settler-culture literature, one would need to go back at least as far as the 1920s – the decade when it first established itself as a professional specialization – and Norman Foerster's *Nature in American Literature* (1923), sometimes said to have "inaugurated the new academic field" of American literature (Mazel 2001: 6).[17] Some Americanists might argue that the origin should be set much earlier, at least as far back as Ralph Waldo Emerson's *Nature* (1836), the first canonical work of US literature to unfold a theory of nature with special reference to poetics.[18] But for present purposes it should suffice to begin with the two precontemporary books of literary and cultural studies of greatest influence for later Anglo-American environmental criticism: in American Studies, Leo Marx's *The*

Machine and the Garden: Technology and the Pastoral Ideal in American Culture (1964), the earliest book listed among the "top fifteen" recommended in *The Ecocriticism Reader*'s bibliography (Glotfelty and Fromm 1996: 395–6), and in British Studies, Raymond Williams' *The Country and the City* (1973), which has been praised as "a masterpiece of ecocriticism *avant la lettre*" (Head 2002: 24).

Marx and Williams both focused on the cultural history and literary instantiation of the intertwined history of attitudes toward nature vs. (for Williams) urbanism and (for Marx) industrial technology. Both dwelt upon the salience and durability of their respective national penchants to identify national essence symbolically with "country" (Williams) or a bucolic "middle landscape" between settlement and frontier or wilderness (Marx). Both also stressed the seductiveness and the mendacity of nostalgia for rurality: how it characteristically expressed itself in the form of wishful prettifying palliatives that disguised the irreversible transformation of landscape wrought by economic power and/or class interest. Both accounts were given further torque and bite by a shared cultural Marxist commitment to conceiving the modernization process as an ironic grand narrative of industrial capitalism's inevitable triumph over the counter-cultures of pastoral opposition (Marx) and traditional local life (Williams).

The importance of these two books and the essays that succeeded them for the subsequent turn in environmental studies lay especially in their identification of the dynamics of the history of what we would now call national imaginaries in terms of a symbiotic opposition between contrasting prototypical landscapes.

Marx and Williams defined the stakes quite differently. Williams concerned himself much more with the actualities of environmental history and landscape transformation than did Marx, who was a leading exemplar of the "myth-symbol" school of American Studies, according to which the key to the dynamics of national history lay in its cultural symbolics. Williams' heroes were endangered country folk and the culture of rural working-class life, and such writers as peasant poet John Clare and regional novelist Thomas Hardy, whose works rendered these most faithfully, despite the threat of cooptation by the stereotypical "green language" of romanticism and the false consciousness implanted by deference to patrons or marketplace. Marx's heroes, on the other hand, were a small group of high canonical literati, from Henry Thoreau to William Faulkner, who practiced a "complex pastoral" that resisted prettified, anodyne mainstream "simple pastoral" by using green tropes to critique advancing machine culture. For Marx, such visions of a lost or possible future golden age had "nothing to do with the environment" per se (Marx 1964: 264). The payoff was entirely political and aesthetic.

Williams more closely anticipated later literature-and-environment studies in his keen interest in the facts of environmental history, in literature's (mis)representation of them, and (in his later essays) the possibilities of the greening of socialism into a "socialist ecology" that might stand as a latter-day equivalent of Victorian poet and culture critic William Morris (Williams 1989: 210–26). Marx, by contrast, was a technodeterminist who declared the demise of antiestablishment pastoral in the first half of the twentieth century and the need for "new symbols of possibility" – although he has since revised that judgment (Marx 1964: 365; 1988: 291–314). But Marx's partiality for complex or critical pastoral, together with the pronounced right-wing tendency of British country writing during the interwar period, helps explain why contemporary American ecocritics have been less quick to share British critics' "cynicism toward the pastoral" as the classist closed circuit that Williams saw it as being. Marx's work has helped energize British ecocritic Terry Gifford's account of an intellectually and politically robust "post-pastoral" mode in contemporary British poetry that calls into question Williams' dismissal of the mode (Gifford 2002: 51–3), and my own argument that "pastoral outrage" at landscape degradation has been key to the "toxic discourse" of recent environmental justice advocacy (Buell 2001: 35–58).[19] It helps also to explain why Scott Hess's critique of "postmodern pastoral," an update of Marx's "simple" or mainstream tradition whereby the machine becomes "no longer a potential interruption but the central site of the pastoral order" (as in virtual imaging technology), nonetheless works round to envisaging the possibility of a "sustainable pastoral" that would not cater to consumerist passivity, but promote more self-conscious "action and participation" through its cognizance of humanity's ongoing interaction with "the non-human forces in which our lives are embedded" (Hess 2004: 77, 95).

Neither Marx nor Williams seems to have been influenced by the other, or by other countries' nature-based nationalisms. (Williams took no interest in American literature, whereas Marx's training and literary research were squarely in American Studies.)[20] More recent environmental criticism within literary studies has likewise generally concentrated on individual nations' literary histories and is only now starting to think intensively in comparatist terms.[21] Of course, Marx and Williams bear no special responsibility for the practice of reading environmental imagination as a barometer of *national* imagination. In this they followed the bias of literary professionalism toward nation-based specialties that marked the work of their own mentors and that still runs strong.[22] Nor is nation-based specialization altogether unjustified in this case. Nations *do* generate distinctive forms of pastoral or outback nationalism (e.g., the myth of the Bush for Australia; the mystique of the far North for Canada; the iconicity of the Black Forest for German culture; the myth of the jungle for Creole cultures of Brazil, Venezuela, and other Latin American nations).[23] Whatever the limits of their analytical horizons, Marx and Williams provided usable models for critical thinking about such national imaginaries, as well as about specific texts and genres.

Their work was not so much directly catalytic for the environmental turn in literary studies, however, as it was retrospectively enlisted once the movement got underway. The work today considered the starting point for American ecocriticism proper, Joseph Meeker's *The Comedy of Survival* (1972, revd. 1997), gives Marx no more than passing mention in the process of denigrating pastoral's anthropocentrism. Jonathan Bate's *Romantic Ecology* (1991) appears

16

to gather a certain amount of energy from Williams, but is mainly concerned to rehabilitate the green language to which Williams himself gave short shrift over against the tendency of new historicism – which reckons Williams as a significant precursor[24] – to dismiss Wordsworth's devotion to "nature" as conservative politics. For Meeker and Bate were committed, as Williams and Marx were not, to the proposition that "an ecological *ethic* must be reaffirmed in our contemporary structure of values" (Bate 1991: 11). Ecocriticism had begun to arrive. But it arrived not as a program so much as a bevy of disparate, semi-intercommunicating practitioners ranging from professional outliers like Meeker to central figures within academe like Bate, who went on to become the general editor of the monumental new *Oxford History of English Literature*.

The Environmental Turn Anatomized

No definitive map of environmental criticism in literary studies can therefore be drawn. Still, one can identify several trend-lines marking an evolution from a "first wave" of ecocriticism to a "second" or newer revisionist wave or waves increasingly evident today. This first–second distinction should not, however, be taken as implying a tidy, distinct succession. Most currents set in motion by early ecocriticism continue to run strong, and most forms of second-wave revisionism involve building on as well as quarreling with precursors. In this sense, "palimpsest" would be a better metaphor than "wave." As has been said of the irregular advance of the idea of sustainable development (or "ecological modernization" as some prefer to call it), the history of literary-environmental studies might be thought of as a loose-hanging "discourse coalition" comprised of semi-fortuitously braided story-lines, each of which encapsulates "complex disciplinary debates" (Hajer 1995: 65).

The initiative that first visibly distinguished ecocriticism from the work of Williams and Marx was the push in some quarters, though

17

by no means all, for closer alliance with environmental sciences, especially the life sciences. This is the standpoint from which the "eco" of "ecocriticism" makes most coherent sense. Meeker reconceives literature under the sign of biology, especially the ethological studies of Konrad Lorenz. He offers an ingeniously offbeat brief for comedy as a mode that values traits humans share with nonhumans – species survival, adaptation to circumstance, community, veniality, and play – as against what he sees as tragedy's anthropocentric haughtiness toward the natural order (Meeker 1997). Since then, others have also taken up the argument that ecocriticism's progress hinges significantly if not crucially on its becoming more science-literate. Specific prescriptions vary greatly, however. Joseph Carroll (1995) and Glen A. Love (2003) look to evolutionary biology for critical models; William Howarth seems rather to favor bringing humanities and science together in the context of studying specific landscapes and regions (Howarth 1996), to which end geology is at least as important as the life sciences (Howarth 1999). Ursula Heise, on the other hand, has recently turned to a branch of applied mathematics, risk theory, as a window onto literature's exploration of the kind of contemporary anxieties underscored by Ulrich Beck (Heise 2002), while for N. Katherine Hayles the prosthetics of environment information technology, artificial intelligence, and virtual reality become crucial in measuring the transit from human to "posthuman" modes of being in the world, and fiction's imagination of these (Hayles 1999).[25]

The story-line encapsulated here is not only one of increasing variety but also of assumed certitudes placed under question. First-wave ecocritical calls for greater scientistic literacy tend to presuppose a bedrock "human" condition, to commend the scientific method's ability to describe natural laws, and to look to science as a corrective to critical subjectivism and cultural relativism. Love is particularly emphatic: the promise of ecocriticism lies in building upon the sociobiology-based "consilience" of disciplines as envisioned by Edward O. Wilson, for whom aesthetic and social theory must ultimately be obedient to evolutionary genetics, whereas "a cultural constructionist position . . . plays into the hands of the destroyers" (Love 2003: 21). From this standpoint, cultural theory's anthropocentric arrogance and ignorant disdain for science cost it the "science wars" that roiled the American academy during the 1990s. From the standpoint of second-wave science-oriented environmental critics like Heise and Hayles, by contrast, the borderline between science and culture is less clear-cut. Both would argue for "a scientifically informed foregrounding of green issues in literature" as Heise (1997: 6) states, but they envisage science's relationship to human culture as a feedback loop in which science is viewed both as objectified discipline and humanly directed enterprise, and the terms of scientistic discourse have significant implications for environmental criticism of literature but do not serve as an authoritative model. The discourses of science and literature must be read both with and against each other.

For a number of other ecocritics, the arrogance of scientism has loomed up as greater hazard than the insouciance of cultural theory in reducing science to cultural construct or the slickness of under-informed literary criticism in its loose "metaphoric transfer" (Heise's phrase) of the lexicon of "eco"-terms. (Of course, the text-as-organism metaphor has a much longer history in critical theory, dating back through new critical formalism to Romanticism, which in turn has much older roots in the mystical idea of the world as text, the *liber mundi*.) Ecofeminist work presents an instructive example of such skepticism. Ecofeminism is itself a multiverse, but inquiry starts from the premise of a correlation between the history of institutionalized patriarchy and human domination of the non-human. As an initiative within literary studies, it has taken shape as an intertwinement of revisionist history of science, with Carolyn Merchant and Donna Haraway the most visibly influential figures; of resistance to androcentric traditions of literary interpretation exemplified by such critics as Annette Kolodny and Louise Westling; of feminist ecotheology inaugurated by Mary Daly and Rosemary Radford Ruether; and of the environmental philosophy of Val Plumwood, Karen Warren, and others.[26] An ecofeminist

19

might claim that the analogy between "woman" and "nature" is inherent, or (increasingly) that it is historically contingent. One might assert, or might disclaim, that environmental ethics properly hinges on an "ethics of care," which women are culturally if not also biologically constructed to undertake more readily than men. One might stake a position within science studies, or one might self-position remotely afield from it, for example as a theologian arguing for the recuperation of maternal images of deity, or as a neopagan advocate for revival of the prehistoric "Goddess" overthrown by the agro-pastoral and monotheistic revolutions. By no means all ecofeminists would position themselves as "anti-science," even many whose particular interests led them away from science as a topic of inquiry. But most would likely sympathize with (if not accept without qualification) the claim that "natural disorder is man-induced"[27] – as well as with the claim that traditions of differential conditioning of the sexes in western history helps explain the instrumental rationalism that made possible modern science and technology and the broader linkage between the history of male dominance and confidence (not confined to scientists) in the knowledge/power of instrumental rationalism to control the non-human environment.

Neither ecofeminists nor any other group of environmental critics hold a monopoly on pondering the question of the objectivity vs. the constructedness of science's methods and findings. If anything, that is the special province of science studies. None has written about it with more brilliance and panache than Bruno Latour. An ethnographer of scientific practices, he gleefully exposes the myth of the "Great Divide" between Nature and Society as an artifact of what he mock-grandiosely calls the modern "Constitution," which he cleverly schematizes as paradoxically ordaining both the absolute separation and absolute authority of both science and politics – thereby ensuring the very opposite: their hybridization (Latour 1993: 13–48).[28] Latour doesn't want to undermine science's authority so much as to redefine it contextually, in such a way as to deny both science's exemption from human agency and its reduction only to that. Science's "facts" are "neither real nor fabricated"; the microbial revolution hinged on a certain kind of orchestrated laboratory performance, without which science history would have taken a different path, but the discovery/invention was not fictitious, either. Latour ingeniously proposes the neologism "factish" (a collage of "fact" and "fetish") to describe this understanding of the "facts" of science: "types of action that do not fall into the comminatory choice between fact and belief" (Latour 1999: 295, 306).[29]

Several second-wave ecocritics have commended Latour as a wholesome antidote to simplistic endorsement either of science's authority over against the claims and frames of literary and cultural theory or of "theory's" purported demolition of science as nothing more than discursive or cultural construction.[30] Not that Latour, who shows scant interest in literature and the arts, will likely become the all-purpose theorist of literary studies' environmental turn. Ecocritical interest in his work betokens, rather, a more reflexive approach to science on the part of those who look to it to energize literary studies (ASLE can here be seen as playing catchup to the Society for the Study of Literature and Science), by provoking a more sophisticated rethinking of the nature and place of "nature" itself. This brings us to the next of our story-lines.

For first-wave ecocriticism, "environment" effectively meant "natural environment." In practice if not in principle, the realms of the "natural" and the "human" looked more disjunct than they have come to seem for more recent environmental critics – one of the reasons for preferring "environmental criticism" to "ecocriticism" as more indicative of present practice. Ecocriticism was initially understood to be synchronous with the aims of earthcare. Its goal was to contribute to "the struggle to preserve the 'biotic community'" (Coupe 2000: 4). The paradigmatic first-wave ecocritic appraised "the effects of culture upon nature, with a view toward celebrating nature, berating its despoilers, and reversing their harm through political action" (Howarth 1996: 69). In the process, the ecocritic might seek to redefine the concept of culture itself in organicist terms with a view to envisioning a "philosophy of organism" that would break down "the hierarchical separations between human beings and other elements of the natural world" (Elder 1985: 172).

Second-wave ecocriticism has tended to question organicist models of conceiving both environment and environmentalism. Natural and built environments, revisionists point out, are long since all mixed up; the landscape of the American "West" is increasingly the landscape of metropolitan sprawl rather than the outback of Rocky Mountain "wilderness"; the two spheres are as intertwined, now and historically, as surely as Los Angeles and Las Vegas have siphoned water from the Colorado basin from the hinterlands for the past century (Comer 1999). Literature-and-environment studies must develop a "social ecocriticism" that takes urban and degraded landscapes just as seriously as "natural" landscapes (Bennett 2001: 32). Its traditional commitment to the nature protection ethic must be revised to accommodate the claims of environmental justice (Adamson, Evans, and Stein 2002) – or (more broadly) "the environmentalism of the poor," as one ecological economist has called it (Martínez-Alier 2002).

This shift has divided but enriched the movement. Certainly it has influenced my own work. It was the most important impetus behind the change of focus from my *Environmental Imagination* to *Writing for an Endangered World*. The earlier book centered on the question of the extent to which (certain kinds of) literature can be thought to model ecocentric values, as exemplified in particular by the directional movement of Henry David Thoreau's career and by American nature writing more generally. In these respects, *The Environmental Imagination* was a representative work of first-wave ecocriticism. Although I believed then and continue to believe that the literatures of nature *do* bear important witness against "the arrogance of humanism" (Ehrenfeld 1978), I found myself agreeing with those who thought the concentration on "environment" as "nature" and on nature writing as the most representative environmental genre were too restrictive, and that a mature environmental aesthetics – or ethics, or politics – must take into account the inter-penetration of metropolis and outback, of anthropocentric as well as biocentric concerns.

It remains to be seen just how far the discourses of urbanism and environmental justice can be coordinated with the discourses of nature and the protectionist agendas they tend to imply. Some significant divisions separate first-wave projects to reconnect humans with the natural world from second-wave skepticism "that more can be learned from the 'black hole' of a weasel's eyes than from, say, the just-closed eyes of a child of the ghetto killed by lead-poisoning from ingesting the peeling paint in his/her immediate environment."[31] According to the former way of thinking, the pro-totypical human figure is a solitary human and the experience in question activates a primordial link between human and nonhuman. According to the latter, the prototypical human figure is defined by social category and the "environment" is artificially constructed. Is there any common ground here to indicate that environmental criticism might grow rather than fall apart from this kind of schism?

I think so. First and foremost because in both instances the understanding of personhood is defined for better or for worse by environmental entanglement. Whether individual or social, being doesn't stop at the border of the skin. If the weasel epiphany sounds too rarefied, set beside the image of the poisoned child this declaration by a Native American writer quoted by an ecocritic/nature writer of more traditional persuasion. "You could cut off my hand, and I would still live . . . You could take out my eyes, and I would still live . . . Take away the sun, and I die. Take away the plants and animals, and I die. So why should I think my body is more a part of me than the sun and the earth?" (K. D. Moore 2004: 58–9). This too has the marks of the first-wave mentality (environment = nature, nature = nurture, the exemplar and the idiom = more or less what one would expect from the paradigmatic "ecological Indian," the model minority sage of green wisdom) (Krech 1999). But the underlying view of the environment-constructed body, of

23

environmentality as crucial to health or disease, life or death, is quite similar.

The image of the poisoned child is also in its own way as much an idealization as the image of the eco-sensitive indigene. Its underlying valorization of "the natural" tends not to be so different from the first wave's as one might suppose. Second-wave ecocriticism has so far concentrated strongly, for example, on locating vestiges of nature within cities and/or exposing crimes of eco-injustice against society's marginal groups. In this there should be enough shared ground for ongoing conversation if not *rapprochement*. Skittishness at modernization's aggressive, accelerating, inequitable transformations of "natural" into "constructed" space is a common denominator crucial to giving ecocriticism, both waves of it, its edge of critique. This is ecocriticism's equivalent as it were to queer studies, with which some environmental writers and critics have in fact begun to affiliate (see Sandilands 1999): to unsettle normative thinking about environmental status quos. Not that there is anything anti-normative about environmental concern as such. On the contrary, environmental concern is more mainstream than homophobia.[32] But not as a high-priority issue. The mainstream view, in the United States at least, is that "the environment" will be society's top problem "tomorrow" – a quarter century from now, say – but not today (Guber 2003: 44, 54). Environmental concern is normal. But *vehement* concern still looks queer.

That is a consensus environmental criticism of whatever stripe is out to disrupt. To adapt the terms of Niklas Luhmann's model of systems analysis, the insistence on environmentality – whether it be the ecological Indian or the poisoned child – interjects the disruptive "anxiety" element that "cannot be regulated away by any of the function systems" that comprise modernized society (the institution of economics, law, etc.) (Luhmann 1989: 127).[33]

Second-wave ecocriticism's revision of first-wave horizons was partially anticipated in several ways. To begin with, the movement's latitudinarian definitions of "environment" increased from the get-go the likelihood that a *de facto* equation of environment = nature

24

would be disputed sooner rather than later. And all the more so because of a certain degree of anticipatory eclecticism within early ecocriticism itself,[34] an eclecticism foreshadowed in some degree by first-wave ecocriticism's pantheon of significant late twentieth-century environmental writers. A preeminent example was Rachel Carson's swerve from her first book *Under the Sea Wind* (1941), a quite traditional performance in the nature writing vein, to *Silent Spring* two decades later, even while carrying over many of the resources and implicit values of the former. That swerve has since been taken further in the self-conscious hybridization of traditional rural-focused nature writing and epidemiological analysis in such post-Carson feminist writers as Terry Tempest Williams and Sandra Steingraber, whose autobiographical narratives of environmental cancer-clusters self-consciously interlace metropolitan and exurban genres and locales. This work brings us to the heart of second-wave ecocriticism's defining concerns. More on that in chapter 4.

The revised and expanded sense of environmentality just noted has altered ecocriticism's working sense of its proper canon more sweepingly than I have so far indicated. Once I thought it helpful to try to specify a subspecies of "environmental text," the first stipulation of which was that the nonhuman environment must be envisaged not merely as a framing device but as an active presence, suggesting human history's implication in natural history. Now, it seems to me more productive to think inclusively of environmentality as a property of any text – to maintain that all human artifacts bear such traces, and at several stages: in the composition, the embodiment, and the reception (Buell 1995: 7–8 vs. Buell 2001: 2–3). These second thoughts seem broadly to typify the directional momentum of environmental criticism. Some of the earlier significant ecocritical interventions already show cognizance of this. I think especially of Robert Pogue Harrison's *Forests: The Shadows of Civilization*, which traces permutations of forest imagination in Western thought and literature, and Louise Westling's *The Green Breast of the New World*, a study of patriarchal misprisions of

25

landscape (together with certain resistances thereto). Both sweep from the ancient Sumerian epic of *Gilgamesh* to the near-present.

Between these two books, significantly, the overlap in the primary texts discussed turns out to be rather slight. Forest phenomenology in the Western high canon and ecofeminism in (chiefly) US literary discourse lead the two authors down quite different paths. Heterogeneity and with it the possibilities for both intense contestation and for ships passing by each other unnoticed are bound to increase exponentially as the consensual understanding of what might count as environmental literature expands. For example, one second-wave appraisal plausibly contends that "ecocriticism becomes most interesting and useful . . . when it aims to recover the environmental character or orientation of works whose conscious or foregrounded interests lie elsewhere" (Kern 2000: 11). What this critic has in mind is landscape semiotics in Jane Austen's fiction, particularly the impact on Elizabeth Bennet of her visit in *Pride and Prejudice* to Darcy's estate at Pemberley, the direct experience of which begins to dispel her dislike of him. Jonathan Bate enlists *Emma*, *Sense and Sensibility*, and *Mansfield Park* with fuller reference to nineteenth-century environmental history in a paired study of Austen and Hardy (Bate 2000: 1–23). But depending on what one means by "environmental character or orientation," one might wish to privilege a completely different set of texts, as with environmental justice criticism's emphasis on contemporary works by nonwhite writers that confront the issue of environmental racism, only a relative few of which were on the radar screens of first-wave ecocritics (Adamson, Evans, and Stein). Here a case for including Austen's fiction in the picture might still be made; but it would require one to foreground rather than mention in passing Edward Said's reading of *Mansfield Park*, which centers on the dependence of the Bertrams' elegant lifestyle on the family estate in Antigua, sustained by slave labor (Said 1993: 84–97).

ASLE's journal, *ISLE*, has reflected these tendencies. It still prints articles on nature writing, Wordsworthian poetry, and pastoral theory. But the last and only number to feature a special section on

Henry David Thoreau was in fact the very first (spring 1993); and the past few years have seen essays on British and American film, Australian place-making, Latin American environmental justice poetry, immigrant autobiography, and a revisionist interpretation of animal encounters in medieval lives of St. Francis as a strategy of Franciscan apologetics.

As this last example suggests, no less striking than the expansion of the range of ecocritical texts and topics has been the reframing of the first-wave's preferred canon. As Lance Newman writes in a provocative essay on "Marxism and Ecocriticism," "nature writing is not a stable form of reaction to a stable problem (the ideologically-driven human domination of nature). It is a dynamic tradition of response to the rise and development of the capitalist ecosocial order . . . how nature writers see and understand nature has everything to do with how they see and understand the society whose relations with it they hope to change" (Newman 2002: 18–19). Newman is *not* making the same claim here about a text like *Walden* that Leo Marx made, namely that Thoreau's interest in the natural world is significant as symbolic theater for political critique and ceases to become of interest to us as the text's interest in natural history becomes more literal. Newman's argument is the obverse: that understanding "ecocentric consciousness" requires a "historical con-sciousness" attentive to the "coevolution of material social and natural systems that has produced the present crisis" of environ-mental endangerment against which nature writing implicitly if not explicitly positions itself (Newman 2002: 21). Taking its cue, as here, from critical theory on the one hand and from the increasing politi-cization of post-Carson nature writing on the other, the newer environmental criticism is likely to continue to press for more cos-mopolitan ways of understanding the work of ecodiscourse in the canon of original concentration, even as it takes in a wider range of literary history so as ultimately to include, in principle, any text whatsoever.

Might this process of cosmopolitanization wind up amounting to a forfeiture of the original mission? To a taming down of first-wave ecocriticism's original schismatic disaffection with business-as-usual literary studies? To the consolidation of environmental criticism as just another niche within the culture of academic professionalism, now that it is on the way to becoming more "critically sophisticated," increasingly more engaged with the other critical games in town? My own response to such concerns, which will take the rest of this book to unfold, is "Probably so, to some extent." But the promise is well worth the risk, both on the intrinsics and the pragmatics – especially if the alternatives are a too narrow conception of enviromentalism and environmentality, and the (re)production of the unemployable.

Right now, as I see it, environmental criticism is in the tense but enviable position of being a wide-open movement still sorting out its premises and its powers. Its reach is increasingly worldwide and from bottom to top within academe: from graduate studies in (some) major university literature departments to courses in entry-level composition. It is wide open to alliances with environmental writers, environmental activists, and extra-academic environmental educators. Not the least of its attractions is the prospect of encompassing all these roles. Increasing critical sophistication may make environmental criticism more professionally cautious and more internally stratified. But its intellectual zest and its activist edge are likely to gain more from its future evolution than they sacrifice.

2

The World, the Text, and the Ecocritic

Environmental criticism strives to "move the notion of environment from abstraction to a tangible concern" (Dixon 1999: 87). That concern leads it to take an exceptionally strong interest in which environmental motifs are selected for what kinds of portrayal. The environmental(ist) subtexts of works whose interests are ostensibly directed elsewhere (e.g., toward social, political, and economic relations) may be no less telling in this regard than cases of the opposite sort where human figures have been evacuated for the sake of stressing environmentality. That Native American poet Joy Harjo sees a statue in the French Quarter of New Orleans as a riderless "blue horse caught frozen in stone," whereas African-American autobiographer Geoffrey Canada sees trees, plants, and other nonhuman life *only* in small-town Maine where he attended college and *never* in the gang-ridden districts of New York City where he grew up and now works – these contrasting stylizations are of potentially equal interest to environmental criticism. The difference in how these two writers make "tangible" "the notion of environment," between Harjo's counterintuitive recuperation of the natural within the forms of urban monuments and Canada's intensification of the polarity between landscapes of urban violence and of privileged collegians, looms up as a significant index of discrepant commitments informed by genre and culture as well as by individual acts of self-conscious response to the specific environments in question.[1]

As these two examples suggest, all artistic work hinges upon the evocation of imagined worlds that may or may not bear a close resemblance to literal or historical environments. This chapter seeks to provide some guidelines for navigating the disparate ways that literary texts evoke and particularize fictive environmentality. The first of the chapter's two main sections explores the general question of how environmental criticism has and should theorize the relation (or disrelation) of word-world to actual world. The second section concentrates more intensively on three complementary approaches to conceiving that relation.

Questions of Mimesis:
Environment as Invention and Discovery

All inquiry into artistic rendition of physical environment must sooner or later reckon with the meta-question of how to construe the relation between the world of a text and the world of historical or lived experience. This must be a concern both for first-wave nature-writing-oriented ecocriticism and for second-wave urban and ecojustice revisionists, whatever their disagreements. No one doctrine rules the field. The majority of ecocritics, whether or not they theorize their positions, look upon their texts of reference as refractions of physical environments and human interaction with those environments, notwithstanding the artifactual properties of textual representation and their mediation by ideological and other sociohistorical factors. They are "worldly" critics, even if not in the same sense that Edward Said had in mind when he assembled the book of essays from which this chapter takes its title (Said 1983).[2] Many environmental critics, both first-wave and revisionist, seek to break down the formal division of labor between creative writing, criticism, field-based environmental studies, and environmental activism. As we saw in chapter 1, ecocritics who teach for a living often combine classroom instruction with some sort of field experience. Motivating this is a conviction that contact (or lack of contact) with actual environments is intimately linked, even if not on a one-to-one basis, with the work of environmental imagination, for both writer and critic. Environmental justice revisionism has recommend "toxic tourism" as a way of reading such "classics of 'toxic nonfiction'" as *Silent Spring*.[3] Even those whose bent is more contemplative than activist are apt to be on guard against the kind of conditioning that reinforces what one critic calls "falling up," or precipitous jumps "from the material terms of the text into . . . the ideological or psychological or whatever, and then staying in abstraction without closely examining the image or plot movement or other material representation which generated" it (A. Wallace 1993: 3).

Accordingly ecocritics, both first-wave and second-wave, often show what superficially seems an old-fashioned propensity for "realistic" modes of representation, and a preoccupation with questions of factical accuracy of environmental representation. One critic approvingly cites late nineteenth-century nature writer John Burroughs' dictum that "the literary naturalist does not take liberties with facts; facts are the flora upon which he lives"; another honors the attempt of Raymond Williams' fiction for its "reinvigorated Lukácsian realism"; a third chides reviewers of Chickasaw novelist Linda Hogan's *Solar Storms* for failing to place this text in its "real historical context" (Hydro-Quebec's environmental injustice and racism during the 1970s against the James Bay Cree and Inuit), stressing how the novel is "grounded in historical fact."[4]

Such disposition to take the word-world linkage seriously at a time when privileging literature's capacity for mimesis and referentiality remains unfashionable has given rise to considerable anxiety and division. At one end of the spectrum, some ecocritics have tended to dismiss the (post)structural revolution as mostly "discover[ing] nothing to read but constructs of self-reflexive language."[5] At the other, some movement insiders have scrupulously absorbed anti-mimetic theory's caveats. One draws a firm line – reminiscent of Leo Marx's simple vs. complex pastoral – between good nature writing that displays an appropriate postmodern reflexiveness toward its own status as textual artifact, and mediocre nature writing that succumbs to naive descriptivism (Fritzell 1990). Another denigrates attempts to recuperate realism as restricting the field of environmental writing, as ludicrously foreshortened in focus ("its practitioners . . . reduced to an umpire's role, squinting to see if a given depiction of a horizon, a wildflower, or a live oak tree is itself well-painted and lively"), and in any case bogus, since "mimesis presumes the *sameness* of the representation and the represented object" (Phillips 2003: 163–4, 175).

Since the latter critic's main target is my own work, I should perhaps recuse myself from attempted mediation.[6] But with a decade having passed since the publication of the chapter in question I make bold notwithstanding. The mimesis debate now seems to me narrowly focused and overblown, though the underlying issues remain as relevant as ever. On the one hand, those who decry ecocriticism's retrogression to a pretheoretical trust in art's capacity to mirror the factical world tend to work from a reductive model of mimesis, which, *contra* Phillips, posits refraction but most definitely *not* "sameness," and from a cartoon version of ecocritical neorealists as doggedly hard-hat positivists. Look closely at those essays on Burroughs, Williams, and Hogan, and we see that the first is perfectly aware of Burroughs' dependence upon metaphor, the second of Williams' realist fiction being written in the service of critical-revisionist history, and the third of the strong ideological/activist edge to Hogan's novel. None of the three critics insists on anything like a one-to-one correspondence between text and world, but rather on a certain kind of environmental referentiality as part of the overall work of the text. On the other hand, ecocritical neorealists limit their horizons insofar as they evade reflexive discussion of the premises underlying such privilege as they accord to dense representations of environmental facticity or appeal to existential immersion, narrative power, and ecological literacy as a means of suturing the divide between empirical world and creative artifact. This not only threatens to short-circuit defense of critical realism, but also to frustrate ecocritical engagement with non- and antirealistic genres that are no less environmentally engaged. Let's look more closely at each of these points in turn.

As to the former, even designedly "realistic" texts cannot avoid being heavily mediated refractions of the palpable world. The basic facts are obvious. Languages are culturally coded symbol systems. Writing is a system of abstract graphic notation. Books are manufactured commodities. Written and even oral expression is subject to severe sensuous limits, being sight and/or sound-biased. All attempts to get the world between covers are subject to an asymptotic limit beyond which environment cannot be brought to consciousness in any event, and to an array of other inhibiting factors, personal and sociocultural, that further contort the attempt to do so: by dominant assumptions as to what counts as a worthwhile environmental topic (or, for that matter, what counts as an environment), by marketplace forces, by reluctance to defy sacred cows or perverse insistence on doing such, by hastiness of composition, and by genre choice, such as traditional nature writing's tendency to sit in the woods and say little about urbanization. The failure of Cuban novelist Alejo Carpentier's composer-protagonist in *The Lost Steps* (1953) to find his way back to the primeval world he has discovered in the Venezuelan backcountry after he has felt compelled to return home to get paper on which to inscribe the music this excursion has inspired in his head elegantly dramatizes the intractable divide between nature and discourse.[7]

Yet it is equally clear that the subject of a text's representation of its environmental ground *matters* – matters aesthetically, conceptually, ideologically. Language never replicates extratextual landscapes, but it can be bent toward or away from them. We can see this in such basic aesthetic decisions as whether or not to foreground local toponymy, vernacularization, and indigenous names for uniquely native species. As Australian ecologist and literary critic George Seddon remarks of the difference between the idioms of contemporary New Zealand environmental writing and Australian, such discursive practices have both a specifically environmentalist agenda and a more broadly cultural one (Seddon 2002).[8] They position readers *vis-à-vis* the represented landscape and culture, according for example to whether they share the text's local knowledge (as when Thomas Hardy has Giles Winterbourne in *The Woodlanders* reproach his long-absent fiancée for forgetting the difference between John-apple-trees and bitter-sweets) or render it opaque (as when Hardy's contemporary, the American local colorist Rowland Robinson, leaves it to a laconic farmer who speaks an almost impenetrable dialect to identify the moment when maple syrup is fully boiled as when "it begins tu luther-ap'n"). [9]

To unpack further the mimetic issues at stake, consider this series of imagined trees:

> We bring about your fertile gardens, your palm trees and vines, your haunts of ample fruits to eat and a tree of trees originating in Mount Sinai, yielding oil that is always there to hand at your meals. (*Al-Qur'ān* 23: 19–20) [10]

> The day is come when I again repose
> Here, under this dark sycamore, and view
> These plots of cottage-ground, these orchard-tufts,
> Which at this season, with their unripe fruits,
> Are clad in one green hue . . .
> (William Wordsworth, "Tintern Abbey") [11]

> At the bottom [of the orchard] was . . . a winding walk, bordered with laurels and terminating in a giant horse-chestnut . . . A waft of wind came sweeping down the laurel walk, and trembled through the boughs of the chestnut . . . what ailed the chestnut tree? it writhed and groaned; while wind roared in the laurel walk, and came sweeping over us . . . Before I left my bed in the morning, little Adèle came running in to tell me that the great horse-chestnut at the bottom of the orchard had been struck by lightning in the night, and half of it split away. (Charlotte Brontë, *Jane Eyre*) [12]

> Most were not aware of the size of the great elm till it was cut down. I surprised some a few days ago by saying that when its trunk should lie prostrate it would be higher than the head of the tallest man in the town . . . How much of old Concord falls with it! The

town clerk will not chronicle its fall. I will, for it is of greater moment to the town than that of many a human inhabitant would be ... Is it not sacrilege to cut down the tree which has so long looked over Concord beneficently? (Henry David Thoreau, *Journal*)[13]

> I must tell you
> this young tree
> whose round and firm trunk
> between the wet
>
> pavement and the gutter
> (where water
> is trickling) rises
> bodily
>
> into the air with
> one undulant
> thrust half its height –
> and then
>
> dividing and waning
> sending out
> young branches on
> all sides –
>
> hung with cocoons
> it thins
> till nothing is left of it
> but two
>
> eccentric knotted
> twigs
> bending forward
> hornlike at the top
> (William Carlos Williams, "Young Sycamore")[14]

> Gumtree in the city street,
> Hard bitumen around your feet,
> Rather you should be
> In the cool world of leafy forest halls

35

And wild bird calls.
Here you seem to me
Like that poor cart-horse
Castrated, broken, a thing wronged,
Strapped and buckled, its hell prolonged,
Whose hung head and listless mien express
Its hopelessness.
Municipal gum, it is dolorous
To see you thus
Set in your black grass of bitumen –
O fellow citizen,
What have they done to us?
(Oodgeroo Noonuccal, "Municipal Gum")[15]

Buzzworm was born and raised near about the corner of Jefferson and Normandie. Said when he was growing up, never noticed trees . . . What's trees? he always wondered. Never sure about trees, even though he learned to spell it, learned to copy the pictures other kids painted in tempera, two brown strokes for a trunk and that green amorphous *do* on top, sometimes with red dots they called apples. Never saw one of those in the neighborhood. It was a puzzlement. No trees in this city desert.

One day, however, he was walking his block like always, and he suddenly noticed that row of poles planted every so many yards into the grass or dirt to one side of the sidewalk. His eyes followed the gray-brown poles up to the sky, and for the first time, he recognized what he believed to be a tree . . . Too high to see if birds live in them. Too high to check for fruit. But he was sure he had the tallest trees of anyone in the class. He thought if you could get to the top of them, you could see everything. Those trees could see everything. See beyond the street, the houses, the neighborhood. See over the freeway. (Karen Tei Yamashita, *Tropic of Orange*)[16]

Even so small a dendritic assortment as this shows both the inescapability of mimesis and referentialism as lenses of critical understanding and the challenge of grasping their textual effects with any precision.

36

None of these passages makes sense without reference to natural history and/or cultural ecology: Middle Eastern people's dependence on olive oil; the craggy massiveness of the mature horse-chestnut, and its use as an estate tree; the status of the American elm as a signature tree in traditional New England communities; the gum as a generic name for a large array of native Australian species often deemed ugly by Eurocentric standards, but cherished by Aborigines for reasons both cultural and ecological; the palm as a banal mark of subtropical environmentality from a US urban planning standpoint, but of far greater ecocultural significance for traditional African cultures (and also Islamic and ancient Hebrew) than the apple tree of Anglocentric culture; the difference between the dense, "dark" English sycamore (sycamore maple, as it is called in the US) and the sparser, lighter, more vertical sycamore of American parlance – for which the New Jersey suburb where Williams lived during the middle of the twentieth century is known even today.[17]

Anything like a full comparative account would also need to recognize a series of discrepant representational axes or continua – particular/general, factical/fictive, literal/figurative, etc. – during which it would also become quickly evident that mimetic particularity and referentialism don't tightly correlate. Thoreau's tree is a fact of history, but also made elaborately symbolic. Williams' is a typical suburban sidewalk or curb lawn sapling – most any young tree would do, perhaps – but his poem is more given over to particularized description of its contours and sweep than are any of the other excerpts. Note too that he provides a calibrated visual surface image of the sapling's spindliness in a formalist arrangement of its visible structure that is as intertextually mannered as Wordsworth's: a bottom-to-top reverse blazon, as against Wordsworth's eighteenth-century prospect poem strategy, as "Tintern Abbey" continues, of fanning out to farther vistas from a fixed point. The same goes for the description of the palm in *Tropic of Orange*, a sardonic rerun of Williams' bottom-to-top method that follows the awakening of a small black ghetto child (who grows up to become a giant,

37

incidentally) to the fact that the asphalt-and-concrete labyrinth in which he lives has trees after all.

Wordsworth and Thoreau's allegedly unique trees both seem indispensable to the *genius loci* as each describes it; but Wordsworth's *thisness* is more purely personal. Thoreau's elm also embodies and witnesses to community history. The Qur'ānic passage makes the most of its tree's *ecological* significance, yet it is the least descriptive. To be understood by the faithful, a minimalist, ideogrammatical *gestalt* suffices. So too, in a negative sense, with the out-of-placeness of Oodgeroo Noonuccal's gum tree. The tree, the gelded cart-horse, and the disconsolately uprooted Aboriginal speaker form a bitter triad of displaced, hemmed-in victims described in telegraphic and symbolic, but also starkly material terms. Thoreau, by contrast, must belabor the case for *his* tree's sacrality with thick description and historical anecdote – far more copious than my excerpt includes – knowing (or at least claiming) that the tree is precious only to him. He can count on his townsmen assigning a certain iconic significance to elms, but not on their sharing his view that the life of a great tree is more important than the life of the average Concordian.

The glimpses of the horse chestnut in *Jane Eyre* are more particularized than either the archetypal olive or Wordsworth's sycamore; but their purport has almost nothing to do with either landscape ecology or cultural significance and almost everything to do with providing seductive/ominous symbolic backdrop to the singular drama of Jane's precipitous acceptance of Rochester's marriage proposal under the tree. The tree's fate is both a stereotypical foreshadowing of the blasting of their hopes soon after and a slightly more subtle anticipation of Rochester's later mutilation. Any large tree might do for that, but a horse chestnut would have been readily understood by Brontë's readers as befitting Rochester's gnarly massiveness better than most.[18] In Yamashita's *Tropic of Orange*, the choice is even more provocative. Any tall tree might dramatize the denatured look of inner-city Los Angeles at ground level, but the palm is an easy regional stereotype for the outlander to grab hold of that is given a couple of extra twists by reason of the demand for palms as adornments in upscale communities (Nabhan 1985: 21), and the chance that the novel has in mind the multiple eco-ritual significances of the palm for traditional African cultures as a source of nourishment and clothing, and as a communal meeting place.[19]

Still more might be said about the different mimetic strategies here in evoking a more or less textured sense of thisness and in appealing to an extratextual, factical ground. No wonder ecocritics want to interrogate the "falling up" simplisms of a critique that supposes that the "mimetic fallacy" is something criticism should outgrow. Not that a single distinctive theory of mimesis and/or reference is likely to command assent from environmental critics across the board. Much more likely will be a continued interest in the matching, or non-matching, of wordscape and worldscape that takes quite varied forms. Precisely how you approach the subject will depend on your preferred starting point. If poetic language is your central interest, then perhaps you will find yourself attracted to Paul Ricoeur's theory of metaphor as a double move of turning away from the denotative in order to enrich the perceiver's return to the world (Ricoeur 1977). If your starting point is the environmental construction of individual acts of expression, then you might look to the plural landscapes thesis derived by nature writer Barry Lopez from the storytelling practices of place-based indigenes: narrative as wrought by the interplay between "outer landscape" and the storyteller's "interior landscape," which by implication is mediated by the cultural landscape (Lopez 1989: 61–72; cf. Buell 1995: 91–4). If your interest is in defining the echo, necessarily belated and reductive, of text to antecedent environmental context or knowledge base, then Leonard Scigaj's neo-Derridean theory of *référance* might appeal (Scigaj 1999: 35–81).[20] If your interest in the text–world relation is spatial rather than temporal, then Francis Ponge's conception of the poetic text as *adéquation* or transposition of the gist of the thing into a different register of verbal and visual arrangement might seem especially compelling.[21] If, on the other hand, you start from the position of wanting to honor literature's witness to direct environmental experience, such as the experience of subaltern victims of environmental injustice whose experience-based testimony is put under question by such official knowledge protocols as the canonical definition of "risk," you might want to enlist Satya Mohanty's critical post-positivism in support (Mohanty 1997).

Though all of these theories posit a relation between text and world, significantly none of them explicitly privileges classical realism's aspiration to make the text a replica of the world. The mimesis police are probably right in complaining that early ecocriticism tended to narrow its sights overmuch in this regard. A disproportionate amount of first-wave energy was probably directed at texts and genres that seemed to provide dense, accurate representations of actual natural environments and not enough to the implications of Leslie Marmon Silko's caveat, issued with the examples of traditional Pueblo pictographs and petroglyphs specifically in mind, that "a lifelike rendering of an elk is too restrictive," as disclosing no more than the surface particularities of a single creature (Silko 1986: 85). As Silko perceives, what Roland Barthes (1986) called the "reality-effect" is not necessarily an ecology-effect.

Barthes himself is a biased witness here, since the only literary "ecology" that matters to him is the ecology of the sign, which he rightly took realism as wanting to disrupt by infusing into narrative a degree of documentary detail that he himself disdains as so much detritus, especially given that "the most realistic narrative imaginable develops along unrealistic lines" (ibid: 148). To some extent, Barthes' astringency is well-founded. Realism's denseness can indeed be tedious and distracting as well as superficial. Realism can heighten the divide between narrative consciousness and the text's represented world even as it purports to serve as bridge. Its "you-are-there" potential can be offset by the alienation produced by descriptive prolixity, which silently declares: "You, dear reader, are watching all this at a further remove even from me, the narrator, who am also watching and recording all this." Finally, as Fredric Jameson remarks of "the great realistic novelists," descriptive objectivism must also be understood in some measure as an ideologized strategy of concealment, in effect if not intent. "Their evocation of the solidity of their object of representation – the social world grasped as an organic, natural, Burkean permanence – is necessarily threatened by any suggestion that that world is not natural, but historical, and subject to radical change" (Jameson 1981: 193).[22] Insofar as the history of nature writing can be told as a story of attempts to salvage and restabilize the shrinking remnant of more-or-less wild nature in the face of modernization through solidification of natural objects, this critique holds for it as well – even if one takes exception to Jameson's underexamined zest for "radical change" and his obliviousness here and elsewhere to environmental issues, as if the "social world" were all that matters. Yet these strictures on realism by no means encompass what nature writing and other genres favored by first-wave ecocriticism are all about, and far less do they define the totality of environmental representation.

To take the narrower point first, with regard to nature writing: whatever ecocritics and *their* critics have sometimes been tempted into suggesting to the contrary, it is not politically monolithic, not hermetically confined to the sphere of the "natural," not necessarily "realist," and neither oblivious nor unsympathetic to the phenomenon of change. The environmental writing of Gilbert White and John Burroughs and Annie Dillard is studiously apolitical, while that of William Cobbett, Mary Austin, Aldo Leopold, Edward Abbey, and Geoff Park is distinctly politicized, and in mutually different ways. As for hermeticism, Rachel Carson's career is especially telling as a study of one writer's rejection of the premise that nature writing should be focused on a space apart from the social, owing to the discovery that there is no space on earth immune from anthropogenic toxification. To some extent, this mid-life switch testifies to the intertial force of a prior convention of separating off human and natural spheres for the delectation of an increasingly (sub)urbanized landless culture. The "romance of natural history," the nature book as self-contained Victorian terrarium: it continues to this day.[23] But it is also the case that traditional nature writing

41

itself is more invested in the interpenetration of social and natural frames of reference than early ecocriticism tended to indicate (Newman 2002).

The most canonical of Anglophone nature books, Thoreau's *Walden*, is a prime instance, and nowhere more so than in a climactic moment that seems at first sight a purely woodland fantasy disconnected from anything that might have been going on in town. In this passage, nature writing's capacity to flout realism and celebrate change looms particularly large: the much-discussed *tour de force* contemplation, in the "Spring" chapter, of the "truly *grotesque*" "architectural foliage" disclosed by the melting sandbank created by the construction of a railway line at the far end of the pond the year before Thoreau moved there.

> I am affected as if in a peculiar sense I stood in the laboratory of the Artist who made the world and me, – had come to where he was still at work, sporting on this bank, and with excess of energy strewing his fresh designs about. I feel as if I were nearer to the vitals of the globe, for this sandy overflow is something such a foliaceous mass as the vitals of the animal body. You find thus in the sands an anticipation of the vegetable leaf. No wonder that the earth expresses itself outwardly in leaves, it so labors with the idea inwardly . . . The overhanging leaf sees here its prototype. *Internally*, whether in the globe or animal body, it is a moist thick *lobe*, a word especially applicable to the liver and lungs and the *leaves* of fat (λείβω, *labor*, *lapsus*, to flow or slip downward, a lapsing; λοβος, *globus*, lobe, globe; also lap, flap, and many other words), *externally* a dry thin *leaf*, even as the *f* and *v* are a pressed and dried *b*. The radicals of lobe are *lb*, the soft mass of the *b* (single lobed, or B, double lobed), with a liquid *l* behind it pressing it forward. In globe, *glb*, the guttural *g* adds to the meaning of the capacity of the throat. The feathers and wings of birds are still drier and thinner leaves. Thus, also, you pass from the lumpish grub in the earth to the airy and fluttering butterfly. The very globe continually transcends and translates itself, and becomes winged in its orbit . . . The whole tree itself is but one leaf, and rivers are still vaster leaves whose pulp is intervening earth, and towns and cities are the ova of insects in their axils.[24]

This passage, which continues on and on for five pages in the standard edition of Thoreau's work, is *Walden's* equivalent of the image of the entangled bank which ends Darwin's *On the Origin of Species*. To be sure, *Walden* is paleo-scientific by contrast: much more a work of romantic *naturphilosophie* or post-Emersonian mysticism than Thoreau's later writings, which are more given over to precise observations of the natural world that, toward the last, show an intelligent, approving, albeit selective, perusal of *Origin of Species*. But all this is a bit beside the point of the *Walden* passage. Note especially here the refusal to separate natural order from social order and the resort to the device of minute observation to create a heaped-up tangle of imagery that defies the protocols of realism. In context, Thoreau makes it quite clear that this "natural" scene has been produced by the humanly engineered embankment. His crypto-evolutionary recognition of change/metamorphosis as distinctive to life-process goes to show that not only earth's forms "but the institutions upon it, are plastic." The rhetoric seems designed to represent that plasticity. The speaker here is acting out his fanciful conception of the kind of primal Artist who strews his fresh designs about with playful excess of energy.[25]

Thoreau doubtless knew that his passage would sound eccentric, even perverse. It's a striking fortuity that he anticipates here the one thing about the normative subdiscipline of ecology that Neil Evernden identifies as conceivably "subversive, if taken literally" – "a plasticity of being which can be disconcerting to orderly minds." For example, mitochondria in the cells of the human body are "quite as independent as the chroloplasts in plants . . . We cannot exist without them, and yet they may not strictly be 'us.'" So are we colonies or organisms, or what? (Evernden 1985: 38–9). Thoreau's transmutations of sand into liver and lungs into leaf into river are a rough-and-ready version of these defamiliarizations. Human body parts erupt from the landscape, as if there were "no end to the heaps of liver lights and bowels, as if the globe were turned wrong side outward." In its own way the denial of species fixity is as disconcerting as Darwin's – and partly because the prose

43

is so much less measured and, well, realistic.[26] And the stakes here are larger than just the demonstration of natural instability. The passage also wants to make this scene a laboratory model for disclosing a law of civilizational instability analogous to the messy logic of the natural: a compound of regulation and randomness, stretching from the permutations of language to the course of empire.

Environmentality Across the Genre Spectrum

As the *Walden* passage begins to suggest, all that might be said about nature writing – or any other genre – *vis-à-vis* realism scarcely exhausts what deserves to be said about texts as environmental representations. Genres and texts are themselves arguably "ecosystems," not only in the narrow sense of the text as a discursive "environment," but also in the broader sense that texts "help reproduce sociohistorical environments" in stylized form (Bawarshi 2001: 73). Indeed, an individual text must be thought of as environmentally embedded at every stage from its germination to its reception. At each stage, how environmentality gets encoded and expressed is always both partial and greater than one notices at first look – the paradox at the heart of what I have called "environmental unconscious" (Buell 2001: 18–27). Insofar as the where of existence precedes the what of social practice, a text's environmental unconscious is more deeply embedded even than its "political unconscious." Regardless of how one comes down on this issue of priority, however, the "active relationship with the Real," as Jameson holds, is not a matter of simply allowing "'reality' to persevere inertly in its own being," but also of the text drawing "the Real into its own texture," "as its own intrinsic or immanent subtext" (Jameson 1981: 81).

Yet this is still a too constricted formulation of the "active relation" between text and world – as if "reality" were to be taken as finally subsumed by textuality. That is part but only part of how art registers environmentality. In the rest of this chapter I want to take

44

up at greater length three other models for thinking about the reciprocity between text and environment: as rhetoric, as performance, and as world-making.

Rhetoric has been of strong interest for environmental critics from the start of the ecocritical movement. This is understandable. Rhetoric comprehends all genres of expression, literary or academic or popular, at the point where the properties of language and the agendas of persuasion meet. As such it not only "represents the world" but also "positions us in relation to the rest of the world" (Brown and Herndl 1996: 215). Depending on the context and the disposition of the critic, environmental rhetoric can thus mean a doctrinaire and sometimes also sneaky foreclosure of alternate options, but it can also (or concurrently) mean an opening up of language's capacity to represent both in the sense of "image" and in the sense of "advocate." Thus one study defines "ecospeak" as "a way of framing arguments that stops thinking and inhibits social cooperation" (Killingsworth and Palmer 1992: 9), whereas another sympathetically unpacks the force of "embedded persuasive rhetoric" in selected nature writers (Slovic 1996: 91). Still another analysis of "greenspeak" takes a studiously neutral approach to weighing the descriptive plausibility, conceptual (in)coherence, and cultural work of metaphor in ecodiscourse: planet earth as "home," "lifeboat," and so forth (Harré, Brockmeier, and Mühlhaüsler 1999: 91–118).

This last study's cautiously hedged conclusions are especially notable in the present context. On the one hand, "languages depend for their survival on an ecological support system," language being "the instrument through which we acquire knowledge about the environment and through which we acquire or change attitudes toward it." On the other hand, some metaphors of normative earth–human relations are decidedly more plausible and productive than others, and it behooves us to "take a similar critical stance on the variety of narrative conventions that shape environmental discourses" (pp. 173–4). This in turn must mean greater self-awareness in enlistment of "objective" scientific research – but bearing in mind as we do so not only its potential relevance to environmentalism

but also the countervailing fact that environmental rhetoric rightfully rests on moral and especially aesthetic grounds *rather than* scientistic. Environmental rhetoric is by contrast a vision of "the fitting
together in a dynamic equilibrium of the human race with all the
other things, organic and inorganic, that grace the outer layers of
the planet Earth" (p. 186).

Not all students of environmental rhetoric would agree with how
these three co-authors frame greenspeak's essential purport. For
them, the "loose collection of dialects" which constitute greenspeak
(p. 177) boils down finally to a vision of deep ecology. Second-
wave environmental critics would define the proper mission of
greenspeak as centered more on environmental equity among
humans than on interspecies harmony. What seems more permanently valuable here is the treatment of rhetoric as environmental
representation in a spirit of skepticism toward rhetoric's propensity
for distortion and overreach, yet receptivity to its potentialities:
descriptive and visionary as well as polemical. Language and environmental rhetoric are seen as distinctive without being separable
from ecocultural context or from "objective" science. That is the
kind of macroperspective that allows one, for example, to affirm,
without falling into either a doctrinaire cultural constructivism or
a doctrinaire objectivism, that a place-based agrarian Chicano community's metaphor of water as "our lifeblood" has better warrant
than a mining company's argument against this traditional understanding of water rights − backed by "expert" testimony and rati-
fied in the end by judicial fiat − that water is a commodity "for
sale to the highest bidder" (Peña 1998: 253–5).

Although students of environmental rhetoric more often than not
approach rhetoric as text, it always also implies performance and
often requires live performance acts, as in the case of public advocacy − in the courtroom, in the boardroom, in the auditorium.
Sometimes the upshot is discouraging, as in the case just mentioned.
Sometimes greenspeak gets results. A study of public testimony considered by the joint Canada–US commission on Great Lakes Water
Quality found that "perceived sincerity was one feature that the

46

commissioners found persuasive" (Waddell 1996: 156). Either way, the continuum that links environmental rhetoric to performance strengthens the link between discourse and world even as it recognizes the non-identity of these domains by its concentration on rhetoric as a means of refiguring the world.

Partly, no doubt, because of the directness of both kinds of link, the environmental rhetoric of nonfictional ecodiscourse has been more fully studied than that of dramatic literature. But the latter is deeply interesting in its own right. Let us start with ecodrama specifically. Modern ecodrama often scripts environmental encounter and embeddedness in what might loosely be called ritual terms, reminiscent of theater's ritual origins. Henrik Ibsen's *An Enemy of the People* (1882), the first canonical modern example, turns on a paradigmatic encounter wrought by the bacteriological revolution. The protagonist Dr. Stockmann is a sturdy "science warrior," as Bruno Latour calls the champions of positivism (Latour 1999: 109),[27] contending against local resort oligarchs who profiteer from their famous spas, the crown jewel of the local economy, the pollution of whose waters Stockmann's cutting-edge research has discovered. Wole Soyinka's surrealistic *A Dance of the Forests* (1960) hijacks a ritual of state (the play was first performed as part of Nigeria's independence celebrations) to create a counter-ritual "gathering of the tribes" in which the corruptions of precolonial Africa's supposed glory days, when wife-stealing potentates were in cahoots with slave-traders, are laid bare and analogized to those of the neocolonial present, when the forest is cut down to produce the self-congratulatory pageant arena and officials are bribed to keep polluting, lethally unsafe vehicles on the road and create hideous accidents.[28] At mid-point, in an anticipation of Leo Marx's machine-in-the-garden *topos* (Marx 1964: 11–16), a deafening, stinking lorry gets driven onstage to the consternation of the forest creatures. The scene eerily foreshasdows the victimization of Nigeria's Ogone peoples by big oil interests publicized by Nigerian writer-activist and eco-martyr Ken Saro-wiwa, who was executed on trumped-up murder charges in 1995.[29]

Environmental criticism has only begun to think about how such texts enact human groundedness in environment. The texts predictably range greatly in tone and focus. On the one hand, the project may be a "comic" dramatization of mind-expanding awareness of the possibilities of life in place, as with the dream that temporarily elevates the humble West Indian charcoal burner Makak into an African prince in Derek Walcott's *Dream on Monkey Mountain* (1967), which also satirizes the Afrocentrism it indulges. On the other hand, ecodrama may tilt toward a dreary fatalism that people would shut out if they could: as with the humble community of Aran Islands fisherfolk depicted in Anglo-Irish playwright J. M. Synge's *Riders to the Sea* (1904), which centers on the anticipated death and stark, numbing funeral of the youngest and dearest drowned son. That this play never takes us outdoors except through the characters' projective imagination and Greek tragedy-style messenger reports signifies much more than a dutiful observance of the traditional unities. In either instance, central to the premise of the text is the performance of a particular kind of eco-cultural commitment.

But to dwell only on plays that directly thematize environmental issues is too confining. Dramatic performance always requires and reproduces physical environments. Not that reading can't. Always the read text is being engaged by at least one solitary mind/body poised somewhere in space; the experience becomes communal via a reading group or formal class; and these reading contexts matter. The ambiance of Andrew Marvell's poem "The Garden" ("Two paradises 'twere in one / To live in paradise alone") will present itself differently to a middle-aged male professor according to whether he engages it in the privacy of his back yard on a delightful summer day or in the give-and-take of an indoor seminar room of undergraduates predictably skeptical about the persona's androcentric prissiness. But in performance, environmentality is underscored and its residual potentialities multiplied. The stark blasted tree in Beckett's *Waiting for Godot* means something different, and equally pointed, when the play is performed in a tight, closed space in postwar Paris, outdoors on a rocky treeless land-scape in Beckett's native Ireland, or again outdoors in a neocolo-nial subsaharan state suffering from desertification.[30] Gogo and Didi's mysterious tie to this non-place, as well as their inability to leave it, takes on more meaning when witnessed in *whatever* kind of environment than on the printed page. To the extent that the prototypical image of the place we live now is increasingly taken to be a degraded landscape rather than a pristine one, *Waiting for Godot's* impoverished environmental scene will only get richer and richer.

To stress drama's portable environmentality might seem to run counter to Leslie Silko's conception of place-and-tradition-based artistry. But presumably she intends her Pueblo example as para-digmatic rather than as uniquely culture-specific, or else it would not amount to anything more than another instance of the single-elk fallacy. Besides, nothing just said is meant to discountenance the environment-effect of original performance conditions, or the attempt to replicate such. No one will read Aeschylus' *Agamemnon* the same way who has seen it performed in the semi-restored ancient amphitheater on the island of Epidaurus, with night falling and the star-winked sea for a distant backdrop. A happenstance gaggle of tourists from 25 countries, none of whom know ancient Greek and most of whom recall the mythic background foggily at best, will of course react differently to a performance of this play in a museumized setting than would an assembly of ancient Athe-nians. But at least such a performance is more likely to stretch them backward toward apprehension of Hellenistic ecoculture more than one I saw a few years later in a small experimental theater with the performers dressed in white tie and tails.

Performances also have a way of producing unplanned but telling environmental effects. The Oregon Shakespeare Festival stages a pas-toral drama on a large tract of land sequestered for the tourist indus-try, contributing to disruption of the local settlement patterns and economy even as the exegetes of Shakespearean drama decry early modern enclosure laws.[31] An open-air performance of *King Lear* is interrupted by the rumblings of a real electric storm – as the temporarily lucid King awakes in Cordelia's arms. *The Importance of Being Earnest* is hastily staged on a terrace near an arbor packed with nasty stinging insects.

From the standpoint of rhetoric, environment figures as a discourse to be measured both against the facts of the case and its own vision of the good. From the standpoint of dramatic performance, it figures as the enactment of human emplacement. But environment can also be figured as that which constitutes the discourse that constitutes it.

The most suggestive attempt of this kind so far, at least for poetry, has been Angus Fletcher's theory of the "environment-poem" (Fletcher 2004: 122–8). "Such a poem," Fletcher explains, "does not merely suggest or indicate an environment as part of its thematic meaning, but actually gets the reader to enter into the poem as if it were the reader's environment of living." This means something more comprehensive than just readerly "identification" with the "world" of the text. The poem is itself to be taken as a world. What's distinctive about the "environment-poetic" is "a special kind of natural ensemble, where drama and story are not the issue, where emotion is subordinate to the presentation of the aggregate relations of all participants." Fletcher posits, over-anxiously perhaps, an anthropocentric imperative ("to render and convince us vividly that any environment exists, the writer must also connect the elements of the scene with humans"), but with two notable stipulations about dramatizing an elastic structure of environmental belonging that decenter human control. First, "the poetry will express the mere existence of those creatures who belong or do not belong"; and second, it "will show how this belonging occurs . . . The least creature among the flora and fauna, 'rolled round in earth's diurnal course / With rocks and stones and trees,' belongs in the manifold and deserves its space, so that the poet's almost unimaginable chorographic persona must be that of a second creator, a demiurge of the scene" (pp. 122, 123, 127–8).[32]

50

I don't know whether Fletcher would be content to see his model extended beyond poetry to include (at least some examples of) other genres, but I think it can be. As formulated, the theory is too restrictive, generated with such touchstones in mind as John Ashbery's wandering associativeness, John Clare's tendency to snaggle his persona in environmental detail, and Walt Whitman's panoramic catalogue rhetoric and attendant collectivization of the persona. Then, too, Fletcher seems to have been overly swayed by Harold Bloom's sturdy bifurcation of English vs. American poetic traditions. Despite the precedence Fletcher accords Clare, Romanticism generally, and neoclassical loco-descriptive poetics as an enabling matrix for the emergence of the environment-poem, he is led to characterize it as a distinctively new world form, arising from Eurocentric settler culture sense of confronting an "empty" landscape.[33] This put the burden on American writers – so goes the now-familiar argument – to create not only art but environment itself, all the more so because of their disposition to define cultural difference in terms of landscape difference. (Fletcher then gives this argument an environmentalist twist by conceiving of imagination situating itself within – rather than bending landscape to – artistic will.) But arguably the same could also be said of many writers, both from the "new" world (Neruda and Walcott, for instance) and the "old" (the Defoe of *Robinson Crusoe*, the Shelley of *Alastor* and *Prometheus Unbound*). Any limitations aside, though, I prefer Fletcher's model to my own more circumscribed definition of "the environmental text" (Buell 1995: 7–8), generated with environmental nonfiction especially in mind. My stipulation that nonhuman environment must be represented as an active presence and player within the text made some astute readers inclined to be sympathetic in principle anxious as to whether it might exclude other genres, especially prose fiction, and thus threaten to paint ecocriticism into a corner by defining its canon too narrowly (see, for example, Head 1998a; Kerridge 2001). Fletcher's environment-poetic recognizes more explicitly how the social landscape figures as part of total landscape.

51

It is especially helpful in guiding us toward and through the kind of text that seems to want to take the environment itself as the text and prefer to have the persona disappear into it as a denizen or actor. Poems like Whitman's "There Was a Child Went Forth" (1855), generically a portrait of the young aesthete, but beyond this and more consequentially a poem about any young child's "ecology of imagination," the widening horizon of environmental belonging ("the first object he look'd upon, that object he became, / And that object became part of him for the day or a certain part of the day, / Or for many years or stretching cycles of years").[34] Or *Canto General* (1950), that testament of land/labor solidarity by Whitman's greatest admirer among the great twentieth-century Latin American poets, Pablo Neruda:

> Here I found love. It was born in the sand,
> it grew without voice, touched the flintstones
> of hardness, and resisted death.
> Here mankind was life that joined
> the intact light, the surviving sea,
> and attacked and sang and fought
> with the same unity of metals.
> Here cemeteries were nothing but
> turned soil, dissolved sticks
> of broken crosses over which
> the sandy winds advanced.[35]

Or such among the distinctive work of Australian poet Les Murray as his seasonal mandala "The Idyll Wheel: Cycle of a Year at Bunyah, New South Wales, April 1986–April 1987," whose stanzas lose themselves in pondering the shared but subtle and elusive resonance of this life-in-place:

> Hobnail and elastic-side, bare and cloven feet:
> you can't know this landscape in shoes, or with ideas
> like relevance. It is a haughty pastoral
> bent fitfully to farming's fourteen-hour days.[36]

The environment-poetic concept starts to become exclusionary when the ecopoem moves either a certain distance in the direction of self-conscious distancing of persona from world or a certain distance toward isolating objectification. The tilt toward symbolic epitome and lyric apostrophe in Oodgeroo Noonuccal's "Municipal Gum" might reasonably exclude it on the former ground. Williams' "Young Sycamore" might be disallowed for the latter. Full of motion as it is, it leans toward becoming a linguistic equivalent of a still life painting, as do many "imagist" poems. Yet it seems harder to deny standing to works like the following from Jorie Graham and Judith Wright, respectively, even though Fletcher might wish to rule them out.

These lines have my breathing in them, yes.
Also my body was here. Why try to disguise it.
In this morning of my year
that will never be given back.
Also those who will not give it back. Whoever they
                              may be.
How quietly they do their job
over this page. How can I know when it's the
case — oh swagger of dwelling in place, in voice —
surely one of us understands the importance.
Understands? Shall I wave a "finished" copy at you
whispering do you wish to come for lunch.
Nor do I want to dwell on this.
I cannot, actually, dwell on this.
There is no home. One can stand out here
and gesture wildly, yes. One can say "finished"
and look *into* the woods, as I do now, here,
but also casting my eye out
to see (although that was yesterday) (in through the alleyways
of trees) the slantings of morning light
(speckling) (golden) laying in
these foliate patternings, this goldfinch . . .
. . .

do not harm him, do not touch him, don't probe
with the ghost your mind this future as it lays itself out
here, right over the day, straight from the font, and yes
I *am* afraid, and yes my fear is
flicking now from limb to limb . . .
. . .
and my mind gathering wildly up to still itself on him.[37]

★

"Sign there." I signed, but still uneasily.
I sold the coachwood forest in my name.
Both had been given me; but all the same,
remember that I signed uneasily.

Ceratopetalum, Scented Satinwood:
a tree attaining seventy feet in height.
Those pale-red calyces like sunset light
burned in my mind. A flesh-pink pliant wood

used in coachbuilding. Difficult of access
(those slopes were steep). But it was World War Two.
Their wood went into bomber-planes. They grew
hundreds of years to meet those hurried axes.

Under our socio-legal dispensation
both name and woodland had been given me.
I was much younger then than any tree
matured for timber. But to help the Nation

I signed the document. The stand was pure
(eight hundred trees perhaps). Uneasily
(the bark smells sweetly when you wound the tree)
I set upon this land my signature.[38]

Meditation on *print* genres (the poem of the woods, the legal
document) and dramatization of the persona's self-conscious anxiety
(Did I get it right?) or remorse (Did I do the right thing?) domi-
nate both poems. But why? In each, delicacies of environmental
conscience and perception are the heart of the matter. The Wright

persona is torn between the claim of national emergency and stewardship to her stand of old-growth trees, torn again by knowing
that the wood "went into bomber-planes." This is not a memory of
a sealed-in-the-past episode but a malaise that has deepened over
time with the conviction that Australian settler-culture's "destruction of the forests . . . has amounted to the biggest environmental
disaster in the history of the occupation of this land without exception" (Wright 1992: 31). The Graham persona is torn between
fragile pride at weaving the woods into her lines and knowing that
neither there nor anywhere is a stable "home" except to obtuse
second parties and her inferior self. Supersensitive alertness to surrounding motion and nuance persists long after the poem is "done,"
in its first articulation. Environmentality worthy of the name means
letting the goldfinch be, not petrifying it into the kind of "golden"
bird the Yeatsian speaker imagines as his immortal body in "Sailing
to Byzantium" – to which these lines elsewhere allude. In both
"Woods" and "A Contract," the impression of persona- and/or doc-
ument-preoccupation is deceptive insofar as each speaker defines
herself in terms of a condition of environmental being to which
she feels herself belong, yet which she also feels as extending beyond
her in ways she can grasp partially at most, yet without which she
feels diminished, frozen, fragmentary: a state of richly suggestive
uneasiness that remains ever active pending the closure that never
comes, so self-exacting is her environmental conscience.

Nor is it poetry alone that should be allowed to count as
environment-poetics, any more than environmental nonfiction
alone. The strategy of converting subjective place-evocation into a
shareable representation of environmentality without bounds is not
the property of any one genre or style. The environmental evocations
in the fiction of Thomas Hardy, Joseph Conrad, Theodore Dreiser,
Virginia Woolf, D. H. Lawrence, John Cowper Powys, Zora Neale
Hurston, Patrick White, J. M. Coetzee, Salman Rushdie (the Sun-
darbans of *Midnight's Children*), Alejo Carpentier, Wilson Harris, and
other modernists and magical realists also qualify as environment-
poetics, according to a generous reading of the category at least.

The *ne plus ultra* of environment-poetics in narrative would seem to be the kind of project that takes on nothing less than the invention of the entire world. Poetry can grasp at this, of course. Milton, Dante, and Whitman are the great premodern examples. Kenneth Koch, a latter-day Whitmanian who made a speciality of teaching children how to write poetry, affirmed in a reading I attended that whenever he sat down to write a poem he felt the urge to name everything in the universe. He got that from Whitman, whose epicenter was Manhattan and Brooklyn but whose ultimate reach was the globe. But the genre that really specializes in world-making is of course utopian narrative, meaning especially for the past half-century what is loosely called science or "speculative" fiction.[39]

Science fiction has taken a long time to win much respect from academic critics, including ecocritics. Many still think of it as pop stuff, not serious stuff. Recently, the situation has started to change, not because literary criticism across the board has become converted to thinking "environment" (*PMLA*'s special spring 2004 issue on science fiction completely neglects its environmental implications) but for a series of other reasons. These include literary studies' increasing interest in popular culture, science fiction's increasingly brainy assimilation of the findings of leading-edge technologies like cybernetics, artificial intelligence, genetics, and body–machine hybridization generally, and – perhaps most decisively – an attendant turn toward experimental narrative modes: its montages with magical realism, the emergence of cyberpunk fiction and film. Meanwhile, with a few notable exceptions (e.g., Elgin 1985; Murphy 2001), ecocriticism has been behind the curve, partly no doubt because of its resistance to nature as artifice. For half a century science fiction has taken a keen, if not consistent interest in ecology, in planetary endangerment, in environmental ethics, in humankind's relation to the nonhuman world.

Indeed, science fiction's claim on environmental criticism is stronger even than that. If the Qur'ānic passage with which we started can be taken as an iconic image of early agro-pastoral piety (the bounty of the fruitful tree emanating from the sacred mountain), the iconic landscape for the era of environmental crisis is the earth as fragile eco-holism, the split image of the green Gaian ball of the 1969 Apollo moonshot, and the *Whole Earth Catalogue* vs. the dystopic image of the ruined, uninhabitable planet, rendered so by human mistreatment (Jasanoff 2004). No genre potentially matches up with a planetary level of thinking "environment" better than science fiction does. Potentially, that is: not always in practice by any means. On the contrary, science fiction's fantasy wonderlands – space travel and star war extravaganzas, melodramas of invaders vs. defenders, post-Frankenstein bionic hybrids – often turn out to be ecology-lite, although the underlying premise of earth rendered destructible by techno-menace is the same age-of-ecological-anxiety premise that drives more sophisticated environmental imaginations today. Even texts with a serious investment in environmental concerns can get seduced by schlock effect. The first of Frank Herbert's *Dune* quartet (1963) is, one face of it anyhow, an intricate investigation of the ecology of a "desert" planet outsiders find uninhabitable but whose despised natives, embroidering upon the template of a "planetary ecologist," are secretly turning into a garden. The book is dedicated to "dry-land ecologists, wherever they may be."[40] This project gets coopted, however, by the novel's intergalactic thriller aspect: rivalries between packs of neo-medieval warriors led by mighty figures backed up by preternatural powers. Amy Thompson's *The Color of Distance* (1997) is a cyberpunk fantasy of a case of successful earthling adaptation to a jungly green planet inhabited by intelligent frog-like beings, starring an ecologist who is stranded on an aborted intergalactic mission. The planet's inhabitants help her develop a protective alienoid body, master their visual "skin-speech," and overcome an array of other culture-barriers large and small, like her aversion to living in trees. But these alien hosts wind up acting too much like familiar human types in amphibian dressups; the strange landscape and tribal arcana threaten to reduce to a checkoff of exotic terms and redundant pseudo-ethnographic trivia, and the plot to an Algeresque success story thanks to motherwit, true grit, and timely help from kind friends.

Yet the failures of these novels are more interesting, ecocritically speaking, than the successes of contemporary art that acts as if no environmental problems existed. For one thing, they show how hard it is to imagine a plausible other or future world. Science fiction continually testifies against itself to how we're probably stuck, whether we like it or not, with the world we've got. So I end this chapter with two further examples that recognize this and take us closer to the high end of what the field has to offer. One is *The Lathe of Heaven* (1971), a somewhat neglected but quite masterful novel by eminent science fiction writer and environmentalist Ursula LeGuin; the other is ethnographer-turned-novelist Karen Tei Yamashita's magical realist *Through the Arc of the Rain Forest* (1990).

The Lathe of Heaven follows traditional science fiction practice in unfolding step-by-step a psychological-realist plot from an "impossible" premise, albeit with some back-and-forthing of time sequence. The protagonist, George Orr, is afflicted by "effective" dreams. If he dreams an event that never happened, it does, and what's more all humanity's sense of history is altered accordingly, so that he alone understands what he's done. He finds the isolation and burden of responsibility unbearable. But the therapist he consults to cure him of this syndrome – arrogant and ambitious, although at heart, the novel stresses, a do-gooder rather than an evildoer – resolves to try to master and control rather than suppress this effective dreaming. At first the doctor manipulates Orr's dreams both for professional self-advancement and to wipe out manifest social evils like racism and pollution. But inevitably he himself succumbs to the Faustian temptation to become the dreamer, fancying that the machine he's been programming with the data from the therapy sessions can do the trick. This almost wrecks the world and reduces Dr. Haber to imbecility. The cataclysmic plot, however, is only a staging-ground for an ecofeminist study of contrasting environmental ethics embodied by contrasting models of maleness, neither of which is altogether demonized or heroized (the aggressive Haber who is principled about changing the world as well as

58

himself for the better vs. the underachieving wimpy sensitive Orr, who is equally convinced that no person has the right to mess with reality), with the balance tilted toward prudence by the creepy Orwellian implication that altering how things are means altering public memory of them too. Beyond this, LeGuin's unfolding of the effective-dream premise makes the novel an elegant reflection on the paradox of eco-apocalyptic discourse. For the environmentalist dreams such dreams precisely in order to render the dream-scenario impotent.

Whereas *The Lathe of Heaven* takes a psychological realist form, *Through the Arc of the Rain Forest* is – or affects to be – a whimsical romp, like a Brazilian soap opera, writes Yamashita in her preface. Its protagonist, Kazumasa, is a Japanese expatriate cyborg yoked since boyhood to a tiny sphere that whirls continuously in front of his forehead, with magnetic powers that can detect metallic substances, powers that make him a living but eventually also a kidnapper's target. The ball itself is the narrator, who (impossibly) continues to function as a "reliable" teller even after it disintegrates: a sendup on the whole idea of narrative voice. But Kazumasa is only one of a cornucopia of characters that include a Brazilian couple who (briefly) make a killing on a startup enterprise in messenger pigeons; a rubber-tapper who invents the ultimate massage therapy, "featherology"; an idealistic ex-pilgrim who becomes a televangelistic faith healer; a three-armed American capitalist; and the three-breasted French ornithologist who (briefly) marries him and bears him triplets. This surprisingly appealing bestiary – appealing because they never quite lose their innocence however venial some of them become – are in the long run, however, little more than shadow puppets in a parodistic boom-and-bust, rape-of-the-Amazon plot, presided over by the three-armed J. B. Tweep's multinational conglomerate. An apocalyptic ending ensues when the huge expanse of the "Matacão" underlying much of the rainforest, a plasticoid substance from which the corporation has extracted a plethora of infinitely profitable commodities, is discovered to be a compacted upwelling of the "landfills of nonbiodegradable material buried under virtually every populated part of the Earth"; and the mega-dump and everything made from it, from fake feathers to skyscrapers, is consumed as frenetically as it was produced by a mysterious bacterium – possibly one of the profuse mutant life-forms that eco-disruption had generated. The revenge of the ecosystem. Amid "the crumbling remains of once modern high-rises and office buildings," "the old forest has returned" – though things obviously "will never be the same again."[41] High-rolling extraction, consumption, and waste; save-the-rainforest sentimentality and global capitalism; local and transnational forms of greed as networked communications systems shrink the world, from paleotechnic pigeons to broadcast media to computerized databanks – all these get crunched together in a lightened-up version of Soyinka's macabre pageant in *A Dance of the Forests*.

Yamashita's eco-apocalypse inverts traditional speculative fiction approaches, which lean toward intense and morally earnest we-must-try-to-save-the-world drama based on techno-gimmickry. For Yamashita, it's also important to laugh at the craziness of so-called civilization because, after all, not that much is likely to be done about it. Both novels, however, offer cautionary metareflections on the potential hubris of science fiction's project of reinventing the world on one's own terms. In this genre, artistic license in principle knows no limit. You are free to invent any world you can imagine. Indeed, *Lathe* and particularly *Rain Forest* indulge this pleasure more extravagantly than Thoreau's "divine artist" in the passage discussed above. But both novelists also make the shadow of the actual haunt the reinvention, as a brake on imagined liberties taken, indeed even as a conscience. In *Lathe*, remaking the world is seen as pathological, in *Rain Forest* as futile. It is this rather than their extravagance of reinvention as such, that makes such novels count as serious works of environmental representation, as ultimate extensions of environment-poetics.

A further difference between them is the comparatively place-bound nature of *Lathe of Heaven*, which largely concentrates on happenings in and around Portland, Oregon, as against *Rain Forest's* far more mobile, quick-cut, transcontinental peripatetics. The implications of this kind of contrast between traditional place-centeredness and postmodern displacement, however, require a chapter of their own.

3

Space, Place, and Imagination from Local to Global

Environmental criticism arises within and against the history of human modification of planetary space, which started in remote antiquity but has greatly accelerated since the industrial revolution, when "environment" first came into use as an English noun.[1] That coinage is one among many markers of the erosive effect of the pace of transformation upon the stability of locale and the assumption of belonging to it. The sense of being environed or emplaced begins to yield to a more self-consciously dialectical relation between being and habitat, such that environment presents itself somewhat paradoxically as a more reified and detached surround, which nurtures or binds as the case may be, even as it becomes less stable. This chapter examines how environmental imagination registers, judges, and seeks to affect this process whereby the significance of environmentality is defined by the self-conscious sense of an inevitable but uncertain and shifting relation between being and physical context. I do so by focusing on the concept of place.

Place is an indispensable concept for environmental humanists not so much because they have precisely defined and stabilized it as because they have not; not because of what the concept lays to rest as because of what it opens up. It is a term of value that even advocates perceive stands in need of redefinition as well as advocacy. One cannot theorize scrupulously about place without confronting its fragility, including the question of whether "place" as traditionally understood means anything anymore at a time when fewer and fewer of the world's population live out their lives in locations that are not shaped to a great extent by translocal – ultimately global – forces. That the concept of place also gestures in at least three directions at once – toward environmental materiality, toward social perception or construction, and toward individual affect or bond – makes it an additionally rich and tangled arena for environmental criticism.

Spaces, Places, and Non-Places

The logical place to start is the distinction between "space" and "place" as geographical concepts. These are not simple antonyms. Place entails spatial location, entails a spatial container of some sort. But space as against place connotes geometrical or topographical abstraction, whereas place is "space to which meaning has been ascribed" (Carter, Donald, and Squires 1993: xii). Places are "centers of felt value" (Tuan 1977: 4), "discrete if 'elastic' areas in which settings for the constitution of social relations are located and with which people can identify" (Agnew 1993: 263). Each place is also "inseparable from the concrete region in which it is found" (Casey 1996: 31) and defined by physical markers as well as social consensus. So we speak of place-attachment rather than of space-attachment. We dream of a "place" rather than a "space" for me or for us, although by the same token we may crave "space" or elbow room for meditation or leisure to fill. "A place is seen, heard, smelled, imagined, loved, hated, feared, revered" (Walter 1988: 142). Those who feel a stake in their community think of it as their place. My residence is "my place" rather than "my space," unlike how an unfamiliar hotel room would feel. Place is associatively thick, space thin, except for sublime "spaces" set apart as "sacred" and therefore both infinitely resonant and at one remove from the quotidian idiosyncratic intimacies that go with "place."

Up to a point, world history is a history of space becoming place. In the beginning, earth was space without form. Then through inhabitance places were created. But modern history has also reversed this process. Whereas of "early human societies" it might be said that "place and society are fused as a unity," with the advent of societies based on economic exchange "the conceptual fusion of space and society is broken" (Smith 1984: 78), making it difficult, if not impossible, for traditional forms of emplacement. In American history the most striking example is the survey ordained by Thomas Jefferson that carved the new nation's vast hinterland into a rectilinear grid for settlement purposes, within and against whose constraints settlers then struggled – and still do – to convert "democratic social space" (Fisher 1988) from real estate into live-able places (Meine 1997).[2] The Native Americans who dwelt there meanwhile lost both space and place, until remanded to federally defined spaces ("reservations") more like internment camps than decent substitutes for the pre-settlement home place or range.[3]

American settler-culture conquest is one of many episodes of the worldwide "production" of "abstract space" during the past several centuries for which aggressive industrial capitalism bears primary responsibility (see Lefebvre 1991: esp. 48–53), but which was under-written by modern socialist regimes as well.[4] As geographer David Harvey puts it, "the world's spaces were deterritorialized, stripped of their preceding significations, and then reterritorialized accord-ing to the convenience of colonial and imperial administration."[5] This process has proliferated the number and forms of displacement. More and more of the world's population strive to take their places with them as they migrate abroad entrepreneurially or languish as involuntary exiles for the right of return. Story and song are often vital to the retention of place-sense under such conditions (Bowman 1993; Bhabha 1994: 139, 155–7). Meanwhile, even the most priv-ileged of earth's first world denizens regularly incur displacement as a tradeoff for upscale relocation from bustling "neighborhoods" to suburban developments of commodious but identically built-and-landscaped tract houses inhabited by strangers.

One effect of these shifts is to reinforce the idea that modern-ization has rendered place-attachment nugatory and obsolete, as the philosophers who helped usher in the scientific and thence the technological revolutions had begun to claim several centuries before. By the end of the seventeenth century, "place" had been reduced at least in theory to "position, or bare point" on "one of the XYZ axes that delineate the dimensionality of space as construed in Cartesian analytical geometry" (Casey 1997: 199).

For contemporary environmental criticism, by contrast, place often seems to offer the promise of a "politics of resistance" against modernism's excesses – its "spatial colonizations" (Oakes 1997: 509). Up to a point it is surprisingly easy to invert the space–place hierarchy and make the case for place as rightfully the primary term, and not just for aborigines or bourgeois sentimentalists. Such assertions as place is "that within and with respect to which subjectivity is itself established," or "places are part of the source of our rational capacities from the very beginning" (Malpas 1999: 35; Preston 2003: 116), carry a self-evident force. Whatever one thinks of the total Martin Heidegger or the total Maurice Merleau-Ponty, it is hard to quarrel with the propositions that being means being-there, or that "to be a body, is to be tied to a certain world" (Merleau-Ponty 2002: 169). "The Kantian subject posits a world," but self-evidently "in order to be able to assert a truth, the actual subject must in the first place have a world or be in the world" (p. 149). Postmodern theory's break from phenomenology's concentration on the subjective experience of the paradigmatic individual has made it still more axiomatic to think of all "knowledge" as "situated." Hence Edward Casey, the leading American phenomenologist of place, claims a revival of place theory in the late twentieth century (Casey 1997: 285–330). Not that he convinces us to think that place and place-attachment in the traditional sense will be reauthorized in the foreseeable future. Most contemporary discussions of situatedness, as Casey realizes, focus on social contextualization; and many of those for whom physical embeddedness is a central issue concern themselves more with "bodies-*as*-places" (see Casey 1997: 323 on Luce Irigiray) than with emplacement within

65

physical environments. Besides, fashionable claims of situatedness are nearly as much disclaimers as assertions.[6]

But even to those for whom *environmental* situatedness is a primary concern, such disclaimers may have their value. As ecofeminist philosopher Val Plumwood cautions, "place sensitivity requires both emotional and critical approaches to place" (Plumwood 2002: 233). Let's start by being critical, then. Those who speak on behalf of place-attachment need to face certain intractable ambiguities inherent in the concept of place.

One is the fraught relation between environment and emplacement. Devotees of place-attachment can easily fall into a sentimental environmental determinism. Obviously "the trick is to achieve the reintroduction of the environmental part while avoiding the determinism part" (Preston 2003: 106), but that's no easy matter. Still more slippery is the question of anthropogenic construction. Place-attachment implies *adaptation*, yet insofar as place presumes inhabitance, "transformation of the physical world is inseparable from [its] becoming" (Pred 1984: 287). Heidegger stresses that "building" worthy of the name demands that "we are capable of dwelling," which in turn presupposes situating oneself responsively within one's environment; but this kind of formulation tends to mystify the fact that dwelling even in his adaptational sense also presupposes building (Heidegger 1975: 148–61).[7] They are "equiprimordial," to use another Heideggerism. So "the circuit and loops of place tie nature and culture together" (Sack 1997: 125).

Not attending to this reciprocity of nature and culture, one misconstrues one's place in space and how it came to be. Heidegger knows that his paradigmatic Black Forest farm was built by peasants two centuries ago; but he is moved to write as if it were the mystical upshot of natural process: "the power to let earth and heaven, divinities and mortals enter *in simple oneness* into things" (Heidegger 1975: 160). The "trouble with wilderness" diagnosed by environmental historian William Cronon is an aporia of like kind for American and other Euro-settler cultures: insouciance to the prehistory of humans "manipulating the natural world on various

scales for as long as we have a record of their passing." What the
first European settlers of North America saw as primordial or
"empty" space, and what their descendants persist in thinking of as
"wilderness," had been somebody's else's place since the first humans
arrived millennia before – and much longer than that, if we allow
nonhumans to count as "somebodies." On the other hand, as
Cronon rightly but tardily adds, to know all this does not make it
any less "crucial for us to recognize and honor nonhuman nature
as a world we did not create, a world with its own independent,
nonhuman reasons for being as it is" (Cronon 1995a: 83, 87). One
can even speak plausibly of finding a place or "home" in "wilderness" – as a therapeutic refuge, for example – provided that one
recognizes "wilderness" to be a relative rather than an absolute term,
as for example Sally Carrighar and Douglas Peacock both do in
their remarkable environmental autobiographies of recovering
from trauma-induced social dysfunction through contact with wild
animals.[8]

In classic US environmental writing, Thoreau's *Walden* both
points the way and shows the characteristic problem of imagining
a life closer to "nature" without falling into doublethink. Again and
again *Walden* yields to the temptation of fancying that the periphery of the town of Concord is tantamount to primordial wilderness, although in the long run the book hews to its core concern
of envisioning reorientation of the spirit as a turning toward the
largely unnoticed wild spots within and at the edges of the home
place. Somewhat analogously, the emergence of contemporary environmental criticism is in part the story of an evolution from imaging
life-in-place as deference to the claims of (natural) environment
toward an understanding of place-making as a culturally inflected
process in which nature and culture must be seen as a mutuality
rather than as separable domains.

The second area of ambiguity I have in mind is the nested quality
of place – the disparate modes of attachment that the term implies.
What counts as a place can be as small as a corner of your kitchen
or as big as the planet, now that we have the capacity to image

earth holistically and modernization has shrunk the planet to the point that it is starting to seem possible to think of "global culture" or "global citizenship." Ecocriticism, however, has tended to favor literary texts oriented toward comparatively local or regional levels of place-attachment. This has so far held as true for its second wave as for its first. Despite environmental justice criticism's grasp of place as more a human than a natural construct and its greater attention to the production of localities by institutionalized macrosocial forces, it has taken a special interest in narratives of representative endangered communities.

Up to a point this centripetal bias is understandable. Compelling narratives of life in place are plentiful and easy to identify with. Earth's woes need instantiation, need highly publicized cases like Bhopal and Love Canal in order to be "driven home" and made mentally manageable. Place-attachment tends to thin out as the territory expands. "Just as the pretense to 'love for humanity' arouses our suspicion," cautions cultural geographer Yi-Fu Tuan, "so topophilia rings false when it is claimed for a large territory. A compact size scaled down to man's . . . sense-bound capacities seems necessary" (Tuan 1990: 101). Moreover, planetary welfare depends upon concern being effectively manifested at every point, not just toward parks or "biosphere reserves" or other large set-asides for conservation places. If every place on earth were cared for as we like to think a "protected" reserve is cared for, then perhaps the health of planet and people might be secured. But taking a good thing too far (place-attachment and stewardship at the local level) manifestly can produce bad results too: maladaptive sedentariness, inordinate hankering to recover the world we have lost, xenophobic stigmatization of outsiders and wanderers.

Besides, does environmental citizenship *really* hinge on staying put? Henry Thoreau and Wendell Berry have clearly thought so, as do environmental critics who stress the virtues of "reinhabitation" (see Snyder 1995: 183–91; Thomashow 1999: 125–30), a commitment by settler-culture to long-term place-based stewardship, conceived as a latter-day equivalent of first people's interdependence with the lands (hence the "re"), a commitment that would atone for prior abuse of indigenes and of land. But writers like Barry Lopez, no less conscienceful or less critical of settler-culture's track record in wasting local environments, have done their best work as roaming ethnographers, gleaning insights more from interdisciplinary study and place-based informants (both native peoples and field scientists in Lopez's case) than from staying put. The fragility of small-island ecology observed in individual early modern settler enclaves in the Atlantic and Indian oceans (Grove 1995: 16–72) needed also to be studied comparatively in order to give rise to the first theories of global environmental endangerment. Bill McKibben must sortie around the globe in order to tell the full story of the threat global warming is likely to pose for coastal and island nations. There is no single answer to the question of whether the more responsible position, if you want to be an environmental writer or critic or activist, is to find a place to which you're willing to commit yourself or to forage around through libraries, labs, and continents with your antennae alert. Even "the goal of place-conscious and place-sensitive culture need not dictate a place-bound, stationary lifestyle of monogamous relationship to just one place" (Plumwood 2002: 233).

Environmental criticism must also confront the proposition that "non-places are the real measure of our time," as anthropological theorist Marc Augé has claimed. In the world of "supermodernity" that "we" (Westerners of privilege) inhabit now, people are born and die in clinical settings, and in between spend much of their time shuttling about through offices, malls, clubs, and transport designed as neutrally benign and predictably interchangeable spaces (Augé 1995: 78–9).[9] And what's more we like it that way. What most fascinates Augé about "the experience of non-place is its power of attraction, inversely proportional . . . to the gravitational pull of place and tradition" (p. 118). His inquiry begins and ends with an urbanely charming anecdote of a hypothetical international business traveler whose sense of comfort and well-being depends upon the efficient timely negotiation of airport and airplane non-places.

It is tempting to write off Augé's self-insulated executive as a different species of being from the writer and reader of books like this one. But the difference is only one of degree. We may think high-mindedly that we disdain non-places while depending on them daily. When writing this chapter, it irritated me no end to be sidetracked for a whole day spent in non-places, owing to the absurd mischance of a lost automobile license plate. Futile retracing of the early morning route I took driving to a suburban medical clinic (itself a non-place), a long wait at the Registry of Motor Vehicles in a shopping mall of another suburb, the cordially antiseptic chambers of my insurance company in a second mall in still another suburb, the mandatory state inspection of my re-registered vehicle in an auto repair shop in still another town, an encounter with the "parking office" at my workplace that monitors employee's vehicles by plate number – that was my wasted day. But what about the place away from which I was unwillingly taken? True, I had been working in the intimate setting of my home, the window in front of my computer screen overlooking a pleasant expanse of wetlands and beyond that conservancy tracts stretching as far as the eye can see. But my cozy sense of emplacement at home and within "nature" hinges on the produced effects of landscape architecture and public conservation measures (local land trusts, the Massachusetts Wetlands Preservation Act, etc.). Furthermore, when I concentrate on writing, all that disappears. I exist for all practical purposes only in the abstract space of ideas and books, my body immobile except for the flicker of fingers at the keyboard.

Of course the further point of this trivial confession is to ironize the dehydration of the non-place. So too with Augé's anecdote. He is perfectly aware of the insouciant narcissism of those "living only indoors, immersed only in passing time and not out in the weather . . . indifferent to the climate, except during their vacations when they rediscover the world in a clumsy, arcadian way [and] naively pollute what they don't know," as Michel Serres sardonically comments (Serres 1995: 28). But the fact that Augé refrains from delivering a testy screed against simulacra makes his study all the more effective in questioning the wholeheartedness of environmental criticism's tendency to privilege experiences of platial thickness. How much does one really desire it, anyway? Perhaps his demonstration goes to show that placelessness is not merely conditioned but also inherent, that as Neil Evernden argues, what distinguishes *homo sapiens* from other species is that we are "natural aliens," creatures without fixed habitat who can locate ourselves pretty much anywhere (Evernden 1985: 103–24).

Or supposing that emplacement *is* at least a residual value even for nomads, must we not welcome tradeoffs between attenuation of place and place-stewardship on a scale as a big as a planet? Can a person committed to life-in-place as value practice environmental criticism without spending long periods of time in offices and in transit? When a person feels out of place, as travelers often do, the next best thing can be a predictably safe space where you feel buffered against the weirding-out effect of a strange locale. Better to travel the world via a succession of non-places than to risk being stranded, robbed, etc. By the same token, however, Augé's non-place theory can be made to testify to the continuing desire *for* place despite appearances to the contrary. To some extent, the attraction of the non-place testifies to felt problems of place-deprivation, to the non-place as a fallback rather than the first priority. There are other forms of being in the world more richly satisfying to me than writing this paragraph, without which it could not have been written. Doubtless some such explanation helps account for why *Walden* scarcely alludes to the large amount of time the author devoted to writing during his 26 months in the woods. But to press the question of how much place *really* matters requires specifying more carefully just what it means to begin with. This in turn requires thinking more rigorously about place as physical environment – whether mainly "built" or "natural" – constituted simultaneously by subjective perception and by institutionalized social arrangements.

Place-Attachment as Phenomenology vs. as Sociology

Several years ago I developed a five-dimensional phenomenology of subjective place-attachment that still makes sense to me (Buell 2001: 64–78). A barebones recapitulation should suffice here.

Place consciousness and bonding involve not just orientation in space but temporal orientation also. At the spatial level, at least three kinds of mental mapping are involved. The most traditional and still prevalent might be imaged as concentric circles of diminishingly strong emotional identification (and increasing anxiety and fear of the unknown) fanning out from the home base or home range close to which most of one's life is led. Traditionally, one's workplace was close to one's home, if not the very same place, as for small farmers and shopkeepers. Travel over long distances was rare; peripatetic peddlers and traders made up a small fraction of humanity, and their arrival in a village was an event. Many of earth's inhabitants still live that way.[10] Most well-traveled cosmopolitans have had neighbors or schoolmates who still do.

Under modernization, however, place-attachment spreads out to look more like an archipelago than concentric circles. The workplace is increasingly outside the home, in extreme cases a country or even a hemisphere away, requiring breadwinners to live apart from their families for long periods. Other dispersed islands proliferate, such as the childhood home one no longer lives near, the homes of relatives or friends one often visits, or – for the affluent – the second home or other getaway place(s) to which they return season after season. Even a relative homebody like myself can count a handful of such dispersed places. Although multiplication and dispersal may lessen attachment to any one, there is no iron rule. Concerned citizens in their home places may prove even more so in second-home communities they care about.

Meanwhile, one also becomes attached to places by the power of imaging alone – a power as ancient as folk stories told at bedtime and the bardic performances that produced the tales synthesized by

72

Homeric epic and *Beowulf*, but greatly augmented by what has been called the "third nature" of media-produced virtual realities (Wark 1994). The places that haunt one's dreams and to some extent define one's character can range from versions of actual places to the utterly fictitious – Alaska's wild north slope, Robin Crusoe's "desert island," the "little house on the prairie" of Laura Ingalls Wilder's children's books, the promised land of the ancient Israelites imagined from Egyptian or Babylonian captivity, the Hopi *Túwanasavi* or origin-place to which the people are called to return. But the fact that the imaginer hasn't been there and maybe never will hardly lessens the intensity of such storied or imaged places to induce longing and loyalty, and in some cases even to influence national behavior and the course of world affairs. It's entirely possible to care more about places you've never been – the Africa or Israel/Palestine of your imagination – than the ones you know first hand.

Place-attachment has temporal dimensions as well. On the one hand, it reflects the accrued platial experiences of a lifetime. My memory of the place where I grew up has affected my response to all the places where I've lived since, and so too I find for those who led a more wandering existence when young. "To have a sense of one's own past," philosopher J. E. Malpas points out, means having "a grasp of one's own present and future in relation to the 'story' of one's embodied activity within particular spaces and with respect to particular objects and persons" (Malpas 1999: 180). Whether and in what sense I experience a particular location as a "place" will be further affected by such factors as how rooted or peripatetic my previous life has been, what kinds of surrounding I am conditioned to feel as familiar or strange, and so forth. So place-sense is a kind of palimpsest of serial place-experiences.

Conversely, place itself changes. It "is not entitative – as a foundation has to be – but eventmental, something in process" (Casey 1997: 337). My boyhood place has been dramatically transformed by suburban sprawl. Yours may no longer exist. Innumerable communities throughout the world that felt or feel like places to many people have been destroyed or created in far less time than my sixty-plus years of existence. By the same token, imagining a place with any fulness requires at least a glimpse of its whole history, such as those afforded by British novelist Graham Swift, New Zealand ecologist Geoff Park, and American environmental writer John Mitchell, who trace, respectively, the making and remaking of the East Anglian fens, the devastation of New Zealand's natural landscape since colonization, and the district of the northeastern US town where the author lives, back through its many generations of inhabitance to its prehuman geologic past.[11]

These five spatiotemporal coordinates permit a critical grasp of place as subjective horizon: its significance for lived experience, and for artistic renditions of such. But since subjects are never completely free agents with unlimited options, place must also be thought of more extrinsically, as an artifact socially produced by the channeling effects of social position as well as by canonical mappings of space.

A short narrative essay by popular southwestern American writer-environmentalist Barbara Kingsolver affords a handy illustration of these two kinds of place-mapping. "The Memory Place" recalls a day spent with her small daughter in a part of Appalachia not far from where she herself grew up. Delighted by the little girl's "This reminds me of the place I always like to think about" ("Me too, I tell her"), the writer reminisces about her own childhood "roaming wooded hollows like these," relishing the contrast between this "scaled down, small and humane" landscape, better "sized for child adventures," vs. "the windswept sandstone canyons I've come to know in the West." As they forage around the local town and the pretty little river that flows through it, the author conveys a sense of local friendliness, worth, and value, but also mounting anxiety about the future of Horse Lick Creek and its endangered species of freshwater mussels, which are partly protected but still vulnerable to strip-mining effects as well as thoughtless misuse by off-road vehicles and the like. "Who will love the *imperfect* lands, the fragments of backyard desert paradise, the creek that runs between farms?" she asks rhetorically at the end (presumably hoping that her readers inwardly respond "We will!"), resolved for her own part to hold "constant vigil over my daughter's memory place."[12]

All five dimensions of place-attachment figure here: small-town Kentucky as original home base, beyond which is invoked an archipelago of other place-attachments including her adopted home, which she describes (somewhat evasively, as we shall see) as "the desert boundary lands of southern Arizona" (p. 180). The author's sense of Kentucky placeness is inflected both by idiosyncratic accumulation of place-experiences and awareness of local changes during the past century. In both respects, place feels more like a verb than a noun. As for virtual imaging, presumably the daughter's memory place epiphany was pre-prepared by maternal storypower. The story counts on its readers to be similarly prepared.

"The Memory Place" depends, then, not merely on a unique performance of place-attachment, but also on appeal to paradigmatic experiences: to the ecology of childhood attachment to special places, which seems especially luminous when they are protected and "natural" (Cobb 1977; Nabhan 1994; Chawla 1994: 21–50); to the "escalator-effect" of pastoral nostalgia that Raymond Williams traces in English back to Anglo-Saxon times, each generation recalling the last as having lived in closer intimacy with our natural surroundings (Williams 1973: 9–12); to the "motherhood environmentalism" that runs strong in ecofeminist environmental ethics of earth care (Sandilands 1999: xiii). From this standpoint, place-attachment in "The Memory Place" starts to look less like a personal than a socially produced imprint. Its backstory of migration from Kentucky to Arizona, from Appalachian rural backwater to Tucson's booming sunbelt metropolis, confirmed by Kingsolver's other writing and *obiter dicta*, was a predictable repositioning, enabled by class advantage. As the child of a locally rooted but well-traveled professional family, a doctor's daughter both of whose siblings became college professors, the author wasn't destined to live out her adult life in a hometown without a bookstore that was also, so she says, "the last place in the country to get the dial system." Staying put would have meant becoming "a farmer or a farmer's

75

wife" at a point in history when farmers were shrinking into a negligible percentage of the national workforce, with growers of tobacco (the local staple) particularly on the defensive. Transplantation from a small town in a state whose economy and rural population were in long decline to an academic center within a burgeoning region made good socioeconomic sense. Those girlhood rambles in rural Kentucky are a precious memory to pass on to her daughter, but permanent return would spell incarceration for them both.[13] It makes no difference that Horse Lick Creek isn't where she actually grew up, that the daughter's memory place had no direct connection with the author's own early childhood environment. For her purposes, the small towns and valleys of eastern Kentucky boil down to the same ecocultural icon.

Seen thus, in terms of its social positioning, the "place" of "The Memory Place" starts to slide back over toward the opposite pole of the place/space continuum. This is not to denigrate Kingsolver's performance as bad faith or self-deception. True, it sentimentalizes by opting for a selective and stereotyped portrayal of the experience of return.[14] But the intermixture of lyricality and typicality works more to its advantage than not in dramatizing its environmentalist point: "Saving this little slice of life on earth – like most – will take not just legislation, but change at the level of the pickup truck" (p. 174). To that end, it can't just be "my" memory place, but also "ours"; shareable: an alchemical transformation of spaces all over the map into places of lived experience worthy of care.

Border and Scale: From Local Culture to Global Imagination

Where environmental writing and criticism intervenes most powerfully within and against standard conceptions of spatial apportionment is by challenging assumptions about border and scale. Three especially important projects have been the reimagination of localized places (as in "The Memory Place"), the reconception of place at the "bioregional" level in critique of provincial and nation-state borders, and experiments in imagining planetary belonging. Up to a point these projects look synchronous, but they can also be at odds with one another and with themselves. Local attachment, for instance, can express itself either as a vision of ties to a particular bounded spot, or of how a metropolitan district can be shaped and reshaped by global demographic and capital flows and still maintain a distinct, albeit malleable, sense of place (Massey 1994: 146–56).

Traditional writing about place tends to interest itself especially in bounded areas of small size. The prevailing tone may be affirming, as in the high-water mark of the American "local color" movement, Sarah Orne Jewett's *The Country of the Pointed Firs* (1896), delicate sketches of a small seacoast town in southern Maine. Or it may be of the provincial gothic sort, as in Barbara Baynton's *Bush Studies* (1902), which satirizes the barbaric harshness of frontier homesteading in New South Wales, particularly for women. In each, the locale is treated as pretty much frozen in time, with allusions to past and future dispensations minimized, though the reader is also given to understand, through such devices as Jewett's ecotouristical narrator, that the "isolated" place sits just beyond the edge of a more cosmopolitan world and is more permeable than it looks.[15] Kingsolver's "The Memory Place" is to that extent a quite traditional portrait of localism, presuming that Horse Lick Creek is likely, for better or for worse, to remain basically what its residents wish it to be, notwithstanding the flow of visitors and the interventions of such translocal agencies as the Nature Conservancy and the National Forest Service.

Contemporary eco-localism is much more likely to be concerned about countering threats to the bounded holistic community from the outside. "We have become a nation of urban nomads," warns Kentucky farmer-poet Wendell Berry, in a typical jeremiad calling for a new "regionalism," meaning "local life aware of itself," that would entail long-term commitment to one's community. For "without a complex knowledge of one's place, and without the faithfulness to one's place on which such knowledge depends, it is inevitable that the place will be used carelessly, and eventually destroyed" (Berry 1972: 67–9). As things stand, "the people of rural America . . . are living in a colony," sucked dry by a national economy dominated by deracinated metropolitan interests that destroys "local self-sufficiency not only in the local economy but also in the local culture" (Berry 1987: 185–6).

Here, as always, Berry writes as if restoration of the old Jeffersonian dream of a nation of self-sufficient small communities might still be achieved even at this eleventh hour. Others are (even) less sure, especially when the issue is systemic environmental injustice of the rich and well-connected against the poor in marginal communities. Such is Lois Gibbs' brief against the Hooker Chemical Company and other powers that be in *Love Canal, My Story*.[16] Even more so the documentary narrative by the Japanese Rachel Carson, Michiko Ishimure, who exposes the scandal of the Chisso Corporation's long attempts to evade responsibility for the diseases, deformities, and birth defects of local fisherfolk and other workers suffering from what came to be called Minamata Disease, caused by mercury pollution from the chemical plant's wastewater. "Even more than the obvious results of a ruthless modernization and industrialization program," she writes, "what we witness now in Minamata, Niigata and other remote rural areas are manifestations of a deeply rooted contempt for the lower strata of Japanese society and the village communities where they lived."[17] The redress proffered thus far seems culpably belated, condescending, and stingy.

The worst-case scenario comes when the afflicted community is not only impoverished and "backward," but also a despised minority group at the mercy of corrupt officials. That is the scenario of Bengali writer–activist Mahasweta Devi's novella "Pterodactyl, Puran Sahay, and Pirtha." Pirtha, a village of "tribals" or indigenes, is threatened with destruction when graft-deprived underlings of an honest government supervisor who tried to stop their profiteering in fertilizers and insecticides sprayed the residents' fields during the dry season so when the rains came their wells were poisoned. The villagers are inherently capable of self-sufficiency even under drought conditions. But they may not survive the combination of outsider malice and their own cultural maladaptiveness, which prompts them superstitiously to blame themselves and resignedly await extinction. Their case is made convoluted to the point of impenetrability by filtration through the consciousness of another outsider, an investigative journalist who is himself a distracted and wounded being, as he struggles to sort through the disparate and elliptical testimony of interlocutors from competing interest groups and the basics of the tribal belief system, and his moving but mystifying contacts with the tribals themselves. But the author insists, understandably, that her tale is representative. If US readers only take notice of what their nation has done to Native Americans they can "understand what has been done to the Indian tribals. Everywhere it is the same story."[18]

In Berry, Ishimure, and Devi, the place under siege is a small, bounded, traditionally holistic community. Other writers apply similar diagnostics to larger scales. In Carl Hiassen's *noir* novels about the rape of nature in the state of Florida, it's a province. Teetering between exposé and escapade, Hiassen satirizes greedy entrepreneurs, corrupt politicians, and imbecile consumeristic tourists, against whom are pitted sympathetic characters driven by environmentalist passions almost as grotesque as those of his villains. A trust-fund millionaire takes bizarrely elaborate revenges on highway litterbugs; a pistol-packing grandmother hires hit men to kidnap from a crooked imitation Disneyland a pair of "endangered" "voles" (which turn out to be rats with tongues dyed to look like a non-existent species faked by the vendor); and an ex-reform governor resigns, takes to the swamps, and turns wild man in order to become a guerilla eco-warrior when developers and legislature collude to frustrate his green agenda.[19]

In Irish playwright Brian Friel's *Translations*, the scale is a whole country, though symbolized by a single parish in the throes of the ordnance survey of 1833 conducted by the British military after annexation. "An English grid is remorselessly imposed on all Irish complexities" as Gaelic place-names are converted by fiat into English "equivalents." The untranslatableness of native toponymy, whose meaning is as deeply encrypted as the stories that go with the indigenous place names laboriously collected by anthropologist Keith Basso from his western Apache informants, is a barometer of the mutual noncommunication leading to the tragic denouement. Indeed, the locals are alienated from their own past: the semi-deracinated native translator is often stumped; his brother and his father, the master of the local hedge school, have a pedantic obsession with the classics; the female lead wants to learn English.[20]

In West Indian poet-playwright Derek Walcott's "The Star-Apple Kingdom," the scale is a multinational congeries of states reduced to a "chain store of islands" by the collusion of neocolonial politicians and transnational entrepreneurs:[21]

> One morning the Caribbean was cut up
> by seven prime ministers who bought the sea in bolts –
> one thousand miles of aquamarine with lace trimmings,
> one million yards of lime-colored silk,
> one mile of violet, leagues of cerulean satin –
> who sold it at a markup to the conglomerates,
> the same conglomerates who had rented the water spouts
> for ninety-nine years in exchange for fifty ships,
> who retailed it in turn to the ministers
> with only one bank account, who then resold it
> in ads for the Caribbean Economic Community,
> till everyone owned a little piece of the sea,
> from which some made saris, some made bandannas;
> the rest was offered on trays to white cruise ships
> taller than the post office . . .

The poem concentrates specifically on Jamaica under the premiership of Michael Manley (1972–80), but its reach is the whole Antillean transnation, to whose "common geological source in the Caribbean seabed" the poem appeals over and against the demeaning version of regional identity in self-prostituting tourist brochures that figure the Caribbean as "a blue pool" where "inflated rubber islands bob" and pictures with "drinks with umbrellas" offer "the same images of service that cannot distinguish one island from the other." Walcott could – and has – made the same point by focusing more intently on one very small patch of ground, as Jamaica Kincaid does when deploring the fact that one can't get the remotest sense of the natural history of Antigua from its gardens, where there isn't a single native tree. All are colonial imports, and everywhere else in the postcolonized world it is the same story.[22]

As Friel and Walcott expand the scale at which modernization rearranges place into commodified "abstract" space (Lefebvre 1991: 48–50), Berry's metaphor of traditional-small-community-as-colony becomes more toothsome and the potential convergence of environmental and postcolonial critique more evident.[23] It becomes even closer in those portions of Berry's writing that acknowledge the sins of the regional past: land abuse and chattel slavery. But for Berry the sense of history usually folds more comfortably back on itself into a monocultural vision of generational continuity of tribe and clan: agrarian, Christian, patriarchal. Whereas for Friel and especially for Walcott the home culture has never *not* been fragmented. "This gathering of broken pieces," Walcott writes in his Nobel Prize acceptance speech, "is the care and pain of the Antilles, and if the pieces are disparate, ill-fitting," that is a virtue; for "they contain more pain than their original sculpture, those icons and sacred vessels taken for granted in their ancestral places."[24]

The new environmental writing and criticism is also always in some sense a post-nationalist persuasion. In this it builds from such precursive work as Leo Marx and Raymond Williams' skeptical unpacking of the consensus myths of nationness in American and British history that appeal to defining iconic images of national territory. Skepticism toward mythographies of national landscape has been intensified both by mounting critique of the perceived ethnocentricity of all such myths and by the increasing awareness that the environmental problems the world now faces "are quite unaware of national and cultural boundaries" (Claviez 1999: 377). National borders by no means regularly correspond with "natural" borders or physiographic units. For the ancient island nation of Iceland, yes. For the demarcation line between the United States and Canada across the Great Plains and Rocky Mountains, no.

Questioning the incongruity between environmental materiality and the imagined territories of cultural nationalism will not spell the end of nation-focused studies, nor should it. The nation form is not going to wither away anytime soon, nor should it until a solider system of world governance is in place. And any imaginable system of the sort would depend greatly on an infrastructure of national units and regional clusters. Nation-scale environmental criticism also continues to make sense insofar as national polities alter the shapes of national landscapes. Over time, ecologically factitious jurisdictional borders may come to look more distinct. Profound differences in industrial regulation as well as wealth distribution make the topographical contrast at the border between the US and Mexico look more distinct today than a century ago, at the time of the first successful airplane flight. Hence the importance, now and in the foreseeable future, of such environmentally oriented studies of national prefigurations of space as Tim Flannery's *The Future Eaters* (species extinction, land abuse, and aboriginal dispossession in Australia) and Jane Holt Kay's *Asphalt Nation* (US spatial reorganization and environmental deterioration wrought by the automotive age). By the same token, it also falls to environmental criticism to expose the ethnocentrism of territory-based myths of "homeland" insofar as they presume "a nationalist vision of the globe and of interstate relations, in which specific communities 'belong' to particular territories and states by a sort of natural right" (Williams and Smith 1983: 509).

Environmental writing and criticism offer the promise of correcting against this by refocusing attention on place at the level of either the region or the transnation. The first commitment is long-standing. For more than two centuries, Anglophone environmental writing has been distinguished by its regional allegiances.

Wordsworth may have become his nation's Poet Laureate, but he was especially a poet of the Lake District. Dickens' environmental imagination operated more at the level of urban and particularly London life than of the nation. Elizabeth Gaskell's *North and South* is a major work of Victorian environmental fiction with a schematic view of nationness as its organizing geographic principle – the polarity between soothing, leafy, southern village life and the fast-paced and polluted but also more exciting industrialized north. But the greatest of all Victorian environmental novelists was Hardy, whose "country" was Wessex. Thoreau's masterpiece was a local book addressed in the first instance to a regional readership ("you . . . who are said to live in New England") that spends much more time analogizing between its place and other landscapes and cultures around the world than it does in contemplating national space or affairs.

So far the new environmental criticism's most distinctive contribution to the taxonomy of place-scales may be the concept of the bioregion. Like ecocriticism itself, bioregionalism as a self-conscious movement began in the American west. According to the two California environmentalists who put the term in circulation, it "refers both to geographical terrain and a terrain of consciousness." A bioregion is determined "initially" by "climatology, physiography, animal and plant geography," etc., typically including a "major watershed"; but its boundaries and "resonance" are confirmed over time by inhabitance of those who have made a long-term commitment to living there (Berg and Dasmann 1977: 399–400). So bioregionalism is neither a species of environmental determinism nor of cultural constructionism, but an attempt to "integrate ecological and cultural affiliations within the framework of a place-based sensibility" (Thomashow 1999: 121). It aims to avoid the extremes of hard-shell localism and the free-floating sentimentalism of fancying one is in tune with "nature" or "Gaia." It is also designedly "not just a rural program," but "as much for the restoration of urban neighborhood life and the greening of the cities" (Snyder 1990: 43); indeed with special attention to city–hinterland relations, including the metropolitan emplacement within watershed districts. The prototypical bioregion's populace is a collectivity of ethnically and economically diverse stakeholders.

Defining a bioregion is not so easy as some bioregionalists make it seem. Is the "Rocky Mountain West" one bioregion, or eight? (McGinnis 1999: xv, 47). How malleable or problematic are a bioregion's borders? What if the different "natural" markers don't cleanly line up? What if plant distribution, for instance, doesn't correspond to watershed or drainage basin topography? Then too the whole idea of "citizenship" in a bioregion rather than an established county, province, or nation-state has a counterintuitive ring, as when Snyder identifies himself as living not in community A, in state B, and country C, but "on the western slope of the northern Sierra Nevada, in the Yuba River watershed, north of the south fork at the three-thousand-foot elevation, in a community of Black Oak, Incense Cedar, Madrone, Douglas Fir, and Ponderosa Pine" (Snyder 1990: 41). But of course that's precisely the point. Snyder knows that the point of thinking bioregionally is not literally to redraw state or national boundaries but, by calling attention to the artifice of "the social construction called California" (Snyder 1995: 223), to provoke within and against ingrained grid-think keener attention to how interaction with topography, climate, and nonhuman life directs not only how people ought to live but also the way they *do* live without realizing it. For "although at first glance it might seem counter to modern appearances, even urban areas sprang into existence, and most often continue to depend, on environmental circumstances that lie just below the level of our awareness. From the time humans located regularly-visited hunting camps and early river farming settlements, human places have been superimposed on environmental settings" (Flores 1999: 44).

What more precisely is one supposed to do with this awareness? Bioregionalists tend to favor an ethic not simply of environmental literacy but also of "sustainability" – of more prudent, self-sufficient use of natural resources such that environmental and human quality will be maintained (and ideally improved) with better human/

human and human/nonhuman consideration both within the bioregion and beyond.[25] But "sustainability" as an ethical position is hard to pin down, not the least of which reasons being that it requires guesswork about what future generations will be like and that it runs contrary to the known fact that nature itself does not remain stable (O'Grady 2003). Besides, even if one sets aside such conundrums for the sake of some rough-and-ready common-sensical definition, the possibility of "sustainable" living in a fast-urbanizing world might seem out of the question. It is hard to quarrel with the proposition that "sustainable city" is oxymoronic. The "ecological footprint" of modern cities in Europe and America – the amount of land required to produce the resources they consume in relation to the land they occupy – is something like 200 times larger, on average (Rees 1997: 306–7). So "by definition" they are "too densely populated with humans to be self-supporting," and the problem will only worsen as humanity continues to urbanize, with the very real possibility of conurbations of 40 million or more in China and India (Martínez-Alier 2003: 50, 47). Meanwhile, "consumers in the high centers of industrial civilization can take for granted the continued supply of mink from the Arctic, teakwood from India and ivory from Africa, without being [held] in the slightest degree responsible for the environmental consequences of their lifestyles" (Guha and Martínez-Alier 1997: 222). If sustainability is applied with any seriousness as a yardstick, it would seem hard to escape Paul Shepard's sour dismissal of modern urban arrangements: "infinite wants are pursued as though the environment were an amnion and technology a placenta" (Shepard 1982: 124).

Yet despite such pessimism, a strikingly hopeful, can-do streak runs through green urban design, from Ian McHarg's models for developing major US cities in greater synchrony with their riverways and other natural systems ("land is abundant even within a metropolitan region confronting accelerated growth") (McHarg 1969: 65), to the utopian "arcology" of Paolo Soleri's visions of massive cities in the desert or afloat, to environmental journalist David Nicholson-Lord's celebration of small-scale green space reclaimed in British cities (humankind "has learnt to reclaim land, reintroduce farming, and tempt back fellow creatures") (Nicholson-Lord 1987: 228), to landscape architect Anne Whiston Spirn's restoration of a buried stream in a poor Philadelphia neighborhood (Spirn 1998: 161–3, 185–8, 267–72), to the "Chicago Principles" worked out between that city's Department of Environment and architect William McDonough, designed to make Chicago "the greenest city in the United States."[26] Why? Partly techno-optimism, no doubt. Then too, with the exception of Soleri, these urbanists are not utopians so much as pragmatic incrementalists, persuaded that *some* benign modification of the bioregion in the direction of restoring or relieving stress from natural systems must be possible, and pleased – maybe too readily – by signs of "gradual 'countrifi-cation' of the city" (Platt 1994: 37) or the mere presence of some kind of "sustainability plan" tied to quantitative indicators like per capita water consumption and incidence of visits to respiratory clinics (Portney 2003: 31–75).

That the sustainable city or metropolitan area is so far pretty much a drawing-board reality with modest gains to show may help account for the fact that the literature of what might be called urban bioregional imagination is still relatively scant and fragmented – although some of Walt Whitman's metropolitan panoramas (like "Crossing Brooklyn Ferry") might count, as well as portions of Joyce's *Ulysses* and Woolf's *Mrs. Dalloway*, the sections of John Edgar Wideman's *Philadelphia Fire* in which the protagonist Cudjoe extri-cates himself enough from personal and environmental labyrinths to perceive that damaged city holistically, and even more so those parts of William Carlos Williams' *Paterson* that imagine "his" city in rela-tion to its hinterlands or as itself a hinterland of greater New York (see Buell 2001: 84–128). Significantly, the form of urban writing so far most often seized upon by ecocritics is the narrative, essay, or poem of discovery of unexpected signs of nature in the city: a vacant lot gone wild, redtail hawks nesting in crevices of apartment buildings, celebration of skyscape or greenways along city creeks and rivers, trees that especially strike the eye, glimpses of roof and back lot gardening. Rather in keeping with the practical effects of green design, this writing tends to feature short takes and small gains at the micro-level. ("Even in my small New York City apartment I can pause to listen to birds sing, find a tree and watch it," writes African American feminist culture critic bell hooks.)[27] I do not mean to denigrate such work. Ecocritics rightly consider it important. Such epiphanies, though, tend to be ventured against a background of enclosure: a particular social or spatial vantage point considerably more foreshortened than the "whole city." Perhaps this is an inevitable concomitant of metropolitan compartmentalization and sprawl. One can easily schematize a metropolis spatially, diagrammatically; but metropolitan life as platial experience more likely entails bonding to a district or archipelago of niches and corridors.

A case in point is a more intensively place-centered example in the same collection as the hooks piece: Sandra Cisneros' "The Monkey Garden," a chapter from her semi-autobiographical novel *The House on Mango Street*. The garden is evidently a small back lot of a nearby house in a Hispanic district of Chicago, profuse in plant life left behind by ex-residents who moved away. It seems a safe, inviting place to play, although the pubescent but shy and proper Esperanza gets disconcerted when kissing games start and hides herself "in the jungle part, under a tree that wouldn't mind if I lay down and cried a long time." This turns out to be the one really green spot in the novel, unless one counts a short mention of the "house on a hill" where her father works as a gardener, or a mini-chapter on "Four Skinny Trees." Overall, the life of a raised-to-be-nice young girl on Mango Street means, often to her distress though sometimes also to her comfort, a severely regulated and circumscribed life. The same goes for her whole family, it seems. Her mother doesn't know what train to take to go downtown. In this respect, the book follows the path of the closest urban equivalent to traditional exurban regionalism: neighborhood/ghetto narrative.[28] The key difference between city writing of this kind and its exurban counterpart, especially if like *Mango Street* it follows its protagonists

87

at the ground-level of their own mental horizons, is that the urbanist concentrates especially on a district rather than envisaging locale in macro-organismic terms. The city as environment, both the built and the "natural" spaces, generally presents itself in pieces to literary and critical imagination. But at least we are starting to see the beginning of incorporation of urban and other severely altered, damaged landscapes – "brownfields" as well as greenfields – into ecocriticism's accounts of placeness and place-attachment. For ecocriticism to recognize "the city" as something other than non-place is itself a great and necessary advance.

Perhaps what especially differentiates modern bioregionalism, be it rural or urban, from traditional regionalism is the sense of vulnerability and flux. In the Little Hintock of Hardy's late nineteenth-century novel *The Woodlanders* (1887), people's lives get traumatically disrupted or extinguished, but the villagers' basic life-rhythms have scarcely changed for years and seem unlikely to do so in the future. Graham Swift's late twentieth-century regional novel *Waterland* (1983) tells the long history of the East Anglian fenlands as a series of reshapings of landscape and social arrangements. The fate of the dynasty of Atkinson brewer-entrepreneurs, and that of the whole region as well, hinges on the extent to which they fathom and take advantage of wider-world political perturbations and technological breakthroughs like the transportation revolution. The difference in perception of the stability and porosity of local cultural arrangements between the two worlds stems largely from the increasing sense that regions remain permeable to shock waves potentially extending worldwide. That is why the bioregional horizon must extend beyond a merely local horizon: the locale cannot shut itself off from translocal forces even if it wanted to.

Richard Powers' novel *Gain* (1998) dramatizes the contrast between traditional and newer conceptions of environmental scale through a two-track, split-scale narrative in which the quotidian life of a real estate broker in a town in the American midwest, told in an old-fashioned realistic mode, alternates with and is finally shattered by the logic of the other plot, which unfolds as a fabulistic

narrative of the 200-year history of a Boston-based soap manu-
factory that blossomed from a small, struggling family affair into a
multinational corporation headquartered in the same town, beauti-
ful in appearance but toxic in its emissions. The protagonist can
hardly believe that the cancer she contracts might have been caused
by tending her own garden, Candide-like, all the while absorbing
the miasma whose salubrity she has been innocently recommend-
ing to her clients. Belatedly she joins the damage suit against the
company, which reacts by merging and moving offshore, presumably to thrive and pollute indefinitely. *Gain* is not a work of self-
conscious bioregional vision or advocacy, but its double-tracked
structure exposes the impossibility of understanding locales without
taking into account the power of destabilizing macro-forces.

As *Gain* also makes clear, the scope of the factors that define a
bioregion is transnational and even global. Starting from his home
base in the west-central part of the state of Vermont, Christopher
McGrory Klyza proposes a four-level map of "bioregional overlays"
of widening scope: the circumjacent watersheds; the "major
drainage basins" extending from there into the major lakes and rivers
bordering or outside the state; the "larger watershed level" of the
Champlain Basin and the Upper Connecticut Valley, which impli-
cates Vermont within systems of transnational watercourses and air
circulation including Quebec, New England, and New York; and
finally "the ecoregional province level" of forestation and climate
extending from the Maritime provinces to the headwaters of the
Mississippi River in Minnesota (Klyza 1999: 92–4). But even Klyza's
largest scale does not fully take into account the spatial reach of
acid rain, airborne species migration both planned and happenstance, ozone depletion, and global warming.[29] His thought experiment nonetheless marks something like the effective outer spatial
limits of bioregional imagination. Perhaps the only major work of
contemporary creative writing that surpasses it in geographical scope
is Barry Lopez's *Arctic Dreams* (1986), which attempts an ecohistor-
ical anatomy of the entire Alaskan and Canadian Arctic as a single
complex bioregion.

As environmental criticism moves to a global level of analysis, it understandably gets more multivocal, contentious, and fraught. Competing models proliferate. James Lovelock, a polymathic British "independent scientist" whose original base of operations was chemistry, has developed a holistic model of planetary life as a unitary superorganism he calls "Gaia," a self-sustaining system highly although not infinitely resilient to anthropogenic disruption. From the standpoint of sociologist Ulrich Beck's techno-determinist holism, by contrast, industrial modernization has permanently destabilized life on earth because technology can no longer control the damage wrought by its own unintended consequences. Since Chernobyl, or thereabouts, the culture of modernization has entered into a second, "reflexive" stage that Beck calls the "risk society," a culture of "radical uncertainty" in awareness that "systemic crashes are now a part of our predictable future."[30] Although nature has been transformed out of existence in the traditional sense of the word, the psychology of risk society paradoxically "forces one to rediscover human beings as natural entities," now that "the desire or need to breathe, eat, drink, etc., which humans share with animals and plants, is becoming a gate that can no longer be barred against hazards" (Beck 1995: 50–1). On the continuum between these nearly opposite diagnoses of the organization of global environment today – Lovelock's durable planet vs. Beck's permanently destabilized environment – are the earth-mappings of a mind-bogglingly disparate array of environmental watchdog and protection organizations – the Worldwatch Institute, the UNESCO Biosphere Reserves program, and many others – offering attempts both from the "left" (e.g., "social ecology") and the "right" (e.g., "sustainable development") to generate managed solutions that might reconcile techno-economic advancement, human environmental welfare, and the limits of earth's resources.[31]

How might environmental writing and criticism reflect, focus, or redirect this proliferation of ecodiscourses on a planetary scale? Two contrasting thoughts suggest themselves. First, literary world-making is a far more ancient pursuit than modern eco-analysis, already manifest in Western antiquity in Herodotus' *History* and Plato's *Timaeus*, antedating modern science and political economy by some millennia. Since early modernity, from More's *Utopia* to contemporary science fiction, its vigor and variety easily match those of global ecodiscourse in any other field. Cyborg theory looks constrained and tepid compared to the hijinks of cyberpunk fiction and film, which reinvent Beck's jeremiads as spectacular exuberance. Yet environmental criticism in literary studies has so far proven less proactive than some other branches of the environmental humanities (e.g., environmental ethics, ecotheology, humanistic geography, and environmental cultural theory) in going global. In literary and also in historical studies, by far the commoner practice is still to work from an archival base in a particular national culture. For the foreseeable future, ecocriticism – whether traditional or second-wave – may well continue to be done less by true comparatists than by critics who concentrate most on the ecoculture(s) they know best and extend the borders of their knowledge as best they can.[32]

As scale and mobility expand, placeness tends to thin out. *Arctic Dreams* is exemplary. It is a migratory work with many platial epicenters that blur together into a gigantic ensemble. In William Gibson's novel *Pattern Recognition* (2003), the protagonist Cayce, whose expertise of spotting the "right" design configurations for the advertising industry makes her a marked woman caught up in a mysterious plot of global scope, transits guardedly through an unending series of Augésque non-places – offices, apartments, subways, airplanes, taxis, restaurants, hotels, internet workstations. Through most of the novel, interaction with natural environments happens only through peephole glimpses of "squares of blue sky, decorative bits of cloud."[33] The great cities of the world become almost interchangeable, "nodal points in a vast communications and market system," as Saskia Sassen calls the world's most powerful megacities (Sassen 1991: 325).[34] In Octavia Butler's diptych of futurist novels, *Parable of the Sower* (1993) and *Parable of the Talents* (1998), in which a devastated United States seeks to recover from disruption caused by civic breakdown aggravated by global warming, emplacement is seen not simply as a now-lost condition but as a trap. Seeking to realize her dream of an "Earthseed" community, the protagonist is at first seduced into trying to create a self-sufficient homesteading enclave, making the members of her band a fat target for high-tech raiders who attack and enslave them. She succeeds only by reconceiving Earthseed in deterritorialized terms as a far-flung network of people whose aim is not to huddle defensively as a small band of survivors but to proselytize the world.

Is a place-responsive ecoliterature of global scope an impossibility, then? Perhaps the correlation between globalism and placelessness is not inevitable. Although globalism *may* suppress place and even extinguish particular places, as feminist geographer Doreen Massey argues it can also construct new platial "'identities' . . . through their interaction with other places rather than by counterposition to them" (Massey 1994: 121). Such identities are more likely to be both "multivocal" and "multilocal" (Rodman 1992) than the closed communities of traditional regionalist imagination. Meanwhile, in literature if not also in literary studies, something like a global sense of place is coming into existence. One resonant example is Walcott's epic *Omeros*, one of the tiny number of truly great long Anglophone poems of the twentieth century.

Omeros is simultaneously a poem about the island-nation of St. Lucia, the author's home place, about the Caribbean transnation, and about the interpenetrating force-fields of the Euro-Atlantic and Afro-Atlantic world. To this end, it intertwines the resources of African orature and island patois with Western literature in the grand style – Dantean *terza rima* with a Homeric plot featuring peasant characters cast as Achille, Hector, Helen, and Philoctete (whose "incurable" symbolic wound, cured in Walcott's mythology as well as the Greek, is the rancor of slavery); a mysterious multi-faced "Omeros"-figure who alternately appears as bum and bard; the poet himself as both a wandering would-be Homer and a Hamlet haunted by the ghost of the father whom he recalls admonishing him, with a gesture toward a line of women porters unloading a ship:

> Kneel to your load, then balance your staggering feet
> and walk up that coal ladder as they do in time,
> one bare foot after the next in ancestral rhyme.

– "rhyme" here encompassing either "the language's / desire to enclose the loved world in its arms; / or heft a coal basket." "There, like ants or angels," the father's voice intones,[35]

> they see their native town,
> unknown, raw, insignificant. They walk, you write;

> keep to that narrow causeway without looking down,
> climbing in their footsteps, that slow, ancestral beat
> of those used to climbing roads; your own work owes them

> because the couplet of those multiplying feet
> made your first rhymes. Look, they climb, and no one knows them;
> they take their copper pittances, and your duty

> from the time you watched them from your grandmother's house
> as a child wounded by their power and beauty
> is the chance you now have, to give those feet a voice.

This encapsulates the challenge the poem takes up, in full awareness of the divide between the educated, expatriated poet and the local life he sings. He can – and here does – give voice to that life; but only by a trick of metaphor can the "ancestral beat" of the women's feet be converted into pentameter triads and his load be compared to theirs. Yet the poem turns this self-consciousness to advantage by widening the circles of place, interlinking them without conflating. It allows the poet to distinguish his polyphonic voice not just from the *vox* (or rather *pes*) *populi* but also from the voice or beat of Western canonical poetics that lures him and that he also sees as necessary to put St. Lucia on the world stage. "All that Greek manure under the green bananas," he recoils at one point. "When would I not hear the Trojan War / in two fishermen cursing in Ma Kilman's shop? . . . when would I enter that light beyond metaphor?" "But it was mine," he adds, "to make what I wanted of it, or / what I thought was wanted": "a hut closed like a wound," and then

> the track from which a man's figure emerges,
> then a girl carrying laundry, the road-smell like loaves,
> the yellow-dressed butterflies in the grass marges. (271–2)

This double consciousness allows *Omeros* both to enlist Homer to the end of making small island events seem immensely consequential – the stuff of myth – and to build a thicker and more palpable realization of island place faithful to what Casey would call the "eventmental" quality of placeness: how it is always coming into being. The poem's grasp of island and regional history does this in another way: its glimpses of time strata from precolumbian through the various dispensations of conquests, and the moments when possession changed hands. St. Lucia becomes the global center of the failed imperial project. "The concept of idyllic nature" alone, Adorno pertinently remarks of the aesthetic of natural beauty, could not do this; it would merely "retain the provincialism of a minuscule island." For "consciousness does justice to the experience of nature only when . . . it incorporates nature's wounds."[36] That is Walcott's accomplishment here.

Shifts in narrative focus provide additional layering to this vision of damaged yet integral and infinitely expansive placeness. *Omeros* becomes simultaneously a St. Lucian poem, centering on a particular island-nation's landscapes, culture, and history; an Antillean poem, a North American-diasporic poem, an Afro-Caribbean poem; a poem of the Atlantic world cutting across the black and the white; and an oceanic poem of global reach.

Omeros takes its hero, the fisherman Achille, on a vision-quest back in time that reverses the Middle Passage and returns him briefly to his African fatherland, where he magically makes contact without quite achieving solidarity with his dead "father" (i.e., ancestor), who ironically but fittingly cannot recall his son's original African name. ("Everything was forgotten," agrees the dreaming

94

Achille, "The deaf sea has changes around every name that you gave
/ us" – even though of course the sea has also enabled this act of
retrieval [137].) Back on the home front, Achille and the other local
figures in the Homerically named ensemble are shown as cannily
aware of the role-play needed to negotiate the various passages they
choose for themselves between a traditional island life and catering
to the tourist trade. The poem in fact begins:

> "This is how, one sunrise, we cut down them canoes."
> Philoctete smiles for the tourists, who try taking
> his soul with their cameras.

Here, simultaneously, the fishermen ply their traditional trade, the
"native" performer mocks it up for the tourists, and the poetic over-
voice hints self-consciously at its own specular outsidership – taking
its own snapshot of the local soul. Local work, life, landscape,
become realized both as navel and periphery of global space and
deep time with a resourcefulness few but Joyce have equaled.

In recognition of the racial and national mix that the Caribbean
has become, *Omeros* often switches over to the perspective of the
aging retired British soldier Plunkett, the poet's one-time school-
teacher, who with his wife has chosen to live out the rest of his
life in St. Lucia. Walcott deploys Plunkett's personal and ancestral
history as a counterpart example of place-attachment complicated
by ethnocultural barriers and world travel to set alongside the poet's
own creolized, troubled, exilic loyalties. This also allows the poem
to personalize the wide-angle lens of imperial history through the
memory of Plunkett's traumatic stint with the British army in North
Africa during World War II and, further back, a forebear's pathetic
death as a pawn in an eighteenth-century West Indian naval battle
over control of the Indies.

Much more could be said about *Omeros* as a work that is centered yet also migratory, global, and world-historical in its evocations of place. But enough has been said to suggest that substantive
acts of reconstructive place imagination on a global scale, both

grounded and expansive, are no mere hypothetical possibility. They are happening now.

Walcott may have been helped by being a Caribbean poet. So at least he himself has affirmed:

> I think the island experience of writers in some way contributes to a larger sense of space, and of time, and even of history in the Caribbean. No matter how minor the Caribbean poet, in a sense he is an epic poet simply because of the scale of what surrounds him. If you live on a rock in Barbuda you are really in an immense ocean . . . and in an immense sky, and that vertical figure of the individual person is within large elements of physical feeling.[37]

Maybe *Omeros* also takes unfair advantage insofar as it romanticizes traditional peasant culture's durability. "To what extent the culture of satellite television now sweeping the Caribbean," one critic muses, "will undermine the distinctness of the culture" Walcott wants especially to celebrate "remains to be seen."[38] But even allowing for the certainty that the Caribbean local–global epic of 2020, if there is one, might well look rather different, *Omeros* bears out the possibility of imagining placeness in multi-scalar terms: local, national, regional, transhemispheric; topographically, historically, culturally. What especially allows Walcott to do so is the very vulnerability and porosity of the postcolonial condition that makes the critic just quoted wonder if his version of place will become obsolescent. In a topical sense, perhaps. But in a deeper structural or generative sense, such postcolonial multivision may have conferred a prescience that will long outlast the future transformations of local culture as committed to print in 1990 by this one particular semideracinated returnee.

4

The Ethics and Politics of Environmental Criticism

Criticism worthy of the name arises from commitments deeper than professionalism. Environmental criticism, even when constrained by academic protocols, is usually energized by environmental concern. Often it is openly polemical. This is entirely understandable in the case of an issue widely recognized as grave, yet not so widely believed to require immediate action. "One must write with a red hot iron to make any impression," as Ralph Waldo Emerson declared about what he knew his readers would agree was the greatest public evil in his nation's history – slavery – but that only a few were as yet prepared to do anything about.[1] Often too, as for Emerson, the animus is directed inwardly as well as outwardly. As with abolitionist rhetoric, the polemical edge of contemporary environmental criticism reflects stress and disputation within the movement as well as resistance from opposing interests.

From a distance, one sees a trend-line of mounting resolve during the late twentieth century to fathom and raise public consciousness about the history, present state, and possible future of the environmental interdependencies between human and nonhuman and within human society, made increasingly unstable and dangerous by drastic alterations in planetary environment. But this generalization is neither broad enough to encompass the sizeable minority of commentators who deny there's an environmental problem,[2] nor calibrated enough to indicate the disputes among those who do. Two related though non-identical forms of polarization that stand out are ecocentric or biocentric[3] vs. anthropocentric ethics (each of varying stripes, with many intermediate positions along the continuum) and health of physical environment as first focus of concern vs. social welfare or interhuman equity as first focus of concern. Graph these along two axes with ecocentrism as the left-hand or western pole of the horizontal axis and health of physical environment at the top or northern pole of the vertical axis, and we have a rough-and-ready means of plotting internal disparities. Greenpeace and Earth First! would be situated somewhere in the northwest, bioregionalism would extend from northwest to northeast, the environmental justice movement would appear in the southeast, and Earthwatch might stand somewhere in the southwest a little below the horizontal axis.

Within specific disciplinary domains like literary studies these fault lines become further fissured by differences over questions not inherent to environmental issues per se, such as whether to think of literary works and their reception in the first instance as individually or as culturally generated, and whether to think of texts in the first instance as linguistic or ideological constructs or as refractions of historical actualities.

Ecocentrism and Its Discontents

What initially made ecocriticism most distinctive from both a disciplinary standpoint and from the standpoint of mainstream, commonsense opinion – and for many still does – was its ecocentric face. An early example was Joseph Meeker's brief for comedy's superiority to tragedy on the ground that its ecology of genre reflected a nonanthropocentric ethos of adaptation to circumstance rather than hubristic defiance of it. A more recent one has been the vision of an "ecological poetics" of interspecies relation (Gilcrest 2002: 9–29), some versions of which press the model of poem as *imago mundi* so far as to claim that "all poems," whether the foreground be nature or the mind, "are landscape poems inasmuch as they refer primarily or secondarily to a visible world" (Cooperman 2001: 182). These claims synchronize with a long tradition of testimony by environmental writers themselves affirming the environmental construction of their literary identity (Lewis 2003: 145–85). Take, for example, Barry Lopez's assertion:

> My imagination was shaped by the exotic nature of water in a dry Southern California valley; by the sound of wind in the crowns of eucalyptus trees; by the tactile sensation of sheened earth, turned in furrows by a gang plow; by banks of saffron, mahogany and scarlet cloud piled above a field of alfalfa at dusk; by encountering the musk from orange blossoms at the edge of an orchard; by the aftermath of a Pacific storm crashing a hot, flat beach. (Lopez 1998)

Though such statements must be taken figuratively – obviously other factors (such as books) also shaped Lopez's artistic development[4] – the aspiration to write and think more ecocentrically than modern humanity's customary mental default position cannot be written off on that account. Lopez, Meeker, Gilchrist, and Cooperman all second the implication of the riddle Ursula LeGuin puts in the mouth of her trickster-fostermother-guru in "Buffalo Gals":[5]

> *Coyote:* "There are only two kinds of people."
> *Girl:* "Humans and animals."
> *Coyote:* "No. the kind of people who say 'There are two kinds of people' and the kind of people who don't.'"

Hence early ecocriticism's partiality for texts and genres that put human figures at the margin and engage in thought experiments that defamiliarize landscapes in tacit suppression (if not downright reproach) of anthropocentrism. For John Clare letting his persona get lost in the minute details of a nightingale's nest ("Snug lie her curious eggs in number five / Of deadened green or rather olive-brown"), as against the lament for one's human mortality that suffuses Keats's "To a Nightingale." For Mary Austin's perception of nearly invisible desert trails from a rat-and-squirrel perspective as "wide and winding roads" that would seem so "to us if they occurred in thick plantations of trees three times the height of a man." For W. S. Merwin's poetic depiction of a grove of trees chopped down from the standpoint of the trees. For LeGuin's imagination of human explorers' panic as they begin to understand the ecology of the landscape of "World 4470," dominated by intelligent plants.[6] One of first-wave ecocriticism's most contrarian moves is its pursuit of an "aesthetics of relinquishment" (Buell 1995: 143–89) that marks environmental writing self-consciously devoted to resisting anthropocentrism, sometimes to the point of wholly eliminating human figures from its imagined worlds.

Ecocentrism's intellectual roots and resultant forms are more various than I have so far made them seem. Among the many influences within modern Western thought alone, three of the most significant have been Darwinian theory, the holistic environmental ethics of the American ecologist Aldo Leopold, and certain strains of modern continental philosophy. Here is my sense of these genealogies in broad brushstrokes. To Darwin, literary and critical ecocentrism owes the definition of *homo sapiens* as an order of being not created providentially but by a "natural" process that cares no more for whether humans survive than for the welfare of any other species, even if humans happen to be the highest stage of evolution yet.[7] Hence Mary Austin's "of no account you who lie out there watching, nor the lean coyote that stands off in the scrub from you and howls and howls."[8] To Leopold, ecocentric thinking owes the concept of "the land ethic," with its ascription of rights to nonhuman life forms. Fusing early ecological theory with an ethical perspective that may take its cue from Darwin's guess that morality originated with the organization of human bands into communities,[9] Leopold extends the conception of community "to include soils, waters, plants, and animals": a "biotic community" in which humankind is "one of thousands of accretions" and species are entitled to existence "as a matter of biotic right"; and where a proposed environmental alteration is not treated as "solely an economic problem" but put to the test of whether "it tends to preserve the integrity, stability, and beauty of the biotic community" (Leopold 1949: 204, 216, 211, 224–5).[10] To modern continental thought, ecocentric environmental criticism owes the term "deep ecology." It was coined by Norwegian philosopher-outdoorsman-activist Arne Naess (1973), although recent discussions of its continental antecedence sometimes refer it back to the later thought of Martin Heidegger, a far more imposing figure in the history of western philosophy.[11] Ecocentric criticism has also been influenced by French phenomenologists Gaston Bachelard and especially Maurice Merleau-Ponty, whose work is focused more on the body emplaced than on the mind giving itself over to dwelling (Casey 1997: 238–42).[12]

Much more could be said about matters of provenance, about such other lines of influence within western thought as Spinoza's ethical monism, and especially about the many non-European sources of inspiration. These include the influence of Gandhi on Naess; the wide impact of various strands of South and East Asian philosophy, particularly Buddhism and Taoism (as for example on Gary Snyder and numerous other American environmental writers); and the influence of indigenous traditions upon artists and writers worldwide.[13] But already it can be surmised that ecocentric thinking is more like a scattergram than a united front. All its strains define human identity not as free-standing but in terms of its relationship with the physical environment and/or nonhuman life forms. That much they share in common. Beyond that the paths divide. Leopold's land ethic has been most influential for advocates of nature preservation; Darwinist criticism, when invoked as a basis for conceptualizing adaptation, competition, survival, and extinction of life forms, has located itself as easily in urban contexts as rural. To late nineteenth and early twentieth-century writers, cities often seemed as much like Darwinian "jungles" as hinterland backwaters did. Partly on that account, Theodore Dreiser, the first major US urban novelist, was more thoroughly suffused by Darwinist thinking (Ernst Haeckl's biologism and Herbert Spencer's social Darwinism, to be specific) than was the last great Victorian novelist, Thomas Hardy, who was less a philosophical materialist than a cosmic fatalist. Naess, Heidegger, Bachelard, and Merleau-Ponty focus on life as experienced by prototypical humans rather than on environmental history or natural processes or social struggle. Even among this particular subset of ecocentric persuasions, both the direction and the salience of the ethical thrust also differ greatly. Leopold's biotic community is avowedly ethical; Merleau-Ponty's phenomenology is not. Darwinian natural selection has sometimes been read as a product of capitalist culture and implicitly as a defense thereof, although it becomes polemically so only in the hands of social Darwinists like Spencer.

Ecocentrism is more compelling as a call to fellow humans to recognize the intractable, like-it-or-not interdependence that subsists between the human and the nonhuman and to tread more lightly on the earth than it is as a practical program. The history of the so-called deep ecology movement, which environmental humanists have often, somewhat misleadingly, used as a catch-all term for ecocentric thinking generally, witnesses to this. Naess originally thought of "deep" ecology, as distinct from what he took to be the "shallow" (i.e., modestly incremental environmental reform efforts designed – as he saw it – to enhance amenities for those already well off), as being a reorientation of thought that hinged on the bringing to consciousness of "the relational, total field-image" of "organisms as knots in the biospherical net or field of intrinsic relations" (Naess 1973: 95). But when he went along with his American admirers' self-help manual approach to making the idea operational, this vision of counter-normative ontological critique tended to give way to a programmatic eight-point platform (formulated in collaboration with George Sessions) that included such provisions as these:

3   Humans have no right to reduce [the] richness and diversity [of life forms] except to satisfy *vital* needs . . .
4   The flourishing of human life and cultures is compatible with a substantial decrease of the human population. The flourishing of nonhuman life requires such a decrease.

7　The ideological change is mainly that of appreciating *life quality* (dwelling in situations of inherent value) rather than adhering to an increasingly higher standard of living. (Devall and Sessions 1985: 70)

Such bottom-line prescriptions made deep ecology an inviting target. What started as a critique of the adequacy of cautiously instrumental approaches to environmental reform seemed now to be defining itself as another instrumental solution – and a sketchy, question-begging one at that. This opened it up to charges of "utopian ecologism" ("There is not a concrete theory of the state, ideology, technology, or the economy here"), as well as reflex anti-modernism, and a consumerist soft anthropocentrism in thin disguise.[14] A doctrine of "Let nature be," combined with plank number four ("The flourishing of human life and cultures is compatible with a substantial decrease of the human population"), has also prompted charges of neo-fascism (e.g., Luke 1997: 13), with Heidegger's unrecanted Nazism often cited as retrospective collateral evidence. This last is a canard. Yes, Heidegger's reverence for living-in-rustic-place-and-letting-nature-be is inextricable from his *Heimat* ideology, but reverence for living in rustic place and letting nature be is not *ipso facto* fascist; the relation between the two is not intrinsic but historically contingent.[15] Still, deep ecology's early penchant for holism as framed by Naess and Sessions in ethico-political terms laid itself open to the charges of indiscriminate lumping and authoritarianism as well as chuckle-headedness. Since then, more carefully nuanced versions have emerged (e.g., Johnson 1991; McLaughlin 1993). But it still remains a vexed question as to whether deep ecology's emphasis on self-realization through human obeisance to nature contradicts its claims of ecocentrism (Soper 1995: 253–9).[16]

Considered as ontology or aesthetics first rather than as a recipe for ethics or practice, deep ecology looks more persuasive. As an ontology, deep ecology and ecocentrism more generally can provide a needful corrective to modern culture's underrepresentation of the degree to which humanness is ecosystemically imbricated. As ecophilosopher Freya Mathews puts it, "to represent us as anything less than" so interconnected "is in fact to *misrepresent* us to ourselves, and hence to interfere with our possibilities of self-realization," which in turn means recognition of one's positioning within "the wider systems of Nature" (Mathews 1991: 156–8).[17] From this position, ethical and political positions can be deduced, but as next-order considerations that need not be thought to affect the force of the basic ontological point, which is in a sense almost truistical. Jonathan Bate makes a similar claim with regard to literary aesthetics:

> It would be quixotic to suppose that a work of literary criticism might be an appropriate place to spell out a practical program for better environmental management. That is why ecopoetics should begin not as a set of assumptions or proposals about particular environmental issues, but as a way of reflecting upon what it might mean to dwell with the earth. (Bate 2000: 266)

Bate may be too solicitous here about cordoning off criticism from politics,[18] but his distinction between poetics as thought experiment and the kind of scrutiny to which ethical or political proposals must expose themselves when put to the test of pragmatic implementation is also crucial. A good test case is Aldo Leopold's *Sand County Almanac*, which attempts to do both and has been hailed as a classic both of modern environmental writing and of ecocentric environmental ethics.

Leopold's argument that the biotic community's welfare should be the standard of right conduct has been highly influential.[19] But the ethic as stated thinly masks major self-contradictions. Who, for openers, is to determine what is best for the biotic community? "Man," of course. In principle only "a plain member and citizen of the land community," humankind will inevitably be its "overseer and guiding force" (Fritzell 1990: 201). *Almanac* famously calls on its readers to think "like a mountain" (129–33), which is literally impossible. Even if it weren't, might not such a mentality amount

104

to forfeiture of one's humanity, as with the title figure in Wallace Stevens' poem "The Snow-Man," who must freeze into a "nothing" in order to achieve zero subjective bias?[20]

If, on the other hand, one reads *Sand County Almanac* aesthetically, as a "relational field" of "embodied dialogue" between persona and environment that is more exploratory than hortatory,[21] then the contradictions look less problematic. From this standpoint, *Almanac* unfolds as a series of experiences, discoveries, musings, and percepts designed to unsettle standard utilitarian assumptions. "Thinking Like a Mountain" (Leopold 1949: 129–33) is one of those: the author's recollection, whether true-to-life or embroidered, of realizing after he had killed a wolf as a young man that the protection of deer against predators in the interest of farmers and sport-hunters wasn't in the larger ecological interest, the interest of "the mountain." As such, the story is a performance of chastened awakening to a deeper grasp of environmental relationships and more like a traditional Protestant conversion narration (Gatta 2004: 59) than a full-dress argument for ecocentrism or any other centrism. And it culminates like a parable in the proper sense, not a story with a tidy moral handed on a plate but a narrative conundrum, with a series of ambiguously insinuating "perhaps"-es that are left to the listener to interpret and apply.[22]

Almanac's last section, "The Upshot," consists of four long chapters more polemical than the sketches that precede it. But even these closing essays ("Conservation Esthetic," "Wilderness in American Life," "Wilderness," and "The Land Ethic") seem designed rather to awaken the sleeping "ecological conscience" than to work out a systematic, self-consistent ethical position. *Almanac*'s ecocentrism is better understood as a provocation to which Leopold resorts than as a settled position in which he rests.

That is in no sense to diminish the seriousness and the significance, here or elsewhere, of urging one's listeners to make a concerted effort to think against anthropocentrism. Indeed, this amounts to nothing less than a new Copernican revolution at the planetary level – this insistence that the world must no longer be thought of as revolving around "us." Reconstructive ecotheology is an even more dramatic example than green aesthetics or green ethics. As Thomas Berry sums up the stakes and promise in his widely influential *The Dream of the Earth:*

> [Humanity's] reenchantment with the earth as a living reality is the condition for our rescue of the earth from the impending destruction that we are imposing upon it. To carry this out effectively we must now, in a sense, reinvent the human species within the community of life species. Our sense of reality and of value must consciously shift from an anthropocentric to a biocentric norm of reference. (Berry 1988: 21)

Berry's influence has been one of the motivating forces behind the single most ambitious scholarly project of this kind. "Religions of the World and Ecology" comprises ten compendious volumes edited by Evelyn Tucker and John Grim on the basis of a multi-year conference series sponsored by Harvard's Center for the Study of World Religions on the ecotheological implications of world religions, including indigenous faiths as well as the "great traditions" of Christianity, Judaism, Islam, Hinduism, Buddhism, and so on.[23] The purpose of this project is not to make these faiths out to be ecocentric in spite of themselves, but to foreground the strains within each that give aid and comfort to a mental reorientation toward green thinking. In this the project succeeds impressively.

The most critically interesting ecotheological moves of this kind are often those, like Leopold's in the conservation field, that pursue their case in awareness of the challenge of pressing against orthodox sectarian boundaries. The "metaphorical theology" of Sallie McFague, for example, takes the form of a series of as-if experiments with various alternative metaphors for God that might supplement or supersede the traditional God the father: God as mother, as lover, as friend, and the earth as God's body. Of the last, she remarks pointedly that since neither it nor the traditional metaphor is fully adequate, "we have to ask which one is better in our time."

Granted, "the metaphor of the world as God's body puts God's absolutism 'at risk.'" But the upside is a "revived sacramentalism" newly conscious of the world and all its beings as infused with God's presence. "We meet the world as a Thou, as the body of God where God is present to us always in all times and in all places" (McFague 1987: 70–7). McFague pursues this line of thinking both aware of its epistemological tentativeness and convinced that, whatever the Truth with a capital "T," the ecocentric reorientation she proposes can make a difference in how humans regard and comport themselves in relation to the world.[24] The writing of Berry, McFague, and other ecotheologians corroborates what Jonathan Bate eloquently says with literary aesthetics in mind: "we cannot do without thought-experiments and language-experiments which imagine a return to nature, a reintegration of the human and the Other. The dream of deep ecology will never be realized upon the earth, but our survival as a species may be dependent on our capacity to dream it in the work of our imagination" (Bate 2000: 37–8).

As one turns back from the domains of theology and literary imagination to the scene of applied ethics and political pragmatics, however, caution is likely to set in. As political philosopher Robyn Eckersley – herself an ecocentrist – prudently observes of her own field, although ecocentrism may be "the most distinctive and philo-sophically radical aspect of green political thought, to insist that this serve as its defining feature" is less "ecumenical" than to define the field as gravitating toward a "general norm" for protection of the "ecological integrity of the earth and its myriad organisms" (Eckersley 2001: 325–6; cf. Eckersley 1992). Likewise, in environmental ethics, although ecocentrism is the most radical position, a much greater share of the field's energy is taken up with debating questions of just how far to liberalize beyond anthropocentrism, and in what way. Should the outer circle of moral consideration be extended to include only "higher" animals, all sentient beings, all forms of life, or somewhere beyond that? Should the basis of the moral calculus be utilitarian, or a neo-Kantian "respect for life," or a democratic-extensionist "rights of nature" model, or an eco-liberal model of imputed "interest," or a feminist ethics of "care," or a neo- or post-Christian ethics of "stewardship"? Even if you respond positively (say) to Berry's creation theology, even if your most central intellectual or citizenly concern is the claim of endangered species relative to pressing social needs, it will be hard if not impossible for you to navigate the politics of environmentalism solely on the basis of a doctrine of ecocentricism.[25]

Complications of Gender

But it is simplifying matters to suppose that different disciplines, discourses, and projects sat in tidy boxes along an ecocentric–anthropocentric continuum. Ecofeminism is a striking case in point. Some varieties of ecofeminism are congruent with deep ecology, especially those which commend a neopagan "immersion in natural surroundings" as a way of getting beyond spirit–matter dualism (Spretnak 1997: 430). Attempts to frame ecofeminism in executive summary terms like "holism, interdependence, equality, and process" understandably come out sounding quite similar to deep ecology.[26] To some degree the two share a common aversion to what philosopher Val Plumwood calls "ecological denial" – of "the reality of our embeddedness in nature" (Plumwood 2002: 97). Yet feminism's conceptual starting point, the significance of gender distinctions, generally puts it at odds with deep ecology's propensity to think in terms of holisms like "nature" or "man" or even "humankind," and with its emphasis on identification of self as fulfilled through its identification with nature. On the contrary, Plumwood retorts, "The basic concept required for an appropriate ethic of environmental activism is not that of identity or unity (or its reversal in difference) but that of *solidarity*," which "requires not just the affirmation of difference, but also sensitivity to the difference between positioning oneself *with* the other and positioning oneself *as* the other."[27] Although the confident tone masks schisms within

108

ecofeminism,[28] undeniably "the politics of solidarity is different from the politics of unity" (p. 202) – and the underlying epistemologies are different, too. This has led to a series of disputes and attempted mediations, from which ecofeminism seems to have emerged in the stronger position even if not on all counts.[29] That is not because all ecofeminists are of one accord about whether anthropocentrism is a less valid key than androcentrism to understanding the phenomenon of human dominance, but because ecofeminism generally, even when it might itself stand accused of overgeneralizing, arguably offers a more calibrated model for understanding issues of cultural division and historical change.

One of the most significant insights for literary studies afforded by approaching the general problem of ecological denial or alienation through the lens of gender is its exposure of the double paradox of "nature" having been andocentrically constructed as a domain for males, in contradistinction to female-coded domestic space, yet at the same time symbolically coded as female – an arena of potential domination analogous to the female body. "The womanizing of nature and the naturizing of woman," in one ecofeminist critic's tart encapsulation (Bullis 1996: 125). That paradox is central to the ideological calculus behind both traditional US wilderness mythography (Kolodny 1975, 1984) and Latin American creole culture exoticization of the jungle (e.g., Sommer 257–79; Wasserman 1994: 207–12), for example. Ironically, this feminist critique of androcentric modes of environmental imagination has had the effect of putting *eco*feminists on the defensive within feminism, as Stacy Alaimo points out in a candid discussion of "Feminist Theory's Flight from Nature" (Alaimo 2000: 1–22). Anthropologist Sherry Ortner's classic article on the ubiquity across place and time of the symbolic equation female : male = nature : culture diagnoses this formation as a scandalous pathology correctable only by a change in the "institutional base of the society" such that women can "be seen as aligned with culture" (Ortner 1974: 87). How then can ecofeminism avoid falling into an androcentric trap, especially when it tries to argue for an ethics of "care," based on women's conditioned or inherent advantage as caregivers, which in turn results from a patriarchially mandated division of labor?[30]

Alaimo's arresting counter-proposal is to recapture that slippery but ideologically potent signifier "nature" as "undomesticated feminist space." In principle this means "recasting nature" in a cultural critique that rattles icons like "mother nature" to the end of developing "nongendered tropes of nature that emphasize continuity between human and nature while still respecting nature's difference" as a domain that "cannot be encompassed by, controlled by, or even entirely known by human culture" (Alaimo 2000: 171, 183). This leads her to a series of readings of a strikingly varied range of women writers who redefine terrain thought to be familiar and push into new territory: how anarchist Emma Goldman used her journal *Mother Earth* to redefine the title stereotype; how Catharine Sedgwick's *Hope Leslie* and Sarah Orne Jewett's female *Country Doctor* partly defy the pieties of American domestic fiction and regionalism, respectively; how Canadian novelist Marian Engel reinvented bodice-ripper, wilderness romance, and animal story/fairy tale conventions in her surrealistic novella *Bear*, about a librarian who contracts a passionate obsession with a bear while cataloguing books on an island estate in Lake Huron. Each act of undomesticated space-creation is understood not as merely metaphorical or symbolic (yes, there is an actual nonhuman world out there); each is also seen as ventured both within and against conventional framings of women's place in relation to environment, so as to refigure the terms of relation.[31] Alaimo holds to the principle of "reciprocal construction" or "co-construction" of the human and the nonhuman environment (p. 158).[32]

The various mutual constructionist theories don't line up neatly. Merchant starts with the image of an active nature responding to "human-induced change" through ecological change (Merchant 1989: 8). Whereas N. Katherine Hayles starts from the side of constructivism, from "concepts [that] derive from representation," which however are constrained by the "unmediated flux" of what we call reality (Hayles 1995: 53–4). But however one defines its dynamics, the reciprocity model pulls us away from the prospect of human *identification* with the nonhuman to which deep ecology and antidualistic versions of ecofeminism are attracted, toward a more sociocentric view according to which humanity's relation to the nonhuman is always socially mediated and considerations of human welfare and equity strongly inflect (if not govern) the adjudication of environmental questions. Predictably, ecofeminists are apt to situate themselves closer to social ecology than to deep ecology (Bullis 1996: 127). Some have even claimed that ecofeminism *is* "a social ecology" (Warren 1996: 33).

In this, Warren may have gone farther than she intended, insofar as the persuasion known at that time as social ecology was generally identified with Murray Bookchin, whose ecologism is far more doctrinaire, environmental-management oriented, and aggressively rationalistic than most ecofeminisms.[33] Today, however, Bookchin's critics and successors are dismantling his fortress and opening it up to deep ecology as well as (even further) to ecofeminism (Light 1998). Social ecology's aspiration to "confront and ultimately eliminate" capitalism, social hierarchy, and the nation-state ("the objective social causes" of "the ecological crisis") is arguably as utopian as the deep ecology that Bookchin was wont to chastise (far more stridently than most ecofeminists have done).[34] But its emphasis on collective practice, social revolution, and democratic equity at the level of small-scale community-building have tended to make it seem a more attractive option to those suspicious of the emphasis that deep ecology generally puts on awakened consciousness and individual transformation, and on humanness as a universal rather than a sociohistorically contingent condition.[35]

However, to dwell overmuch on how ecofeminism situates itself in relation to "social" vs. "deep" ecology risks losing sight of a point of greater importance: the broader shift in environmental criticism that ecofeminism's predilection for the more sociocentric path bespeaks. Just as feminism was moved by minority and "third world" feminisms during the 1980s and 1990s toward autocritique of its prior focus on Western white middle-class concerns, so during the

111

past decade some ecofeminists have been among the leaders in a broader initiative to push environmental criticism toward substantive engagement with issues of environmental welfare and equity of more pressing concern to the impoverished and socially marginalized: to landscapes of urbanization, racism, poverty, and toxification; and to the voices of witnesses and victims of environmental injustice. This at all events seems to be the most dynamic movement within environmental criticism right now, at least in the United States; and it is taking the ethics and politics of ecocriticism in a still more sociocentric direction. To refer back to the graph metaphor with which this chapter started, the winds of ecocritical doctrine have been shifting from northwest toward the southeast. One sign of the times is *The Environmental Justice Reader* (Adamson, Evans, and Stein 2002), a gathering of critical and social analyses, profiles of exemplary movements, activist testimonies, interviews, and pedagogical papers organized in tripartite fashion (Politics, Poetics, Pedagogy) that is designed as a corrective update to the largely first-wave essays collected in *The Ecocriticism Reader* (Glotfelty and Fromm 1996), which the editors of the new anthology rightly hold is still taken as a standard point of entry for outsiders looking for guidance as to what the movement is all about.

The Challenge of Environmental Justice Revisionism

The difference in preferred approach to environmental writing is quite clear. To begin with, the conception of canon differs markedly. For the purposes of *The Environmental Justice Reader*, American environmental writing effectively starts with Rachel Carson's *Silent Spring*, not with Thoreau or Frost or even Leopold. Contemporary writers of special interest on which the contributors have written here and elsewhere include Japanese American Karen Tei Yamashita (whose two major novels explore, respectively, Amazonian rainforest destruction in transnational context and postmodern inner-city

Los Angeles as a nodal point of transpacific and especially California–Mexico contact zones), Acoma poet-critic-activist Simon Ortiz, Chickasaw poet-novelist Linda Hogan (especially her work on environmental racism in northern Quebec and on clashing native vs. mainstream US canons regarding treatment of endangered species), and Chicana fiction writer Ana Castillo (death by workplace poisoning and AIDS in a New Mexican town) – rather than (say) A. R. Ammons, Gary Snyder, Barry Lopez, or even Terry Tempest Williams.

Simply changing direction doesn't mean you'll carry the day. I've called this new wave a vanguard, but some of the authors themselves express frustration that more headway hasn't been made sooner, despite signals of big-tent receptivity from the ecocritical community at large. "The lack of a strong environmental justice component within the field of ecocriticism should be felt as a deep crisis," one contributor warns. For in order to bring "environmental justice into ecocriticism," a few more articles or conference sessions won't suffice. There must be "a fundamental rethinking and reworking of the field as a whole, just as environmental justice theory and practice is leading to a fundamental rethinking of all environmental movements" (Reed 2002: 157).

This may indeed be ecocriticism's greatest challenge during the first part of the twenty-first century. Yes, we should live as if nature mattered, as the subtitle of Devall and Sessions' (1985) manual for deep ecology admonishes. But unless ecocriticism can squarely address the question of *how* nature matters for those readers, critics, teachers, and students for whom environmental concern does not mean nature preservation first and foremost and for whom nature writing, nature poetry, and wilderness narrative do not seem the most compelling forms of environmental imagination, then the movement may fission and wane.

Will this happen? Who can say for sure? What I want to stress here is my belief that it need not happen, although the kind of rethinking needed will require expansion of critical horizons all around.

113

Several considerations give one reason to expect that ecojustice revisionism will continue to gather force. First is the strong commitment within ecocriticism from the start to the interdependence of academic study and environmental practice, even if not the same kind of practices environmental justice revisionists call for. Second, the most often-cited embodiment of the "Principles of Environmental Justice," set forth in a multi-point statement by participants in the 1991 First National People of Color Environmental Leadership Summit held in Washington, DC, incorporates much that is basic to traditional environmentalism as well. Take, for example, the first and final provisions:

1 Environmental justice affirms the sacredness of Mother Earth, ecological unity and the interdependence of all species, and the right to be free from ecological destruction.
17 Environmental justice requires that we, as individuals, make personal and consumer choices to consume as little of Mother Earth's resources and to produce as little waste as possible; and make the conscious decision to challenge and reprioritize our life-styles to insure the health of the natural world for present and future generations.

To affirmations like these, ecocritics of all stripes would readily assent. Elsewhere, these Principles do certainly break from traditional protectionism. Provision 4, for example – "Environmental justice affirms the fundamental right to political, economic, cultural, and environmental self-determination of all peoples" – seems directed at least partly against expropriation of native land in order to create parks for the privileged, a worldwide phenomenon (see Spence 1999; D. S. Moore 1996) with European antecedents, such as the enclosure movement in early modern Britain. Nor do traditional environmentalist agendas make mention of the issues of "informed consent" to vaccination and experimental medical procedures practiced on people of color (no. 13) or worker safety, including "the right of those who work at home to be free from

114

environmental hazards" (no. 8). But at the turn of the twenty-first century serious environmentalists of virtually all stripes would likely subscribe to most if not all the 17 Principles.[36]

A third ground of optimism lies in the congruence between the ecojustice revisionist focus on community issues and narratives of community *vis-à-vis* first-wave ecocriticism's analogous emphasis on the local and regional. In each case, furthermore, sociocultural reformation and aesthetic awakening are commonly seen as intertwined with issues of ecological literacy.[37] A fourth consideration is the advancing realization that the story of environmental history needs to be told in recognition that the history of conservation and preservation movements is not disconnected from the evolution of urban and workplace environmentalism and such issues of environmental inequity as winners vs. losers in the protectionist sweepstakes.[38] Finally, the sheer moral force of ecojustice revisionism's critique of the demographic homogeneity of traditional environmental movements and academic environmental studies, including early ecocriticism, should not be underestimated. Indeed, this has been a simmering anxiety for the ecocritical movement from the beginning. The contributors to *The Environmental Justice Reader* may underestimate how strongly that tide will continue to run in their favor.

As for impediments, two may be especially consequential, other than simply the inertial resistances of prior commitments and internal solidarity on both sides. One is the sensitive question of how closely "environmental justice" should be seen as tied to the problem of "environmental racism." Certainly in the US and probably also worldwide, racial and ethnic minorities have been subjected to disproportionate environmental immiseration. Certainly within the US and perhaps also worldwide the awareness of this has been pivotal in attracting sizeable numbers of minority activists and scholars to engaging (some) environmental issues. Yet it remains a "contentious issue" as to "which groups or populations to include under the environmental-justice umbrella. Should income or regional location count as much (if at all) as race or ethnicity in environment-justice schemes?" (Rhodes 2003: 18). The preamble to the 1991 Principles calls specifically for "a national and international movement of all peoples of color," but its 17 points are generally couched in universalizing form ("mutual respect and justice for all peoples") (Merchant 1999: 371). Conversely, *The Environmental Justice Reader's* opening editorial statements define environmental justice initiatives broadly, as attempts "to redress the disproportionate incidence of environmental contamination in communities of the poor and/or communities of color" (Adamson, Evans, and Stein 2002: 4); but the ensuing historical sketch focuses solely on the emergence of minority opposition to environmental racism.

Any thinking person who has lived though the civil rights era in US history should understand the pragmatic historical reasons for these mixed signals. Nonetheless they pose a challenge for understanding precisely what "environmental justice" does or should mean, especially in broader global and historical contexts. On the former point, a leading student of "the environmentalism of the poor" in global context, Catalan ecological economist Joan Martínez-Alier, finds the US environmental justice movement something of an outlier insofar as US "environmental justice" concerns boil down to the problem of "environmental racism," especially in African American, Hispanic, and Native American communities (Martínez-Alier 2002: 168–72).[39] How, for example, does one frame the eco-martyrdom of Nigerian writer-activist Ken Saro-wiwa in defense of his Ogone homeland against transnational oil interests and the authoritarian neocolonial Abaja regime that supported them? In a laudable extension of *The Ecocriticism Reader's* attempt to move beyond a US-centric perspective, *The Environmental Justice Reader* treats this as a case of environmental racism (Comfort 2002). Martínez-Alier, by contrast, cautions that "Ken Saro-wiwa did not use the language of 'environmental racism' against the military government of Nigeria" but "the language of indigenous territorial rights and human rights." In this particular case, a middle ground might be that Saro-wiwa did invoke both moral universals *and* Ogone's ethnic, although not racial, minority

116

status. But Martínez-Alier's broader point remains pertinent: that "ecological distribution conflicts are fought with different vocabularies," with "the language of 'environmental racism'" less broadly applicable across the board in a global context than definers like disempowerment and poverty (Martínez-Alier 2002: 172).

One of the most prominent American scholar-activists investigating environmental racism, African American sociologist Robert Bullard, lent support to this view when he remarked at an Australian conference on environmental justice that "environmental racism is just one form of environmental injustice" and elaborated a five-point "environmental justice paradigm" beginning from "the principle of the 'right' of all individuals to be protected from environmental degradation" (Bullard 1999: 34–5). Other conferees also tended to conceive of environmental justice in broad distributional terms not limited to specific racial or ethnic groups (see Dryzek 1999: 266), such that, for example, disproportionate geographical distribution of fallout from the Chernobyl explosion of 1986 was seen as an issue of environmental injustice (Shrader-Frechette 1999). Altogether, the greater the push toward framing the issue of environmental justice on a global scale, as this international conference attempted to do, the greater may be the tendency to think of racism as a frequent but not ubiquitous cause of environmental injustice.[40]

Likewise, when a student of grassroots environmental movements worldwide like Martínez-Alier turns his attention to US environmental justice historiography, he sees it as an idiosyncratically national phenomenon that the "official birth" of the movement should have become identified with a 1982 North Carolina African American community's resistance to the siting of a waste dump in its backyard, rather than credit the late 1970s Love Canal toxification protest as the takeoff point (Martínez-Alier 2002: 172). Strictly speaking, he is wrong to claim that the story has only been told one way. The catalytic significance of Love Canal and its primary spokesperson Lois Gibbs' achievement in creating a national network out of scattered local protests have in fact been quite fully documented (e.g. Szasz 1994: 5, 69–83). But it is also true that US environmental justice historians have often preferred to marginalize this episode for the sake of emphasizing the significance of minority protests since the 1982 Warren County incident, which "began to forge the connection between race, poverty, and the environmental consequences of the production of industrial waste" (Di Chiro 1995: 303). *The Environmental Justice Reader* follows this lead by deferring to the orthodoxy of the 1982 inception, by omitting mention of Love Canal, and by concentrating overwhelmingly on cases of eco-oppression of minorities. The most salient exception confirms the general approach: a white ecocritic's poignant essay interweaving an autobiographical account of his and his late sister's battles against what seems to have been environmentally induced cancer, with critical discussion of (white) ecologist, environmental writer, and cancer-survivor Sandra Steingraber's *Living Downstream* (1997), which brings a wide array of cancer-cluster narratives (including her own) to bear in an assessment of the state of epidemiological knowledge about environmental causation and a stringent critique of the reluctance of powers that be to consider such evidence, particularly the testimony of local or folk epidemiology from underresourced communities (Tarter 2002). The essay is troubled by Steingraber's silence on the question of differential toxification according to race, which to his mind seems to exclude her work from the domain of environmental justice proper, although he finds her book otherwise compelling.

Such hesitancy is understandable in an era when ecocritics are still only starting to explore minority canons, when minority ecocritics are still very few in number, when minority scholars with strong environmental interests of any sort still seem self-conscious of being thought eccentric by their communities (see Peña 1998: 14), and when in real-life US environmental controversies the appeal to minority group membership can be a necessary survival strategy (see Pulido 1998).[41] At such a historical moment, one might argue that it is a virtue for critics from the dominant subculture to take pains to stress the difference between their positions and those for whom ecocultural struggle or immiseration has been compounded by having been racially or ethnically marked as social others. Co-editor Joni Adamson's monograph on environmental justice issues in Native American literature is a model of such self-awareness (Adamson 2001). Still, in the long run, for ecojustice revisionism to become a transformative rather than simply dissenting force within environmental criticism, a fuller engagement of the affinities as well as the differences between the archives of white and minority environmental imagination will likely be necessary. At least two specific paths suggest themselves: two discourses or genres in terms of which the imagination of environmental justice issues in contemporary minority communities might be situated within environmental writing more generally, to the illumination of both.

One just indicated is environmental illness narrative – perhaps of cancer especially, although the gamut includes many other kinds of bodily as well as psychic wounding, of both individual and community. A number of the literary texts cited in the Poetics and Pedagogy sections of *The Environmental Justice Reader* fall into this category. It has a long history, never yet examined comprehensively, which the *Reader*, whose concentration is much more presentist than its predecessor, does not trace back before Carson. A number of these texts are written from and/or about nonwhites, including many Afro-Atlantic slave narratives and Native American autobiographical narratives of the eighteenth century onward that dramatize landscapes of racist confinement in which victims are penned, cheated, and driven to death, as well as spaces of refuge or relief from these. But this is only a portion of the full archive of what has claim to count as environmental justice writing. In US literary history, many narratives of immiserated immigrants of every stripe would also have good claim, for example. The most famous of these is the exposé in Upton Sinclair's *The Jungle* (1906) of gross mistreatment of suffering workers in the Chicago meatpacking industry, focusing on a particular family of Lithuanian victims, who get maimed or killed off one by one.

Well before the apogee of US immigration narrative, early industrial Euro-American factory literature was already dramatizing

119

analogous cases of mistreatment of white workers. Friedrich Engels' *Condition of the Working Class in England* (1845) is the classic documentary work. The very extensive literary archive includes Herman Melville's "The Tartarus of Maids" and Rebecca Harding Davis' "Life in the Iron Mills"; autobiographical narratives by female millworkers in the American northeast; and among Victorian novels, to name but two examples, Charles Dickens' *Hard Times* and Elizabeth Gaskell's chapters in *North and South* on the pathetic death of a tubercular Manchester factory worker's daughter befriended by the protagonist, a proletarian double of her own mother, who is also quietly dying from the polluted atmosphere that weighs upon the city. And a half-century before any of these, William Blake's poems of lost, innocent child laborers, the chimney sweep and little black boy, as well as some of the most graphic passages in his *Jerusalem* and other prophetic books, already broach environmental justice issues.

As *The Environmental Justice Reader* anticipates, the ultimate scope of such inquiry would not just be Anglo-American or Anglophone but, in principle, worldwide, encompassing such texts (and their underlying contexts) as Michiko Ishimure's *Paradise in the Sea of Sorrow* and Mahasweta Devi's "Pterodactyl, Puran Satay, and Pirtha," both mentioned in chapter 3. Or the pioneering literary naturalism of Émile Zola, particularly *Germinal* (1885), which stands behind the long tradition of American fictional naturalism from Norris and Dreiser through John Steinbeck and Richard Wright. For Ishimure and Zola, race is basically a non-issue; for Devi it is crucial; but all three should surely count as environmental justice writing.

So too for literature that takes up the partially overlapping predicament of what Gadgil and Guha, in their environmental history of India, call "ecological refugees," by which they mean specifically land-based peoples (including but not limited to ethnic minorities) reduced to welfare or beggary by displacement from their home communities (Gadgil and Guha 1995: esp. 4, 32–3). This is another prevalent concern in literary texts favored by contemporary ecojustice revisionists, such as Linda Hogan's *Solar Storms*.

It too offers itself as a nexus of a more comprehensive rereading of eco-literature, globally as well as historically, especially if one broadens from narratives of community, like Hogan's Cree or Indo-Anglian novelist Raja Rao's *Kanthapura*, the story of a fictional village obliterated and dispersed for Gandhist resistance to the British Raj, to include also such symptomatic narratives of environmentally displaced individuals as the Shoshone medicine man in Mary Austin's *Land of Little Rain*, or Ivar the landwise but socially maladaptive Norwegian homesteader in Willa Cather's novel *O Pioneers!*, who as his frontier community modernizes must become the heroine's ward.

The literature of ecological refugeeism stretches back even further in time than environmental illness narrative. The literature and aesthetics of the British enclosure movement date back nearly half a millennium, as the work of Raymond Williams and his successors has shown. "It is not easy to forget," Williams remarks, "that Sidney's *Arcadia*, which gives a continuing title to English neo-pastoral, was written in a park which had been made by enclosing a whole village and evicting the tenants" (Williams 1973: 22). Indeed so – once you've learned the fact. This is the kind of history with which contemporary-focused ecojustice revisionism needs to be put in conversation in order for it to become as transformative as it deserves to be.

To rethink the history of environmental reimagination from these perspectives need not mean rejecting ecocriticism's traditional genres but, rather, seeing them in new ways. It need not simply be a matter of calling attention to blind spots like the silence of Edward Abbey's *Desert Solitaire* or – for that matter – Leslie Silko's *Ceremony* on the subject of nuclear contamination of their respective imagined places, important though that kind of critical work also is.[42] The dialogue is more complicated than that. On the one hand, the prettily quaint elegiac couplets of Oliver Goldsmith's eighteenth-century poem *The Deserted Village* ("But times are altered; Trade's unfeeling train / Usurp the land and dispossess the swain") take on new resonance when considered as a reflection on ecological refugeeism.[43] This could be a Chinese village destined for flooding by the Three Gorges Dam. It could be a Hispanic or Native American agricultural village taken over by big ranching or recreational interests. On the other hand, Rachel Carson's achievement as foremother of contemporary environmental justice writing is enhanced as one realizes that she arrived there through a gradual process of reluctantly quarreling – but never completely breaking – with the nature writing conventions that inform her earlier books. The success of *Silent Spring* was in no small measure dependent on the stylistic strategies as well as the public prestige she had previously acquired as an award-winning nature writer.[44]

Even Thoreau's *Walden*, the most canonical text in all of US environmental literary nonfiction, might be productively rethought in terms of an uneasy mediation between the prideful standoffishness of the author's voluntary simplicity experiment and his inability to ignore the genuinely impoverished, extruded Irish and black denizens of the Concord outback. In "Baker Farm" and "Former Inhabitants," Thoreau tries to put these individuals, both living and dead, in their places and offer his own example as a superior counterculture, rather like the way he has previously rebuilt the makeshift shanty of an Irish railroad-worker into a cleaner, trimmer cabin of his own. But he cannot help also acknowledging his interdependence with these outcasts. They are a mocking echo, impossible to romanticize in the way he romanticizes Native Americans elsewhere in *Walden*, of his own half-confessed, half-suppressed inability to balance his own accounts and his awareness of being thought a failure, driven to a state of dependent squatterdom in the eyes of many in his community. Obviously, it would be absurd to claim Thoreau as a refugee of the kind Gadgil and Guha have in mind: the multitudes of landless poor crowded into India's urban slums. But to think of the *Walden* persona, through an environmental justice lens, as struggling with concerns of poverty, downward mobility, and chagrin at being socially reduced to the equivalent of an ethnic other helps both to define the book's mental limits – the presumption of the still-comparatively privileged, subsidized Yankee likening his predicament to that of a wandering Native American basket-peddler – and to mark off what makes *Walden* a more searching ecocultural inquiry than much of the latter-day voluntary simplicity literature partly inspired by it.

Since I have lingered mostly so far on examples from US writing even while commending the importance of thinking globally, for my final examples I shall turn to two works of Australian writing that further suggest how environmental justice concerns can play back and forth across dominant and marginalized subcultures. The first is the opening portion of a protest poem against bicentennial complacency, "Celebrators 88," by aboriginal author Kevin Gilbert, the second a novella by Queensland feminist-regionalist writer Thea Astley, "Inventing the Weather" (1992), told in the first-person by a suburban woman who finds temporary solace after fleeing a failed marriage with a philandering real-estate developer by joining a group of three nuns working on an unauthorized mission to assist a small colony of displaced Aborigines on a remote coast. Here is the passage from "Celebrators 88":

> The blue-green greyish gum leaves
> blew behind the bitter banksia that bent
> in supplication silently bereaved
> bereft of the black circle that once sat
> around its base to stroke and chant the songs
> that made the rivers flow and life wax fat
> the legends and the river now replaced
> by sheep torn gullies and a muddy silt
> that sluggishly and sullen in retreat
> throws up its mud to signal its defeat . . .
> (Kevin Gilbert 1988: 198)

Gilbert and Astley are both hard-bitten ironists in different registers: his rhetorically impassioned, hers dryly laconic. For both, the story of Australian "development" since white settlement boils down to a story of greed, waste, and degradation, whose worst scandal is the plight of the Aborigines. Against this, both fashion sharply

123

different discourses of righteous indignation vs. self-reflexive liberal guilt, that reflect the lines of division between the internationally prominent, well-educated white *literata* vs. the convicted felon of primary school education striving to help build the small, embattled aboriginal intellectual community but wanting to make his voice heard across racial lines. Gilbert's persona confidently aligns his voice with "the black circle," while Astley's narrator feels constrained to declare *her* solidarity at a scrupulously self-critical distance, confessing her initial reluctance to push against the race barrier she knows she will never transcend, and constantly questioning her motives for wanting to be there. She is a sincere supporter of aboriginal rights, but she knows that *her* main motive right now is self-recovery. She's haunted by its triviality compared to the nuns' lifetime commitment. She insists on bringing her self-focused, semi-estranged children to this place, but is guiltily aware of this act of attempted consciousness-raising as a ploy to win back their allegiances that will likely annoy the nuns and the residents. She entertains the idea of remaining herself, but senses all the time that she doesn't belong.

"Inventing the Weather" is a counterpart to "Celebrators 88" rather than a completely different project. They share a common adversary: Julie's husband Clifford could have been one of Gilbert's "thieves a'crouch above the pilfered purse." Each might also be said to respect the other's position. If that seems a strange thing to say about Gilbert's poem, consider how "Celebrators 88" is scripted to appeal across race lines to mainstream concern for *both* aboriginal displacement *and* environmental degradation.

Both texts also show how environmental justice commitments can coexist with an ecocentric persuasion, although this plays itself through differently in each case. Gilbert's poem is unabashedly neoprimordialist. It harks back to presettlement days before sheepfarming and exploitative irrigation, when the intact circle sang the songs that made the rivers flow, and (in a subsequent passage) laments the sun "now veiled in smog so spirits cannot peek." Perhaps this is a "strategic" essentialism that can't be taken at face value –

124

as some have claimed of Native American invocations of the authority of "mother earth."[45] Yet the fate of both people and land do seem for Gilbert to be bound together, as with Native American claims that "most of us think of the earth as our mother; we talk to the waters, to the big plant world and the little plant world, the four-leggeds" (Adamson, Evans, and Stein 2002: 43).[46]

As for Astley's "Inventing the Weather," it too distressedly imagines natural environment and aboriginal culture as coordinate victims. In the bush, moreover, Julie is also overtaken at intervals with something like an ecocentric consciousness, although this is far from being the solidarity-producing sense of belonging that Gilbert ascribes to his imagined ancestors. The place feels more alien than inviting. She experiences "terror Australis, the fear of those unending spaces, the wild unenclosures." The tropical landscape of the mission seems to "flaunt a superiority to human endeavour that is crushing." Could the Romantic poets "have written their more extravagantly maudlin bits under a sky of ripe cobalt, temperature one hundred degrees in the shade?" In a neo-Conradian twist, the bush takes its revenge on Clifford, who to Julie's horror suddenly turns up at the mission intent upon developing the pristine beachfront but then just as suddenly disappears into the surrounding forest, joining "that long roll call of trackers who had challenged jungle."[47]

Neither text adheres consistently to any of the forms of ecocentric ethics discussed at the beginning of this chapter. Yet, for whatever reasons, for both authors, an anthropocentric cultural politics of environmental justice seems to demand appeal to ecocentric scenarios: the primordialist fall from Eden narrative in Gilbert's case, the Darwinian revenge of nature narrative in Astley's. But perhaps there is no self-contradiction here after all. Perhaps appeals to the nature of natural order have a rightful, even fundamental, place in the literature of environmental justice, in framing what justice and injustice mean. "What makes humans exceptional in comparison to other animals," Martínez-Alier observes, "is not only our talking and laughing and our evolving cultures but our potential for enormous and historically increasing *intra-specific differences* in the exosomatic use of energy and materials" (Martínez-Alier 2002: 70–1). In other words, not greater tool-making capacity per se so much as greater production of environmental inequalities that sophisticated tool-making permits *homo sapiens* to indulge is what makes this species stand out among life forms. This defines the perversity of a social order that produces gross inequalities in such a way as to fuse bio-centric and anthropocentric perspectives, making them difficult to prise apart.

Indeed, the two concerns are inherently interwoven, insofar as "nature," to quote another ecojustice scholar-activist, "is the lived environment common to humankind and otherkind wherever both kinds live and work and love and eat." But the "wherever," he knows, covers an enormous range of positions. "Nature is the lead-filled air breathed in by schoolchildren in toxic urban killing fields; nature is the pristine landscapes and watersheds that still survive in rural parks and wildlands" (M. Wallace 1997: 306). Given the disparity in what might legitimately be felt as "nature" or "environment," the divisions I have surveyed seem bound to persist for a long time to come, if not forever.

This is a point worth special emphasis at the end of a chapter that has arranged its materials somewhat too neatly in order to make them manageable. My one-two-three series of deep ecology, ecofeminism, and environmental justice has relegated a number of significant ethico-political positions to the sidelines, most notably the discourses of animal and other nonhuman rights and a range of discourses of local–global interaction from liberal green reform to anticapitalist critiques of consumerism. I have simplified chrono-logically too, extracting a too-tidy narrative of "from (relatively) ecocentric to (more) sociocentric environmentalism" out of a messier and more pluriform critical scene. Deep ecology has not in fact been displaced by ecofeminism or social ecology, nor has eco-justice revisionism displaced them, nor do any of these positions – important and representative though all three of them are – cover the whole range of environmental criticism. Furthermore, the way

126

I have imagined ecojustice revisionism intertwining with prior ecocritical emphases outlined in the latter portion of this chapter is likely to be criticized by both sides, as being an attenuation of core environmental justice concerns and as restricting ecocriticism's agenda overmuch to issues of social justice and equity. But these two pronouncements I do make with confidence. First, that environmental criticism in literary studies is increasingly moving – albeit irregularly – in the direction of extending the concept of environment beyond the arena of the "natural" alone and in the process is becoming increasingly sophisticated in its address to how, in both literature and in history, "natural" and "social" environments impinge on each other. Second, that with regard to ethico-political persuasion, just as in the arena of environmental public policy, so too in humanistic environmental criticism, the soundest positions – whether or not they happen to carry the day – will be those that come closest to speaking *both* to humanity's most essential needs and to the state and fate of the earth and its nonhuman creatures independent of those needs, as well as to the balancing if not also the reconciliation of the two. Serious artists do both. So too must we critics.

5

Environmental Criticism's Future

I hate conclusions. A good book, essay, course, or lecture should open up its subject, not shut it down. Conclusions are chronically hamstrung by the temptations to reach closure or attempt prophecy in the narrow sense of prediction. Temptations to pronounce judgment become all the more irresistible when the subject is a fast-burgeoning movement with which one is identified. But yielding to them under such circumstances is all the riskier. In the mid-1980s, when I first started lecturing and writing on environmental issues, I had no idea that the as-yet unborn ecocritical movement would even come into being, let alone take the course it has. So what authorizes me to predict its future now? Even supposing I were right, this book would then amount to a kind of epitaph in advance and portend what I believe is *not* true: that environmental criticism has no more surprises in store.

A better stab at future-oriented assessment is to take stock of where environmental criticism now seems to stand with respect to the typical challenges or crises that critical movements can expect to face. These include at least four: the challenge of organization, the challenge of professional legitimation, the challenge of defining distinctive models of critical inquiry, and the challenge of establishing their significance beyond the academy. By these criteria, the progress of environmental criticism in the field of literary studies has been on the whole encouraging but mixed.

In the first area the gains have been impressive. The Association for the Study of Literature and Environment has evolved from a small caucus to a worldwide network in less than a decade, with a burgeoning number of conferences and publication venues worldwide. Although this organizational achievement has come at the cost of siphoning a certain amount of intellectual energy into administrative busywork and repetitive intratribal exercise-piece performances, the gains have more than offset these predictable hazards of bureaucratization, in no small measure because of the emphasis that ASLE has put on opening its fora not only to dialogue among scholars but also with artists and activists. More on that below.

The challenge of professional legitimation, by contrast, still has not been met, although the situation is changing slowly for the better. Environmental criticism in literature and the arts clearly does not yet have the standing within the academy of such other issue-driven discourses as those of race, gender, sexuality, class, and globalization. Only a handful of graduate programs in literature make ecocriticism a specialty of the house. For every US college or university job advertising for expertise in literature-and-environment studies today there are several in queer theory and many more in ethnic studies. Were a comparative survey made in the year 2005 of departments of history and departments of literature as to the desirability for a specialist in the environmental field, it would surely be found that environmental history is deemed more central to its discipline than ecocriticism is to its. On the other hand, the quality of the best work now published in ASLE's flagship journal, *ISLE*, is at least equal to that of the articles published in *Environmental History*, the journal of the American Society for Environmental History, even though the latter (both the journal and the organization itself) has been in existence twice as long; and there seems to be no serious lack of publishing venues elsewhere for critical articles and books on environmental issues. The presses that make a *speciality* of environmental criticism tend still to be of the second rank, but they have also gained in visibility and standing as the result of those commitments. Meanwhile, an interest in environmental issues

129

seems more a plus than a minus for young academics in literature who are willing to work within the preexisting grid of literary studies, even when expertise in environmental studies per se has not been expressly advertised for.

Willingness to work within the preexisting grid – this brings us to the third challenge. Environmental criticism in literary studies has, thus far, not changed literary studies or environmental humanities so much as it has been increasingly absorbed therein. This in spite of the fact that first-wave ecocriticism, as we have seen, gathered much of its original takeoff energy from disaffection with critical theory-as-usual. But its durability so far rests on its having introduced a fresh topic or perspective or archive rather than in distinctive methods of inquiry. In this respect, environmental criticism, not only in literary studies but also throughout the human sciences, cannot (at least not yet) claim the *methodological* originality that was injected into literary studies by (say) new critical formalism and by deconstruction. Just as environmental ethics, which (like environmental history) is twice as longstanding as ecocriticism, tends to remain bound to such extrinsic but field-sanctioned models as utilitarian, deontological, and ontological critique, so too with environmental criticism's characteristic ways of reading literary texts. Both for first-wave and second-wave inquiry, the conceptual originality has consisted in such breakthroughs as the foregrounding of neglected (sub)genres like nature writing or toxification narrative; in the exegesis of environmental subtexts through historical and critical analyses that employ ready-to-hand analytical tools of the trade together with less familiar ones eclectically derived from other disciplinary bailiwicks; and in the identification or reinterpretation of such thematic configurations as pastoral, eco-apocalypticism, and environmental racism.

These are far from being trivial achievements, however. On the contrary, to succeed in changing the subject or in changing the archive is every bit as important in the evolution of critical inquiry as a revolution in critical theory as such. The most important legacy of feminist and black studies probably lies, likewise, in having made the case for serious attention to these domains of inquiry rather than in any radical shift in critical methodology associated with them. The likelihood that this will be environmental criticism's legacy too seems all the more probable given the interdisciplinarity of which it necessarily partakes, and in even greater measure insofar as all branches of natural science are potentially of greater inherent relevance to it, as well as the whole range of "human" sciences. (A discourse of nanotechnology of some relevance to the phenomenon of environmental-aesthetic perception seems more plausible than, say, a minoritarian nanotechnology.) There are so many contexts in which environmentality can be instructively framed from the vantage point of literary studies that no one approach may prevail for long. And if not, why complain? It will have been achievement enough if environmentality becomes seen as indispensable to how one reads literature – whether the specific project at hand be the environmental literacy of a text, its way of situating itself locally and/or globally, its attention or inattention to the nonhuman sphere, or its ideological valence(s) with regard to receptivity or opacity to social justice issues.

I certainly do not mean to discourage methodological self-consciousness and innovation. That would be untrue to what I like to think has been the spirit of my own work. I mean only to suggest that a new critical paradigm is not the be-all or end-all that it is often thought to be. Field-defining paradigms are after all made to be broken. Edward Said's *Orientalism*, cited in chapter 1, is a good example. Its forceful, erudite exposé of presumptuous misconstructions by European authorities on the non-west drove home powerful but reductive images of west-non-west dualism and an intellectually silenced non-west that had then to be questioned and taken apart, a process to which Said himself contributed in *Culture and Imperialism* (1993) and a long series of essays before and after. His long-range contribution lay more in opening up for literary studies – and beyond – a hitherto underexamined dynamic of manifest, mounting importance for both western and non-western worlds, than in his specific model for exploring it. Human

131

imbrication in environmentality is another example of an area under-explored in literary studies before 1990 and certain to become much more so in this new century, whatever form inquiry may take. Indeed, no issue of global proportions is more crucially important than this.

But how much will environmental criticism in literary studies matter to those outside its own disciplinary cloister, let alone to the lay world outside the academy? With respect to this, the fourth challenge, the answer so far looks more encouraging in the pedagogical arena than in that of critical discourse. As teachers and citizens, ecocritics of both first and second waves have been highly inventive, indeed exemplary, in breaking down classroom walls to send students into the field, in inspiring them to move on to postgraduate destinations of various sorts in the environmental area, in joining forces with artists and activists, and sometimes in undertaking significant creative or activist endeavors themselves. On the other hand, the market for ecocritical publications so far has been chiefly academic, and within academia chiefly largely confined to professors and students of literature, with relatively modest lateral percolation effect.

To some, this discrepancy is bound to seem ironic and disturbing. For one thing, academic humanists in general, in the United States at least, seem for reasons more complex than this book can explore more desirous of becoming public actors than ever before in my professional lifetime. But more specifically, as seen in chapter 4 and from what has just been said about pedagogy and citizenly commitments, the path of environmental criticism tends to signal a reformist or transformationist aspiration in light of which the very thought of casting one's thoughts into an academic discourse directed chiefly toward other academics may seem dispiriting. That is doubtless a key reason why ecocritics often turn to what Slovic (1994) and others have called narrative scholarship, which casts critical analysis in the form of autobiographical narrative.

Yet there is nothing inherently shameful whatever about the present situation. Far from it. A strong argument can be made for the proposition that intra-field impact followed by trickle-down percolation is what serious academic work should seek in any case. Without that, the second and third challenges – of professional legitimation and of changing the direction of inquiry within the field – will never be successfully met. Said's *Orientalism* would never have had the impact it did without being a first-rate work of scholarship and intellection, despite its allegoristic limitations. The same holds for the inaugural works of new historicism, such as Stephen Greenblatt's *Renaissance Self-Fashioning*. I myself believe that environmental criticism at the turn of the twenty-first century will also come to be looked back upon as a moment that did produce a cluster of challenging intellectual work, a constellation rather than a single titanic book or figure, that established environmentality as a permanent concern for literary and other humanists, and through that even more than through acts of pedagogical or activist outreach helped instill and reinforce public concern about the fate of the earth, about humankind's responsibility to act on that awareness, about the shame of environmental injustice, and about the importance of vision and imagination in changing minds, lives, and policy as well as composing words, poems, and books. There! That is my prophecy.

Glossary of Selected Terms

anthropocentrism   The assumption or view that the interests of humans are of higher priority than those of nonhumans. Often used as an antonym for biocentrism or ecocentrism. Anthropocentrism actually covers a multitude of possible positions, from the positive conviction (strong anthropocentrism) that human interests should prevail, to the belief that zero-degree anthropocentrism is not feasible or desirable (weak anthropocentrism). So it is entirely possible without hypocrisy to maintain biocentric values in principle while recognizing that in practice these must be constrained by anthropocentric considerations, whether as a matter of strategy or as a matter of intractable human self-interestedness. Insofar as anthropocentrism might imply other primates as well as *homo sapiens*, homocentrism is more precise, yet much more rarely used. *See also* anthropomorphism, biocentrism, deep ecology, ecocentrism.

anthropomorphism   The attribution of human feelings or traits to nonhuman beings or objects or natural phenomena. Anthropomorphism implies an anthropocentric frame of reference, but the two do not correlate precisely. For example, a poet's choice to personify a bird or tree might betoken what Victorian critic John Ruskin called the "pathetic fallacy," a projection of human desire to make nature sympathize with humankind; or, oppositely, it might be done in the interest of dramatizing the claims or plight of the natural world. Often, both motives are at play in, say, animal stories and animal folklore. *See also* anthropocentrism.

biocentrism   The view that all organisms, including humans, are part of a larger biotic web or network or community whose interests must constrain or direct or govern the human interest. Used as a semi-synonym for ecocentrism and in antithesis to anthropocentrism. But even most self-identified biocentrists or ecocentrists recognize these ethical paradigms as ideals toward which to strive, rather than actualities likely to be implemented in practice. *See also* anthropocentrism, ecocentrism.

bioregion, bioregionalism Bioregionalism is a philosophy or vision, originating in the American west during the 1970s, of life in place conducted in so far as possible in deference to the ecological limits of the place where one lives. From the perspective of ecology, a bioregion or ecoregion is a geographical area of similar climate where similar ecosystems and groups of species are found on similar sites. Bioregionalism, however, views a bioregion not only as a territory defined by natural markers, such as watersheds, but also as a domain of consciousness and as a focus of citizenly allegiance that challenges conventional political boundaries. Bioregionalism aspires to respect and restore natural systems while satisfying basic human needs in sustainable ways, believing that geographical units of relatively small scale are likeliest to promote such engagement. Chapter 3 discusses the concept (and its vulnerabilities) in more detail. *See also* ecology, place, reinhabitation, sustainability.

brownfields A term coined by environmental analysts in the early 1990s to denote toxic sites, the opposite of affluent suburban and exurban "greenfields," particularly in inner-city areas, that pose health hazards and require remediation (Shutkin and Mores 2000: 57–75). "Brownfields" is also used more loosely to characterize anthropogenically degraded landscapes, particularly in urban and industrial zones. The maldistribution of brownfields sites in poor and minority neighborhoods, and the threat of further degradation, has been key to galvanizing the environmental justice movement. As ecocriticism has taken an increasing interest in urban environments, brownfields as well as "greenfields" have become more important to its agenda as well. *See also* environmental justice.

culture Raymond Williams (1983: 87) rightly calls culture "one of the two or three most complicated words in the English language." "What is culture, anyway?" Jamaica Kincaid shrewdly asks. "In some places, it's the way they play drums; in other places, it's the way you behave out in public; and in still other places, it's just the way a person cooks food."[1] Environmental critics often emphasize its derivation from Latin *colere*, whose denotations include "cultivate, respect, till, take care of." From this standpoint, "a culture is a network of neighborhoods or communities that is rooted and tended" (Snyder 1990: 179). "In all its early uses," culture "was a noun of process: the tending of something, basically crops or animals" (Williams 1983: 87), or "skilled human activities through which non-human nature is encompassed and transformed."[2] In this sense culture can be seen as arising from (if not dependent on) agriculture (Berry 1977: 39–48).

Culture's beginnings as a noun, denoting a life-state as distinct from life-process, and its association with institutions of various strata of civility (as in high culture or folk culture), seem to date from the early modern period but not to have become fully institutionalized until the nineteenth century

(Williams 1983: 88–90). Culture as noun has thus during the past several centuries evolved in increasing distinction from nature (considered as non-built environment): from an understanding of the two domains as symbiotic, to the notion of culture as a marker of the divergence of the social from the natural. Nature writer Edward Abbey encapsulates the traditional understanding of culture-as-noun in defining culture as "the way of life of any given human society considered as a whole," "an anthropological term referring always to specific, identifiable societies," and including "all aspects" of such – economy, art, religion, etc.[3] This holistic "one society, one culture" mentality now looks simplistic, however, in light of contemporary recognition that actual societies are at least as likely to be marked by cultural difference and/or hybridization as by "a" common culture. By the same token, although culture has tended to be thought of in terms of traditions passed down through the generations, clearly cultures also evolve, whether one thinks of them in holistic or in multi-stranded terms. Williams usefully distinguishes between three cultural phases or dispensations, which typically also overlay: the residual, the dominant, and the emergent (Williams 1977: 121–7).

In modern times, culture has also become a term for characterizing the socialization-effect of particular roles, as in the "culture of professionalism" or the "culture" of the corporate world. One of the marks of the culture(s) of environmental criticism today is that the place of culture in relation to nature has become a matter of lively debate. Many join Snyder and Berry in pushing to redefine culture and cultural practices so as to reconnect them more closely with nature; but as noted especially in chapter 4 (above) an increasing number of critics approach environmental issues from the standpoint of cultural studies, conceiving of nature, particularly under modernization, predominantly in terms of its manipulation or reinvention by human culture. *See also* ecocriticism, nature.

cyborg A mid-twentieth-century coinage, deriving from "cybernetics," denoting an organic (typically, human) being altered by mechanical means. Since the mid-1980s the idea has been given greater circulation and bite through the influence of Donna Haraway's "Cyborg Manifesto" (1991: 149–81), in which "cyborg" signifies not one but three "crucial boundary breakdowns": between organisms and machines, between humans and nonhumans, and between the physical and the nonphysical. Haraway's vision of a cyborg as "a kind of disassembled and reassembled, postmodern collective and personal self" (p. 163) is framed particularly as a socialist-feminist myth of identity to liberate women from the bonds of the natural; but its intended reach is more sweeping: to envisage "a way out of the maze of dualisms in which we have explained our bodies and our tools to ourselves" (p. 181). In this view, we are all cyborgs now.

136

Glossary of Selected Terms

deep ecology As discussed in chapter 4, a term introduced by Norwegian philosopher Arne Naess to distinguish Naess's biotically egalitarian vision of "organisms as knots in the biospherical net or field of intrinsic relations" from "shallow" environmentalist campaigns against "pollution and resource depletion" chiefly for "the health and affluence of people in the developed countries" (Naess 1973: 95). (Naess further distinguishes deep ecology from "ecosophy," meaning a personalized version of the former.)

Deep ecology envisages, then, a relational understanding of selfhood "based on active identification with wider and wider circles of being" (Mathews 2001: 221). This biospherical inclusiveness, together with deep ecology's rapid transformation from a philosophical position to a movement that has tended "to avoid philosophical honing" (Hay 2002: 42), has been responsible for its being sometimes used as a synonym for ecocentric persuasions generally. Yet the emphasis deep ecology typically attaches to realization of (a transformed) self through identification with nature has provoked some to argue that it is actually anthropocentric relative to ecosystem-based or respect-for-nature ethics (Katz 2000). Ecofeminists have also criticized the lumping tendency in deep ecology's conception of humanness that leads it to elide or marginalize gender difference and the history of patriarchy, though some have also tried to mediate between the two (e.g., Mathews 1999; Salleh 2000).

Deep ecology's biotic egalitarianism, together with the recognition of affinities between deep ecology and Heidegger's thought, and pronouncements by some deep ecologists that overpopulation and ecosystemic imperilment are more pressing problems than human poverty and disease, have incurred charges of antihumanism or ecofascism (e.g., Ferry 1995). Zimmerman (1997) has persuasively replied to these, both by acknowledging that Nazism *did* combine "eugenics with mystical ecology" (p. 241), from which Heidegger cannot be shielded, and contending that charges of ecofascism against latter-day deep ecology are groundless, that deep ecologists from Naess on who have engaged in activism have done so from the left rather than the right. *See also* ecocentrism, ecofascism.

ecocentrism The view in environmental ethics that the interest of the ecosphere must override that of the interest of individual species. Used like the semi-synonymous biocentrism in antithesis to anthropocentrism, but whereas biocentrism refers specifically to the world of organisms, ecocentrism points to the interlinkage of the organismal and the inanimate. Ecocentrism covers a range of possible specific ecophilosophies (Hay 2002: 34–5 identifies at least five). In general, ecocentrists hold that "the world is an intrinsically dynamic, interconnected web of relations" with "no absolute dividing lines between the living and the nonliving, the animate and the inanimate" (Eckersley 1992: 49). The origins of modern ecocentric ethics are traceable to Aldo Leopold

137

(Merchant 1992: 75), inventor of the concept of the "land ethic," which "enlarges the boundaries of the community to include soils, waters, plants, and animals" (Leopold 1949: 204). *See also* biocentrism.

ecocriticism Ecocriticism is an umbrella term (see chapter 1 for more detail), used to refer to the environmentally oriented study of literature and (less often) the arts more generally, and to the theories that underlie such critical practice. Thus, for example, an ecocritic *may* be an ecofeminist, but only a fraction of ecofeminists would generally be thought of as ecocritics. It can apply to hybrid genres of "narrative scholarship" (Slovic 1994) that blend the "creative" and the "critical" (e.g., Snyder 1990; Elder 1998; Marshall 2003). First (and still most commonly) used in the US, the term has spread worldwide. Insofar as ecocriticism gestures toward biological science and to the "natural" as against the "built" environment, it might be thought too restrictive to encompass the actual range of critical practices, relative to such terms as literature-and-environment studies (which does not explicitly signal "natural" environment) or environmental criticism (which better implies the wide interdisciplinary range of methods so-called ecocritics employ). Notwithstanding, ecocriticism remains the preferred term for environmental literary studies worldwide, although green studies is sometimes favored in the UK. It also has the intrinsic advantage of implying the tendency of such work for thinking ecologically in the metaphorical as well as scientistic sense of focusing on how artistic representation envisages human and nonhuman webs of interrelation.

This book distinguishes between "first-wave" ecocriticism and "second-wave" or revisionist ecocriticism, in recognition of a growing diversification of critical method and a broadening of focus from an original concentration on such genres as nature writing, nature poetry, and wilderness fiction toward engagement with a broader range of landscapes and genres and a greater internal debate over environmental commitment that has taken the movement in a more sociocentric direction, as discussed in chapters 1 and 4. It would be a mistake, however, to suppose that ecocriticism has unfolded in a tidy, sequential manner, with a new dispensation displacing the old. For example, new-wave environmental justice ecocriticism both takes issue with and builds upon earlier ecocritical practice (e.g., Adamson 2001).

ecofascism A term used to stigmatize a social Darwinist biologization of the human that countenances authoritarian regulation of society according to the supposed laws of nature. Though often (and reductively; see Bramwell 1985, 1989) associated specifically with Nazism, ecofascism has recurringly marked Western and particularly German thought since Ernst Haeckl, a Darwinist who coined the term "ecology" in 1866 (Biehl and Staudenmaier 1995). *See also* deep ecology.

138

ecofeminism (or ecological feminism) is an umbrella term for a range of theoretical and practical positions that share the view that the "twin dominations
of women and nature" (Davion 2001: 234) are artifacts of patriarchal culture
instituted in antiquity and (as argued most influentially in Merchant 1980)
intensified by the epistemological dualism and rational instrumentalism of the
scientific and technological revolutions. The term was coined in the 1970s by
French feminist Françoise d'Eaubonne, but the movement first developed in
the United States in the 1980s and has since spread worldwide to comprehend
a great "variety of regional, ethnic, and cultural ecofeminisms."[4] On environmental issues, ecofeminist persuasions range from anthropocentric to anti-
anthropocentric, from liberal to radical. As in feminism generally, the question
of essentialism vs. constructivism has been much debated (e.g., whether to consider gender difference as innate or culturally contingent), with the tilt tending
in constructionism's favor when the argument takes an either/or form, but with
an increasing sense that the dichotomy may be a false one if only because in
certain instances essentializing either cannot be avoided or may be of positive
strategic value (Carlassare 1999; Sturgeon 1997). An analogous divergence holds
between cultural ecofeminism and social/socialist ecofeminisms, the former
placing more primary emphasis on transformation of values and consciousness
that tend to presume "woman" or "motherhood" as a fixed category, the latter
on "a socioeconomic analysis that treats nature and human nature as socially
constructed, rooted in an analysis of race, class, and gender" (Merchant 1992:
194).

ecological conscience, ecological consciousness *See* ecology.

ecology, ecologism Ecology is the study of the interactions between organisms and the environment. During the past century, the field has evolved into
a congeries of theoretical and applied foci, including such disciplines as population biology, ecosystem ecology, conservation biology, landscape ecology, and
restoration ecology.

Meanwhile, especially for non-scientists, ecology has also taken on an ethico-
political connotation as its premise of the interconnection among life forms
has been seized upon by environmentalists as the basis of various green reform
movements (Worster 1977). These may, like social ecology, claim scientific
warrant, or may, like deep ecology, be attempted revolutions in consciousness
or value having no ground in science except for the general ecological principle of the interrelatedness of things.

Even as non-scientists have looked to ecology as authorizing holistic thinking about environmental interrelatedness, some scientists and historians of
science have charged ecology with an excess of such thinking, including ecosystem theory itself (see Golley 1993: 185–205), as being insufficiently
grounded scientifically, even if fertile heuristically. On the other hand, some

practicing ecologists have sought to energize lay environmentalism by applying ecology's master metaphors of interrelatedness to the social sphere. Particularly influential here has been Aldo Leopold, who defined ecology as "the science of communities" and coined the term "ecological conscience" to refer to "the ethics of community"; that is, the ethics of living in accord with the welfare of the ecological community (Leopold 1991: 340). Whether or not you question the soundness of such cross-disciplinary transfers (see Phillips 2003: 3–82), or take satisfaction in the fecundity of ecological frames of reference for thinking in other fields, will depend a good deal on the relative importance you place on precision of thinking vs. historical impact.

Etymologically, the Greek *oikos* – signifying "household" in the comprehensive sense of residence and grounds, as well as family – is the root of both "ecology" and "economy." This provenance, together with economy's originally cosmic implication, connoting the divinely appointed order of things, has prompted some modern environmental writers like Wendell Berry to call for a reorientation of the secular (or "little") economy in accountability to the "great" economy (Berry 1987: 54–75). *See also* deep ecology, ecofeminism, environmental justice, social ecology.

ecology movement *See* environment, environmentalism, social ecology.

economy *See* ecology.

ecosophy *See* deep ecology.

ecotone A transition area, of varying size, between two adjacent ecological zones, particularly different plant communities, such as forest and grassland. The ecotone has some of the characteristics of each zone and often additional species not found in either. Also used in a metaphorical sense by ecocritics (as in the journal, *Ecotone*, ed. David Gessner) to imply the synergy of discrepant perspectives.

environment, environmentalism, ecology movement The verb environ ("to surround") is of medieval provenance. Environment as noun was introduced during the first third of the nineteenth century (*OED* credits Thomas Carlyle with first usage: see chapter 3, above), initially to denote cultural milieu but then often with primary reference to physical surroundings specifically. Environment can denote the surroundings of an individual person, a species, a society, or of life forms generally. To Estonian biologist Jakob von Uexküll we owe the related concept *Umwelt*, denoting the individual organism's perceptual world (Evernden 1985: 79–83).

Environment and environmentalism are widely used, as in ecological science, to apply to natural environment(s) specifically. But, more commonly (as in this book), environment comprehends both "built" and "natural." For this same reason, however, and/or because environment is thought by some to imply an anthropocentric center (e.g., Serres 1995: 33), some critics prefer to use "nature" or "natural environment" to specify what they take to be especially significant or pivotal about the environing world. Yet in no ecocritical use does environment imply the same degree of controlled arrangement usually implied by "landscape." Thus, Richard Kerridge observes how, in Hardy's novels, "landscape becomes environment, constantly developing and being seen from a complex mixture of perspectives."[5]

"Environmentalism" is a term of ethically dubious origin. In the early twentieth century, environment "referred mainly to the external social influences working on the individual (as opposed to genetic endowment)" (Worster 1999: 165), and environmentalism was coined to denote the view that culture and/or character is determined by environment rather than heredity. This is ironically the *only* denotation given in the 1987 *OED* Supplement. It has long since been eclipsed, however, by the use of environmentalism as an umbrella term that may stretch to cover any environmental reform movement, whether anthropocentric or ecocentric, radical or moderate, although some activists, such as environmental justice advocates, would want to disassociate themselves from any implication that environmental ills are more fundamental than social ills such as poverty and racism.

The borderline between environmentalism and "ecology movement," another umbrella term that covers a range of environmentalist issues and ideologies, is also blurry. Ecology movement seems to be a term of European origin, associated with the rise of green party movements, but still uncommon in the United States. More consistently than environmentalism it is identified with a radical edge of some sort, whether politicized and confrontational like Greenpeace or movements still more incendiary, or countercultures like Wiccan neopaganism. Even though some would consider it redundant to speak of "radical environmentalism," environmentalism as a general noun is often chastised as mere establishmentarian incrementalism by those staking out more radical positions, including mutually antithetical critics, such as Norwegian philosopher Arne Naess, who coined the term "deep ecology," and American eco-anarchist Murray Bookchin, who claims to have invented "social ecology." For Naess, what is conventionally called environmentalism is a "shallow" mode of reformism (Naess 1973: 95); for Bookchin, it connotes "a mechanistic, instrumental outlook" (Bookchin 1999: 154). *See also* deep ecology, ecology, environmental justice, landscape, social ecology.

environmental criticism *See* ecocriticism.

environmental justice As discussed in chapter 4, environmental justice is a rapidly growing grassroots movement, which started in the US around 1980 as a series of community-based resistances against toxification of local environments and the siting of waste dumps and polluting industries that discriminate against poor and otherwise disempowered communities, particularly minority

141

communities seen as victimized by what has come to be called environmental racism. In contrast to mainstream environmentalism, whose traditional support base has been predominantly the white educated middle class, with the leadership of major organizations until quite recent times predominantly male, the public health and anti-discrimination agendas of environmental justice activism have enlisted strong leadership and support from minority groups and from women across the color line. US environmental justice advocates do not see this movement as narrowly national, but as part of a worldwide "attempt to broaden the definition and scope of environmentalism to include the basic needs of poor and politically less powerful groups."[6] These many international environmental justice movements, however, have their own distinct histories, in many if not most cases evolving independently of the American movement (e.g., see Guha 1989a; Shiva 1988), with race sometimes figuring as a less salient issue in global context relative to poverty and human rights claims than in American struggles (Martínez-Alier 2002). *See also* ecology, environment, social ecology.

environmental racism   *See* environmental justice.

environmental unconscious   A neologism (introduced by Buell 2001: 18–27) to refer to the necessarily partial realization of one's embeddedness in environment as a condition of personal and social being. Environmental unconscious implies both the potentiality for a fuller coming-to-consciousness and a limit to that potentiality.

environmental writing, environmental literature   Terms sometimes used as virtual synonyms for nature writing, but always with the intent of suggesting a more encompassing range of reference, if not also a wider range of genres. Environmental writing usually (though not always) denotes nonfictional prose. Texts in any genre can count as environmental literature. *See also* ecocriticism, nature writing.

factish   A neologism (introduced by Latour 1999), compounded from "fact" and "fetish," designed particularly as a reinterpretation of the former: to make "obvious that the two have a common element of fabrication." Factish is not meant to imply the reduction of facts to "mere" constructs, but rather "to take seriously the role of actors in all types of activities" (ibid: 306).

Georgic   *See* pastoral.

green studies   *See* ecocriticism.

homocentrism   *See* anthropocentrism.

land ethic   *See* ecocentrism, ecology.

landscape   A polysemic term whose chief modern usage in English derives from early modern Dutch *landschap* painting. Landscape may refer "to the appearance of an area, the assemblage of objects used to produce that appearance, [or] the area itself."[7] Landscape typically refers to rural rather than urban contexts, and typically implies a certain amplitude of vista and degree of arrangement, whether the referent is an artifact or an actual locale. But what is called landscape *may* be messy or chaotic rather than orderly, foreshortened as well as panoramic, urban as well as exurban. In all cases, landscape implies the totality of what a gaze can comprehend from its vantage point. Although the "scape" of the English noun implies a reified "thereness," landscape should also be thought of as shaped by the mind of the beholder, as well as by sociohistorical forces, a connotation that the German *Landschaft* captures better. *See also* environment.

narrative scholarship   *See* ecocriticism.

nature, naturalize   Raymond Williams rightly deems nature "perhaps the most complex word in the language" (Williams 1983: 219). He identifies three principal denotations: nature as essential character of something; nature as the "inherent force which directs the world," as in the capitalized Nature of classical mythology or eighteenth-century Deism; and nature as the material world, sometimes but not invariably including human beings. In this third sense (our main concern here), nature is loosely used to denote "what man has not made, though" (Williams shrewdly adds) "if he made it long enough ago – a hedgerow or a desert – it will usually be included as natural" (p. 223). What looks like nature, then, is in fact often naturalized.

Especially after two centuries of industrial revolution, nature may no longer exist any more in the traditional sense of entities unmodified by human influence. Indeed, for millennia nature has been subject to such modification. So to insist that a thing is natural in the sense of being primordial is arguably to mythologize or obfuscate. On the other hand, arguably nature still has value as a relative term, in the sense that (say) icebergs are more "natural" than statues of national heroes in public squares, even though the former may have broken off from glaciers as a consequence of anthropogenically induced global warming and the latter may be constructed entirely from "natural" substances like granite.

Philosopher Kate Soper usefully distinguishes three levels of thinking about nonhuman nature: nature as a "metaphysical" concept ("through which humanity thinks its difference and specificity"), as a "realist" concept (referring to the structures, processes, and powers "operative within the physical world"), and as a "lay" or "surface" concept (referring to "ordinarily observable features of the world"). She argues that green thinking invokes the last especially, but at different points all three are invoked (Soper 1995: 155–6 ff.).

Cicero was the first to contrast "first" (or primordial) nature with the "second nature" that humans create by irrigation, damming, and so forth (*De Natura Deorum*, ii. 152). In modern times this distinction has been reinvented and updated by (certain) Marxist thinkers in recognition that under capitalism nature is more complexly mediated, by exchange value as well as use value. But neo-Marxists have since argued that global capitalist hegemony has made the first/second nature distinction obsolete, that "the production of nature, not first or second nature in themselves, [is] the dominant reality" (Smith 1984: 58; he wisely adds that "the production of nature should not be confused with *control* over nature"). Second nature continues to be used, however, in a related but nontechnical sense to denote action or attitudes that habit and/or culture have naturalized. Meanwhile, the advent of sophisticated imaging and information technology has led to the introduction of the concept of a "third nature," or nature as technologically reproduced (Wark 1994).

Distinctions between first, second, and third nature make best sense in language-cultures where there is a strong tradition, whatever the empirical facts, of dualistic thinking about nature as an autonomous domain. This is by no means universally the case, however. It is not true, for example, of many non-western traditions (see Silko 1986: 87, 92–4), which imply more of a fusion of the human and nonhuman than does the English "nature" (in Williams' third sense).

nature writing Succinctly definable as "literary nonfiction that offers scientific scrutiny of the world (as in the older tradition of literary natural history), explores the private experience of the individual human observer of the world, or reflects upon the political and philosophical implications of the relationships among human beings and the larger planet."[8] Nature writing has been of central interest for ecocriticism from the movement's beginnings, particularly during what I have called its first wave. Historically, nature writing has focused on exurban locales, though it can be practiced in urban contexts too, as eco-critics increasingly stress (e.g., Bennett and Teague 1999; Dixon 1999, 2002). *See also* environmental writing, environmental criticism.

pastoral, anti-pastoral, post-pastoral Traditional pastoral, dating from the poetry of Theocritus, is a stylized representation of rusticity in contrast to and often in satire of urbanism, focusing in the first instance on the life of shep-herds. In the early modern and romantic eras, as in seventeenth-century English country house poems and in Wordsworthian lyric, pastoral becomes more mimetically particularized, and more given over to representation of country ways that are being displaced by enclosure and/or urbanization. A concurrent instance of this turn from fictive Arcadia toward material referent was for the sites of European colonization to be conceived in pastoral terms, as areas of natural and even edenic possibility. This pastoralization of "new worlds," in time, helped give rise to different forms of pastoral nationalism on the part of post-colonial intelligentsias, such as the US cult of wilderness and the Négritude movement in Francophone Africa and the Caribbean (Buell 1995: 53–82). Such practices, however, particularly in the case of European settler cultures, are also reflective of and historically interdependent with "old world" tendencies from Britain to Russia to imagine nation in terms of country or hinterland.

144

Pastoral's ideological valence, as these last reflections suggest, has become increasingly complicated, though it was never wholly straightforward to begin with. Pastoral is originally and predominantly a high-cultural, hegemonic formation; but oral epic tradition, starting as early as the traces of it in Homer's *Iliad*, contains lyric passages that celebrate the natural world. In the literature of early modern natural history and travel and in such Neoclassical poems as James Thomson's *The Seasons* (1730–48), pastoral starts to fuse with a georgic poetics of work, but in high culture they tend to fuse on pastoral terms, such that canonical Anglophone poetry and painting, for example, typically imagine landscapes that are spaces of aesthetic pleasure contemplated at leisure rather than working landscapes, landscapes indeed that tend to delete workers in order to enhance the idyll. This has given rise to a tradition of anti-pastoral exposure of pastoral euphemism (Gifford 1999: 116–45). On the other hand, Leo Marx (1964) distinguishes in the history of British–American literary culture between a dominant strain of simple pastoral, wishfully oblivious to and tacitly complicit with the advance of technoculture, and complex pastoral, which uses pastoral to politically oppositional ends; and Buell (1995) argues, building to some extent on this analysis but disputing Marx's judgment that pastoral is not really "about" nature but about culture, that US pastoral imagination can embed or prepare the way for ecocentric thinking. Gifford (1999: 146–74) somewhat similarly charts in modern Anglophone literature a "post-pastoral" aspiration to recuperate nature without false consciousness, recognizing both that "retreat informs our sense of community" and that humankind must "improve our relationship with our neighbors on this planet."

place, placeness, non-place Discussed extensively in chapter 3, place is succinctly definable as space that is bounded and marked as humanly meaningful through personal attachment, social relations, and physiographic distinctiveness. Placeness, then, is co-constituted environmentally, socially, and phenomenologically through acts of perception. Place connotes not simply bounded and meaningful location but also dynamic process, including the shaping of place by outside as well as internal influences (Agnew 1987: 28–37). By contrast, "non-place" (a term introduced by Augé) is neutrally engineered space such as an airport or a hotel, designed to provide security for the displaced without the thick platial identity connoted by place. Place and space are not antonyms, either. Although arguably they "require each other for definition" (Tuan 1977: 6), and although from the standpoint of humanistic geography "the experienced richness of the idea of place" stands in contrast to "the detached sterility of the concept of space,"[9] space does not in and of itself require the idea of place (as a physical geographer would be quick to point out), whereas physical place is located within space. Nor does place always bear a positive connotation relative to space. Contemporary theorists agree that place can become regressive and repressive when it is thought of in essentialized terms as an unchanging unitary entity, as in ethnocentric appeals to *Heimat* or local patriotism. See chapter 3 for more specific discussion of dimensions of place. *See also* space.

reinhabitation A term coined in the 1970s to denote "learning to live-in-place [*sic*] in an area that has been disrupted and injured through past exploitation [by generations of settler culture.] It involves becoming native to a place through becoming aware of the particular ecological relationships that operate within and around it. It means undertaking activities and evolving social behavior that will enrich the life of that place, restore its life-supporting systems, and establish an ecologically and socially sustainable pattern of existence within it" (Berg and Dasmann 1977: 399). This gloss has proven durable. In environmental criticism, poet-ecocritic Gary Snyder has been particularly influential as a definer and spokesperson (e.g., Snyder 1995: 183–91). Reinhabitation presupposes a prior indigenous dispensation (hence the "re-" prefix and the "becoming native" stipulation) that lived more lightly on the land and in that sense should be looked back to as a model, and a commitment to an ecologically sustainable lifestyle that involves both ecological literacy and involvement in a place-based community. *See also* bioregionalism, place.

restoration ecology (ecological restoration) The theory and practice of remediating anthropogenically modified landscapes so as to make them better approximate an earlier, more unspoiled condition. This involves not only historical and technological challenges, but also ethico-philosophical ones (Higgs 2003). For example, what should be the *status quo ante* to which the landscape is to be restored? Who is to have ownership over such decisions? *See also* ecology.

social ecology, ecological socialism Social ecology is a tradition of theory and reform practices that view "societies and their environments as biophysically linked systems."[10] It disowns industrial capitalism, but advocates enlisting science and technology to the end of creating ecologically sustainable human communities. It has strong regionalist as well as eco-communitarian tendencies. In the past half-century, social ecology was especially associated with American eco-anarchist Murray Bookchin, who in fact claimed to have "formulated" the "discipline" (Bookchin 1999: 154). But its roots go back at least a century earlier (Clark 1997: 4–8), and arguably Lewis Mumford deserves to be called the "pioneer American social ecologist" (Guha and Martínez-Alier 1997: 200). John Clark, one of social ecology's emerging spokespersons, has sought to build bridges with deep ecology as well as socialism, replacing Bookchin's insistence on humankind's superiority on the evolutionary ladder with a holistic vision of "evolutionary processes of human and planetary self-realization."[11]

"Socialist" ecology or ecological socialism (or ecosocialism) is by contrast more squarely rooted in Marxist thinking, though also in critique of preexisting state socialisms that have ignored or worsened ecological crisis, as well as the ecological destruction wrought by capitalism. It insists that "the basic socialist principles – egalitarianism, eliminating capitalism and poverty, resource distribution according to need and democratic control of our lives and communities – are also basic environmental principles" (Pepper 1993: 234). As such, ecological socialism is more avowedly anthropocentric than social ecology and more antithetical to "the bioethic and nature mystification" of deep ecology (ibid: 232). "Environment" is seen as "*socially* determined rather than something before which we must humbly 'submit'" (Eckersley 1992: 127). *See also* deep ecology.

space   Considered relative to place (as chiefly in this book), space denotes areal form in the abstract, whether literal territory or metaphorical (as in "a space of meditation"), carrying the implication of locational specificity of some sort without any particular affect. But space is not value-neutral. Spatial practices – cartography, territorial definition, and land apportionment, for instance – inevitably express the values and agendas of those in charge of them, as for instance with medieval European maps centering on Jerusalem, modern world maps that center on Europe, and the "democratic social space" made possible by the late eighteenth-century mapping of the US hinterland into rectilinear parcels. In colonization of the hinterlands of the US, Australia, and elsewhere, the concept of *terra nullius* – the land as "empty" or pure space – was historically used as a pretext for conquest and denial of aboriginal land rights.

In a similar spirit, modern social theory uses space to refer to socially institutionalized conceptions and practices in the marking and apportioning of territory. One influential formulation is Henri Lefebvre's account of space as a "product" of sociohistorical processes such that premodernity's landscape of what Lefebvre calls "absolute space" (comprised from socially sanctified "fragments of nature located at sites which were chosen for their intrinsic qualities") has been reproduced by the forces of modern capitalism into "abstract space," which is at once homogenized ("the earth, underground resources, the air and light above the ground – all are part of the forces of production") and fissured according to innumerable specialized functions (Lefebvre 1991: 48, 347).

According to this way of thinking, space, spatial practice, and even place acquire a taint of suspicion. Even the creation of benign sites of refreshment like health facilities or environmental sanctuaries are seen as hegemonic manipulations. A notable instance is Michel Foucault's theory of "heterotopias," defined as "real" places which (he suggests) can probably be found within every culture, that function "as something like counter-sites," as "a sort of simultaneously mythic and real contestation of the space in which we live." Although one might think of heterotopias as counter-cultural sanctuaries (and to some extent Foucault does), the paradigmatic modern cases for him are "heterotopias

147

of deviation," institutions like rest homes, hospitals, and prisons "in which individuals whose behavior in relation to the required mean or norm are placed" (Foucault 1984).

sustainability, sustainable development   "Sustainable" and "sustainability" are terms long used in both applied ecology and economics to denote a mode of subsistence and more specifically a rate of agricultural or other crop-yield that can be maintained without detriment to the ecosystem. In the 1930s, Leopold writes of the "sustained yield" of responsible forestry practice as against over-harvesting (Leopold 1991: 186). So-called sustainable agriculture is a latter-day initative that envisages more rigorously ecosystem-responsible practices than traditional conservationist measures.

The 1987 "Brundtland Report" by the World Commission on Environment and Development, *Our Common Future*, fuses the economic and ecological connotations in its influential outline of a scenario for sustainable development to ensure that humanity "meets the needs of the present without compromising the ability of future generations to meet their own needs." This formulation has proven both influential and controversial. One key point at issue is whether what is called sustainable development can meet the requirements of sustainability. As discussed in chapter 3, sustainable development has become a mantra for eco-economic optimists, a source of concern for those in the developing world who fear that an ethic of sustainability may be invoked to keep their economies down, and a target of attack by environmentalists who hold that the term is oxymoronic and in practice gives permission for economic interests (development) to override sustainability. With such disputes in mind, some distinguish between "strong" and "weak" sustainability in recognition that the economic and ecological perspectives do not easily line up.

UMWELT   *See* environment, environmentalism.

wild, wildness, wilderness   Wild, wildness, and wilderness all share the sense of "undomesticated." Wildness and wilderness can be used synonymously, as in Gerard Manley Hopkins' poetic plea that the burn and braes of Inversnaid be preserved: "O let them be left, wildness and wet; / Long live the weeds and the wilderness yet."[12] But wilderness literally refers to a spatial area, whereas wildness is a term of quality rather than location. Wildness is arguably "everywhere: ineradicable populations of fungi, moss, mold, yeasts, and such that surround and inhabit us" (Snyder 1990: 14).

As a descriptor of human rather than animal traits, "wild" traditionally bears the equivocal or pejorative connotation of "disarranged" or "bewildered" (as in "driven wild"), or implying unfitness for civil society ("wild man"). Wild's modern usage as a term of value, as in the passage from Snyder's "Etiquette of Freedom" just quoted, deliberately inverts these senses. Hence the bite of Henry Thoreau's assertion: "In Wildness is the preservation of the world,"[13] which later

148

became the motto of the Sierra Club, co-founded by John Muir and now one of the leading US mainstream preservationist organizations. Thoreau is often misremembered as having written "wilderness," but his primary interest was not in wilderness as such but in discovering and honoring the evidences of the wild near at home, in "the tonic of wildness" as an antidote to hypercivilization.[14] Wildness is a quality humans share with nonhuman entities ("We are wildness – soil, water, oxygen, sunlight": K. D. Moore 2004: 95), whereas wilderness denotes *terra incognita*, typically of large size, the abode of beasts rather than humans: a place where civilized people supposedly do not (yet) dwell. Before white settlement, Europeans notoriously viewed the Americas and Australia as "empty" wilderness, whether fearsome or edenic, and therefore ripe for the plucking.

In modern times, wilderness has also acquired a statutory definition, as codified in the US by the 1964 Wilderness Act, to denote large parcels of basically undisturbed land without permanent human inhabitants – in order to create which, aboriginal dwelling, hunting, and religious practices have often been abridged. In the Anglophone world, the US has taken the lead in setting aside large tracts as wilderness areas (Dunlap 1999: 275–305).

Notes

1 *The Letters of John Keats*, ed. Hyder Edward Rollins (Cambridge, MA: Harvard University Press, 1958): 1, 224.

Chapter 1   The Emergence of Environmental Criticism

1 These generalizations encapsulate almost four decades of controversy touched off by Lynn White's "The Historical Roots of Our Ecologic Crisis" (White 1967), which pinned responsibility for technodominationism on Judaeo-Christianity. White's thesis has been disputed by biblical scholars, theologians, and environmental ethicists, who have convincingly exposed its tendentiousness without having permanently laid the charge to rest. Many of the responses have been collected by Timothy Weiskel, "The Environmental Crisis and Western Civilization: The Lynn White Controversy" (http://ecoethics.net/bib/1997/enca-001.htm). Adjudication is complicated by sharp variance between the different creation accounts in Genesis 1–2 by the scribes known respectively as "Priestly" and "Jahwist," the former being much more dominationist than the latter. Here I especially follow the analysis of Theodore Hiebert, "The Human Vocation: Origins and Transformations in Christian Traditions," *Christianity and Ecology: Seeking the Well-Being of Earth and Humans*, ed. Dieter T. Hessel and Rosemary Radford Ruether (Cambridge, MA: Harvard University Press, 2000), 135–54, a concise follow-up to Hiebert's *The Yahwist's Landscape: Nature and Religion in Early Israel* (New York: Oxford University Press, 1996).

2 Victor D. Montejo, "The Road to Heaven: Jakaltek Maya Beliefs, Religion, and the Ecology," in *Indigenous Traditions and Ecology: The Interbeing of Cos-*

mology and Community, ed. John A. Grim (Cambridge, MA: Harvard University Press, 2001), 177; Manuka Henare, "*Tapu, Mana, Mauri, Hau, Wairua:* A Mäori Philosophy of Vitalism and Cosmos," in the same volume, 198. Montejo's Mayan source is the *Popul Vuh*, Book III, Chapter 1 – a post-conquest transcription.

3   Here I adapt Raymond Williams' useful distinction between residual, dominant, and emergent cultures (Williams 1977: 121–7) – useful in part because Williams does not minimize the difficulty of distinguishing "emergent" from "dominant" or from copycat "facsimiles of the genuinely emergent cultural practice": 126. As we shall see, especially in chapter 4, it is no small matter to distinguish what is and is not genuinely radical in environmental criticism.

4   See, for example, the 1994 forum, "Defining Ecocritical Theory and Practice," posted on the ASLE website (www.asle.umn.edu/archive). Only one of the sixteen contributors made a point of strongly emphasizing the potential significance of urban writing and landscapes. Overwhelmingly, "environmental" literary study is here seen to be a matter of "the ways that the relationship between humans and nature are reflected in literary texts" (Stephanie Sarver, "What Is Ecocriticism," 1994 forum).

5   For presentations of this philosophy of teaching in action by two participants in that discussion, see Elder (1999) and Tallmadge (2000).

6   This from Australian ecocritic Bruce Bennett's recollection of a conversation with environmental writer Barry Lopez as "we walked along a line of cork oaks by the Swan River at Matilda Bay." See Bennett, "Some Dynamics of Literary Placemaking," *ISLE*, 10 (summer 2003): 99.

7   Quotation from Elder (1999: 649). The essay as a whole describes one such pedagogical experiment. The ASLE website, *ISLE*, and *Green Letters* make clear the movement's intelligent commitment to environmental education in the broadest sense. See, for example, Terry Gifford's notes from a 2000 Taiwan conference session led by him and two American ecocritics, Scott Slovic and Patrick Murphy: "Introducing Ecocriticism into the University Curriculum," *Green Letters*, 4 (spring 2003): 40–1.

8   The bibliography of *The Ecocriticism Reader* lists Snyder's bioregional manifesto, *The Practice of the Wild* (1990), as one of its "top fifteen choices" (Glotfelty and Fromm 1996: 397). Phillips' otherwise caustic assessment of what he takes to be early ecocriticism's high-minded simplisms ends by commending Ammons' book-length poem *Garbage* for its wily, sardonic, self-reflexive perceptiveness (Phillips 2003: 240–7).

9   Henry David Thoreau, "Walking," *The Norton Anthology of American Literature*, 6th edn., ed. Nina Baym et al. (New York: Norton, 2003), B: 1993.

10 Thomas Nagel, "What Is It Like to Be a Bat?" *Philosophical Review*, 83 (October 1974): 435–50.

11 Timothy Morton's (2000) study of Romantic-era consumerism in the case of the spice trade is a good example of such internalization, even though it makes only passing reference to Foucault.

12 For further insights into ecocritical understanding of the relation of narrative and critical practices, see the introductions, notes, and selected interviews in Satterfield and Slovic (2004).

13 See Buell (1999: 700–4) and Reed (2002: 148–9) for (non-identical) taxonomies of discrepant practices.

14 This is in no sense meant to denigrate the efforts and impact of such particular individuals as Scott Slovic (University of Nevada-Reno), *ISLE's* editor during the period of its emergence into a journal of real significance, and a catalytic influence on the creation of ASLE chapters in Japan and Australia.

15 See Jay Parini, "The Greening of the Humanities," *New York Times* (Sunday magazine), October 29, 1995, pp. 52–3 – an article that was significantly cut and altered by editorial fiat from the author's original version. Its provocative, editorially bestowed subtitle is "Deconstruction is compost"; and some of the interlocutors are reduced to misleadingly simplistic sound bites like "Literary theory wasn't real. Nature is tangible."

16 The Texas A & M University faculty group hosting the 1980s visiting lecture series on new historicism, that led to Jeffrey N. Cox and Larry Reynolds (eds.), *New Historical Literary Study: Essays on Reproducing Texts, Representing History* (Princeton, NJ: Princeton University Press, 1997), expressed bemusement and frustration at the reluctance of their guests, among whom I was privileged to be one, to confess to being new historicists. "It seems there are more discussions than actual examples of it," the editors remark (p. 6).

17 *American Literature*, the original flagship journal in the field, annually offers a prize in Foerster's name for the year's best essay in *AL*.

18 The first item in Mazel's (2001) anthology of "early ecocriticism" dates from 1864.

19 This is not to imply agreement on all points, of course. For the most recently published of a series of exchanges, see Marx (2003) and L. Buell (2003).

20 Marx does devote a limited amount of attention to the pastoral formation as a transplanted Eurocentric desire, particularly in his discussion of "Shakespeare's American Fable," *The Tempest* (March 1964: 34–72), and Williams' final chapter ("Cities and Countries") sketchily anticipates post-colonial studies by imagining Britain and its colonies as a symbolic oppo-

sition of metropolitan and outback (pp. 289–306). See also Marx's thoughtful review of *The Country and the City* (Marx 1973: 422–4).

21 An auspicious exception is *The Green Studies Reader: From Romanticism to Ecocriticism* (Coupe 2000), a British counterpart to Glotfelty and Fromm (1996), which includes a range of British and American ecocritical work together with relevant continental theory. Of course, these items are juxtaposed rather than critically compared at any length.

22 For Williams, the most significant precursor in the present context was F. R. Leavis, and the key book was Leavis and Denys Thompson, *Culture and Environment: The Training of Critical Awareness* (1933). For Marx, it was Perry Miller, and the key works were certain essays collected in Miller's *Errand into the Wilderness* (1956) and (posthumously) *Nature's Nation* (1967).

23 As to US literary studies, Mazel (2001: 5–6) overstates, but not by much, in remarking with Norman Foerster in mind (and quoting the subtitle of Devall and Sessions 1985), that "it was only by reading literature *as if nature mattered* – by practicing an early ecocriticism – that American literary criticism came to be professionalized."

24 Catherine Gallagher and Stephen Greenblatt, *Practicing New Historicism* (Chicago: University of Chicago Press, 2000), 60–6.

25 Some ecocritics might consider Heise or at least Hayles to be scholars of "literature and science" rather than ecocritics, but both have published in ecocritical venues and Heise in particular has taken a significant part in ASLE forums and conferences.

26 Strictly speaking, "ecofeminism" is a French invention, the term having been coined by Françoise d'Eaubonne (in *Le Féminisme ou la mort*, 1974). But the movement is of Anglophone origins (Merchant 1992: 184).

27 Conley (1997: 132), paraphrasing Luce Irigiray.

28 Latour dedicates *We Have Never Been Modern* to Donna Haraway, whose briefs on behalf of hybrids ("monsters," "cyborgs") respectfully cite Latour (Haraway 1991: 149–81, 295–337).

29 For Latour on the microbial revolution, see *The Pasteurization of France* (Cambridge, MA: Harvard University Press, 1988).

30 Clarke (2001: 152–4) states this case "affirmatively" (Latour attempting to move "beyond the culture of denunciation"); Phillips (2003: esp. 30–4) states it negatively (Latour as exposing the stupid extremisms of scientistic arrogance and postmodernist denial).

31 Bennett (1998: 53). He refers here to a passage from Annie Dillard's *Pilgrim at Tinker Creek*, not so much to chide the book itself (which he teaches to urban students) but to rebut environmental critic Neil Evernden's claim, citing the same passage, that one's place in the natural world can be

found only through direct contact with the "ultrahuman" (Evernden 1992: 118–23).

32 William Schneider, "Everybody's an Environmentalist Now," *National Journal*, 22 (April 28, 1990): 1062.

33 The mordant Luhmann views ecological anxiety mainly as a "self-inductive" form of "self-certainty" in its own right, rather than as a reliable mechanism for ameliorating "the relation of society to its environment"; but he grants it the power to disrupt business-as-usual norms by creating a climate of critical self-reflexive moralism (Luhmann 1989: 129–31).

34 For example, Glotfelty and Fromm's *The Ecocriticism Reader* (1996) includes Cynthia Deitering's 1992 essay "The Postnatural Novel: Toxic Conscious-ness in Fiction of the 1980s" – right after Scott Russell Sanders' first-wave "Speaking a Word for Nature." The treatment of Don DeLillo's *White Noise* in both these essays, in turn, has been seized upon by one ecojustice revi-sionist as an indicator of how much further ecocriticism needs to go in the direction of pinpointing "the invasive, pervasive effects of corporate capi-talism" and the workings of "the racial–class dynamic" (Reed 2002: 151), according to which Sanders' essay is judged clueless and Deitering's com-mendable but underconceptualized.

Chapter 2   The World, the Text, and the Ecocritic

1 Joy Harjo, "New Orleans," *Harper's Anthology of 20th Century Native American Poetry*, ed. Duane Niatum (San Francisco: Harper Collins, 1988), 287; Geoffrey Canada, *Fist Stick Knife Gun: A Personal History of Violence in America* (Boston, MA: Beacon Books, 1995), e.g., 57–8 vs 157–8: summer as the most dangerous time in the South Bronx for teens, vs. the gently wind-blown foliage of Brunswick, Maine, seeming to whisper: "Child, fear no more. Hear the sound of peace."

2 Said's *The World, the Text, and the Critic* (1983) was specifically concerned to further the "Foucaultian shift" from poststructuralism's linguistic turn to emphasis on texts as *socioculturally* embedded social interventions. But his broadest claim, that "a text in its actually *being* a text is a being in the world" (p. 33) is congruent with environmental criticism, both traditional and new.

3 Reed (2002: 153), citing Di Chiro (2000).

4 Ralph Lutts, "John Burroughs and the Honey Bee: Bridging Science and Emotion in Environmental Writing," *ISLE*, 3 (fall 1996): 90; Head (2002: 30); Jim Tarter, " 'Dreams of Earth': Place, Multiethnicity, and Environ-mental Justice in Linda Hogan's *Solar Storms*," in Tallmadge and Harrington (2000: 140–1).

5   John Elder and Robert Finch, "Introduction," *The Norton Book of Nature Writing* (New York: Norton, 1990), 25.

6   Phillips (2003: 159–84) focuses on my "Representing the Environment" (see Buell 1995: 83–114), in a strenuous critique that I have found instructive at certain points, but that overall strikes me as an overwrought reduction of book to chapter, chapter to monolithic claim, and "realism" to monolithic formation.

7   A further irony of this novel is that even though the narrator succeeds in his original mission to confirm that human musical expression begins with primitive instruments which represent nonhuman sounds (a coincidental reinvention of the correspondence theory of language's origins that fascinated earlier North American writers from Emerson through Pound), his own furthest point of penetration is a model village founded by an outsider. He never reaches the domain of a still-more remote, ferocious indigenous group that, the novel makes clear, would disconfirm the image of primal life as edenic.

8   Seddon refers specifically to Park (1995), in whose work he finds "around a dozen non-standard English words on every page," symptomatic of an "evolving New Zealand sub-language" (p. 252) intended to make national expression more Pacific and less omni-British through hybridization with indigenous usage. Seddon stresses both the progressiveness and the opacity-insularity of this turn.

9   Thomas Hardy, *The Woodlanders* (1887) (London: Macmillan, 1974), 56; Rowland Robinson, *Uncle Lisha's Shop: Life in a Corner of Yankeeland* (New York: Forest and Stream, 1902), 150.

10 *Readings in the Qur'ān*, ed. Kenneth Cragg (Brighton: Sussex, 1988), 99.

11 William Wordsworth, *Poems*, ed. John O. Hayden (New Haven, CT: Yale University Press, 1981), 1: 358.

12 Charlotte Brontë, *Jane Eyre*, ed. Richard Dunn (New York: Norton, 2001), 211–19 passim.

13 *The Journal of Henry David Thoreau*, ed. Bradford Torrey and Francis Allen (Boston, MA: Houghton, 1906), 8, 130–2.

14 William Carlos Williams, *The Collected Earlier Poems* (New York: New Directions, 1966), 332.

15 Oodgeroo Noonuccal (Kath Walker), "Municipal Gum," *Inside Black Australia: An Anthology of Aboriginal Poetry* (Gilbert 1988: 100).

16 Karen Tei Yamashita, *Tropic of Orange* (Minneapolis, MN: Coffee House Press, 1997), 31–2.

17 Jerry Cheslow, "If You're Thinking of Living in Rutherford; A Patriotic Town with an Easy Commute," *New York Times*, November 4, 2001. It is unclear whether Williams is referring specifically to the indigenous

American sycamore or (much more likely) to the London Planetree, a hybrid between the former and the Oriental Planetree of southeastern Europe and Asia Minor. On the ritual significance of palms in subsaharan Africa, see n. 19 below; for Islam and Hebrew scripture see, for example, Nathaniel Altman, *Sacred Tree* (San Francisco: Sierra Club Books, 1994). For both the contemporary-secular and traditional indigenous significance of palms in southern California, see Nabhan (1985: 21–34).

18   The authoritative turn-of-the-nineteenth-century work on the dendritic picturesque, William Gilpin's *Remarks on Forest Scenery*, 3rd edn. (London: Cadell and Davies, 1808), describes the horse-chestnut as "a heavy, disagreeable tree" whose form is "commonly unpleasing," although its very heaviness, "in itself a deformity, may be of singular use in the composition" of a landscape (1: 64, 5). This fits (Jane's view of) Rochester quite well indeed.

19   See, for example, this reminiscence from the eighteenth-century Afro-British slave narrator James Albert Ukawsaw Gronniosaw of his boyhood community in Bournou (around Lake Chad): "Our place of meeting is under a large palm tree; we divide ourselves into many congregations as it is impossible for the same tree to cover the inhabitants of the whole City, though they are extremely large, high and majestic; the beauty and usefulness of them are not to be described; they supply the inhabitants of the country with meat, drink and clothes." *A Narrative of the Most Remarkable Particulars in the Life of James Albert Gronniosaw . . .* (1777), in *Unchained Voices: An Anthology of Black Authors in the English-Speaking World of the 18th Century*, ed. Vincent Carretta (Lexington: University Press of Kentucky, 1996), 34.

20   "A text informed by *référance*," Scigaj (1999: 38) explains, involves a three-stage process of "a self-reflexive acknowledgment of the limits of language," but nonetheless "referring one to nature, to the referential origin of all language," and "in most cases achieving an atonement or at-one-ment with nature." The theory needs refinement: its second and third stipulations claim too much as to the grounding of language in nature and the capacity of the text to return one there. But the sequence envisaged seems convincing.

21   Francis Ponge, *The Voice of Things*, ed. and trans. Beth Archer (New York: McGraw-Hill, 1974); Ian Higgins, *Francis Ponge* (London: Athlone Press, 1979), 51–66; and Sherman Paul, *For Love of the World: Essays on Nature Writers* (Iowa City: University of Iowa Press, 1992), 19.

22   Ideological critiques of realism diagnose its political valences differently, ranging from the model of realist narration as will-to-dominance, as actively complicit with the modernization process, as bourgeois reification, as an

expression of anxiety to restore a threatened or lost social control. The prevalent diagnosis, in any case, is that the realist formation is conservative rather than progressive. This consensus might be of course disputed as reflecting (post)modernist parallax. When anti- or post-realist modes are in fashion, realism is easier to stigmatize as unprogressive than when Scott and Dickens and Eliot were contending with the romantic and sentimental modalities that function as recessive brakes on their own realist experiments.

23 The quotation serves both as the title for one of many books by prolific Victorian naturalist writer Philip Gosse and the basis of Lynn L. Merrill's illuminating *The Romance of Victorian Natural History* (New York: Oxford University Press, 1989).

24 Henry David Thoreau, *Walden* (1854), ed. J. Lyndon Shanley (Princeton, NJ: Princeton University Press, 1971), 306–7.

25 Richard Grusin, "Thoreau, Extravagance, and the Economy of Nature," *American Literary History*, 5 (spring 1993): 30–50, comments insightfully on the striking contrast in *Walden* between Thoreau's conceptions of human vs. natural economy.

26 James Krasner's study of post-Darwinian prose, fictional as well as non-fictional, finds that "the confusion that the multiplicity of external objects implicit in Darwinian theory causes for" these writers "is often expressed in a desire to order the landscape into an accurate and intelligible vista" (Krasner 1992: 28). Thoreau, for his part, never ceased to hope that his data might define a cosmically coherent material universe; but his relish for minute particulars, and his trust in the inherent value of collecting them, superseded that desire.

27 Latour would not necessarily want to argue against the validity of Stockmann's findings, only against his hubris.

28 Soyinka's critique by no means implies idealization of animistic primordialism, however, as Biodun Jeyifo argues in *Wole Soyinka: Politics, Poetics and Postcolonialism* (Cambridge: Cambridge University Press, 2004), 134–7.

29 See especially Ken Saro-Wiwa, *Genocide in Nigeria: The Ogone Tragedy* (Lagos: Saros International, 1991), and *Ogoni's Agonies: Ken Saro-Wiwa and the Crisis in Nigeria*, ed. Abdul Rasheed N'Allah (Trenton, NJ: Africa World Press, 1998).

30 I adapt this example from Joseph Roach's observations on *Godot* performance history in a 2001 lecture delivered at Harvard University.

31 For detailed analysis of this case, see Sharon O'Dair, "Shakespeare in the Woods," *Class, Critics, and Shakespeare: Bottom Lines on the Culture Wars* (Ann Arbor: University of Michigan Press, 2000), 89–114.

32 Fletcher quotes from one of Wordsworth's "Lucy" poems, "A Slumber Did My Spirit Seal" (Wordsworth 1981: 1, 364).

33　On Bloom's, and post-Bloomian, accounts of "the American sublime," see Bloom, *Poetry and Repression: Revisionism from Blake to Stevens* (New Haven, CT: Yale University Press, 1976), 235–66; Mary Arensberg (ed.), *The American Sublime* (Albany, NY: State University of New York Press, 1986); Rob Wilson, *American Sublime: The Genealogy of a Poetic Genre* (Madison: University of Wisconsin Press, 1991), esp. ch. 1.

34　Walt Whitman, *Leaves of Grass: Comprehensive Reader's Edition*, ed. Harold W. Blodgett and Sculley Bradley (New York: New York University Press, 1965), 364. For the ecology of childhood imagination in this context, see Cobb (1977), Chawla (1994), and Nabhan (1994).

35　Pablo Neruda, *Canto General*, trans. Jack Schmitt (Berkeley: University of California Press, 1991), 299.

36　Les Murray, *Collected Poems 1961–2002* (Potts Point, NSW: Duffy and Snellgrove, 2002), 282.

37　Jorie Graham, "Woods," *Never* (Harper Collins, 2002), 10.

38　Judith Wright, "Document," *Collected Poems 1942–1985* (Manchester: Carcanet, 1994), 242.

39　Science fiction is both a borderland (in montaging with magical realism, for instance) and a subdivisible omnibus term (cyberpunk novels and films are a postmodern branch, for instance).

40　See Gough (2002) for comparative discussion of *Dune* in relation to *Silent Spring* and the fiction of Ursula LeGuin.

41　Karen Tei Yamashita, *Through the Arc of the Rain Forest* (Minneapolis, MN: Coffee Table, 1990), 202, 212.

Chapter 3　Space, Place, and Imagination from Local to Global

1　"Environ" as verb is of medieval provenance. *OED* credits the first usage of "environment" as one's surrounding (1830) to Victorian critic of machine culture Thomas Carlyle. Carlyle's first recorded use of the term has nothing specifically to do with environmental issues as we conceive them today (an 1827 essay on Goethe, referring to the lovelorn young Werther as a creature of his intellectual and cultural milieu). But the underlying stance of Carlyle's 1829 "Signs of the Times" is the same: the "Mechanical Age" commits people to a logic of reification such that "our happiness depends entirely on external circumstances." See *The Works of Thomas Carlyle*, ed. H. D. Traill (London: Chapman and Hall, 1896–9), 27: 67. Ralph Waldo Emerson, after a memorable 1833 visit to Carlyle, paid tribute to his coinage in a way that shows clear understanding of "environment" in the modern sense: "Drawn by strong regard to one of my teachers I went to see his person & as he might say his environment at Craigenputtock." See *The Correspondence of Emerson and Carlyle*, ed. Joseph Slater (New York: Columbia University Press, 1964), 97.

2   Environmental writer William Least Heat Moon's essay on the township of Hymer in Chase County, Kansas – "With the Grain of the Grid," *PrairyErth (A Deep Map)* (Boston, MA: Houghton, 1991), 279–87 – offers an inventive, droll, and poignant portrait of how midwestern settlers made their rectilinear plots into habitats through a combination of modification and self-adjustment – a creative seconding of Meine's (1997) systematic analysis of the challenges the gridwork poses to midwestern farm life. For Fisher (1988), on the other hand, "democratic social space" implies a synergy of ideological, technological, and spatial determinism that make for an irreversible conquest of place by space. It "requires an ever more sophisticated and effortless system of transportation alongside a less and less developed sense of place, region, or home," reducing place to "the crossroads of one or another system of movement" (p. 64). This comports with Cronon's history of the organization of the American hinterlands into a vast system of commodity and capital flows around Chicago as hub (Cronon 1991: 55–259).

3   On the links between the history of national park and American Indian reservations, see Spence (1999). The recent outmigration from the middle plains by the settler-culture population (leaving many counties from eastern Montana and western North Dakota to northern Texas at below frontier levels), combined with the marked increase in the Native American population, testifies both to the challenge of turning abstract space into liveable space and the pertinacity of place-sense once it is embedded.

4   Whether capitalism or socialism is more environment-unfriendly has been much debated. Both have so far failed miserably from a biocentric standpoint (McLaughlin 1993: 14–62). Neither Adam Smith nor Karl Marx was an environmentalist. On the one hand, "free world" consumer culture has left a bigger "ecological footprint," while industrialized socialist nations have worse pollution records, due partly to comparative suppression of dissent. On the other hand, capitalist cultures have taken the lead in eco-philanthropy, whereas socialist theory offers the stronger critique of environmental inequity and of human domination of environment. Both left-leaning "ecosocialist" initiatives (e.g., Williams 1986; Pepper 1993) and free-market-oriented "sustainable development" or "ecological modernization" programs (e.g., Hajer 1995; Mol 2001) have been advanced as responses to runaway production and resource extraction.

5   David Harvey, *The Condition of Postmodernity: An Enquiry into the Origins of Cultural Change* (Oxford: Blackwell, 1989), 264.

6 "To announce one's situatedness," David Simpson remarks, "appears to preempt the accusation that one is not being inadequately self-aware, and at the same time to provide a limited authority to speak from a designated position. It is at once defensive and aggressive, and in this way it fits the needs of a world-condition that requires the subject's self-descriptions to be at once abject, made by others, merged into prior formulations, and at the same time to bear all the marks of a recognizable *agency* and *responsibility*." David Simpson, *Situatedness, or, Why We Keep Saying Where We're Coming From* (Durham, NC: Duke University Press, 2002), 195.

7 Hence Lefebvre's complaint that Heidegger's "obsession with absolute space" "stands opposed to any analytic approach and even more to any global account of the generative process in which we are interested" (Lefebvre 1991: 122).

8 Sally Carrighar, *Home to the Wilderness: A Personal Journey* (Baltimore, MD: Penguin Books, 1974); Douglas Peacock, *Grizzly Years: In Search of the American Wilderness* (New York: Holt, 1996). Peacock found grizzly-watching in the American outback a way of coping with his trauma as a medic during the Vietnam War, which left him unable to lead a "normal" social life. Carrighar was traumatized by girlhood as a privileged but unwanted child, during which her mother actually tried to kill her. (Carrighar's *Icebound Summer* (1953), ironically dedicated "To My Mother," contains a chapter, "Unsentimental Mother," on how a typical young hair seal is briefly reared and then traumatically abandoned by its mother to the unended mercies of a Darwinian "Mother Nature.")

9 Augé cautions also that "place" and "non-place" are not discontinuous but bipolar: "the first is never completely erased, the second never totally completed; they are like palimpsests on which the scrambled game of identity and relations is ceaselessly rewritten." Augé's dichotomy of place/non-place rather than the more familiar place/space seems designed to underscore that sites which might be thought of as thin, abstract, affect-neutral space can be sites of strong attachment.

10 Nomadic tribesman excepted, of course. But here too a version of the same point applies. Even if there is no one single home base, the home range is limited.

11 Graham Swift, *Waterland* (New York: Vintage, 1992); Geoff Park, *Ngā Uruora (The Groves of Life): Ecology and History in a New Zealand Landscape* (Wellington: Victoria University Press, 1995); John Mitchell, *Ceremonial Time: Fifteen Thousand Years on One Square Mile* (Garden City, NY: Doubleday, 1984).

12 Barbara Kingsolver, *High Tide in Tucson: Essays from Now or Never* (New York: Harper Collins, 1995), 170, 178, 180.

13 This overview is synthesized from Internet-posted biographical material (chiefly www.kingsolver.com and George Brosi's "Barbara Kingsolver" at www.english.eku.edu), as well as Kingsolver's "In Case You Ever Want to Go Home Again," *High Tide*, 35–45.

14 Comer (1999: 137–51) presses this point insistently with reference to the "southwestern kitsch" of one of Kingsolver's most popular novels, *Animal Dreams*.

15 *Pointed Firs*, Richard Brodhead astutely remarks, "is oriented toward a place, but it establishes this place not in its own terms but as a place to come *to*, a place literally of resort for a narrator who comes from afar." See Brodhead, *Cultures of Letters: Scenes of Reading and Writing in Nineteenth-Century America* (Chicago: University of Chicago Press, 1993), 145. Baynton achieves counterpart effects through ironized third-person narration and, in two of her half-dozen studies, plotting a laborious and traumatic journey into the bush through the consciousness of her female protagonist.

16 Lois Gibbs, *Love Canal: The Story Continues* (revision of her 1982 *Love Canal: My Story*) (Gabriola Island, British Columbia: New Society, 1998), 26, makes clear that her original image of "a lovely neighborhood in a quiet residential area" has been permanently destroyed.

17 Michiko Ishimure, *Paradise in the Sea of Sorrow: Our Minamata Disease*, trans. Livia Monnet (Ann Arbor: Center for Japanese Studies, University of Michigan, 2003), 328–9.

18 Mahasweta Devi, *Imaginary Maps*, trans. Gayatri Chakravorty Spivak (New York: Routledge, 1995), xi. This text has indeed found its way onto the syllabi of US courses in environmental justice literature, alongside Native American and other minority literatures; see Jia-Yi Cheng Levine, "Teaching Literature of Environmental Justice in an Advanced Gender Studies Course," in Adamson, Evans, and Stein (2002), 370, 373.

19 The grandmother and the millionaire figure in *Native Tongue* and *Sick Puppy*; ex-Governor Tyree (alias Skink) appears in the whole series of (so far) five novels.

20 Quotation from Declan Kiberd, *Inventing Ireland* (Cambridge, MA: Harvard University Press, 1996), 719. Friel makes a number of his leading characters impressively, indeed obsessively, literate in Latin and Greek as well as Gaelic but unable or unwilling to speak English. Presumably the double-sided implication is that Mediterranean high culture flourished in Ireland earlier than England but that in the age of Great Britain cultural pride and linguistic separatism are fated to make Irish as "dead" a language as the classical. "He essentially degaelicizes his depiction of the historic Irish speakers," one critic suggests, "to dispel the nationalist myth of a past Gaelic purity, predicated upon the Romantic belief in an *echt* Irishness": see Scott

Boltwood, " 'Swapping Stories About Apollo and Cuchulainn': Brian Friel and the De-Gaelicizing of Ireland," *Modern Drama*, 41 (winter 1998): 578. However, at least some of the traditional community-financed so-called hedge schools, which the British system was soon to replace, did teach "the classics of an advanced standard": see J. J. R. Adams, "Swine-Tax and Eat-Him-All-Magee: The Hedge Schools and Popular Education in Ireland," *Irish Popular Culture, 1650–1850*, ed. James S. Donnelly, Jr. and Kerby A. Miller (Dublin: Irish Academic Press, 1998), 97.

21 Derek Walcott, *Collected Poems 1948–1984* (New York: Farrar, Straus, 1986), 390.

22 Citations from Patricia Ismond, *Abandoning Dead Metaphors: The Caribbean Phase of Derek Walcott's Poetry* (Jamaica: University of the West Indies Press, 2001), 276; Walcott, "The Antilles: Fragments of Epic Memory," *What the Twilight Says* (New York: Farrar, Straus, 1998), 81; Jamaica Kincaid, *My Garden* (New York: Farrar, Straus, 1999), 135.

23 See Roy Osamu, "Postcolonial Romanticisms: Derek Walcott and the Melancholic Narrative of Landscape," *Ecopoetry: A Critical Introduction* (Salt Lake City: University of Utah Press, 2002), 207–20; and especially George B. Handley, "A Postcolonial Sense of Place and the Work of Derek Walcott," *ISLE*, 7 (summer 2000): 1–23.

24 Derek Walcott (1998: 69) ("The Antilles"). A key difference between Walcott's aesthetic and Friel's play is that Walcott envisages Antillean art as "restoration of our shattered histories" (ibid), whereas Friel wants to shatter specious holistic images of Irish cultural primordialism. But these are both representative postcolonial strategies.

25 Bioregionalism and sustainability are partially convergent but not synonymous. In environmentalist circles, sustainability once especially implied ecosystem-responsive, small-scale agricultural practices that set a value on resource and energy self-sufficiency that might (but does not necessarily) entail the bioregionalist propensity for thinking of geographical units as possible cultural units. But since the late 1980s, with the rise of the concept of "sustainable development" as a code phrase for striking a balance between ecological responsibility and economic interests, sustainability rhetoric has been stretched beyond the agricultural context to apply broadly to economic systems that show promise of being able to operate within ecological limits.

26 Quotation from Chicago Mayor Richard Daley, "The Chicago Principles" (www.mcdonoughpartners.com). See also "Metropolis Principles FAQ" (www.chicagometropolis2020.org) and Jim Slana, "Dear Bill McDonough," *Conscious Choice*, April 2002 (www.consciouschoice.com). For analysis/critique of Soleri, see Luke (1997: 153–76).

27 bell hooks, "Touching the Earth," in Dixon (2002: 32).
28 Sandra Cisneros, *The House on Mango Street* (New York: Vintage, 1984), 94–8; rpt. in Dixon (2002: 164–7). For discussion of the longstanding resemblances between these subgenres, see Stephanie Foote, *Regional Fictions: Culture and Identity in Nineteenth-Century American Literature* (Madison: University of Wisconsin Press, 2001).
29 Not to mention the question of institutionalized social differences in the various jurisdictional entities, as eco-anarchist (and Vermonter) Murray Bookchin is quick to point out (September 20, 1995 "Comments on the International Social Ecology Network Gathering," section X, http://dwardmac.pitzer.edu/Anarchist_Archives/bookchin/clark.html).
30 Quotations from Beck, Giddens, and Lash (1994: 5–6) and Willms (2004: 135); but see especially Beck (1992). At times Beck seems to want to limit risk society or reflexive modernization to advanced technological societies, but the overall vision is "the self-created possibility, hidden at first, then increasingly apparent, of the self-destruction of all life on this earth" (Beck 1995: 67).
31 Social ecology is especially associated with Murray Bookchin; but this is by no means the totality of what has been claimed as social ecology (see Light 1998), much less of "ecological socialism" (see Pepper 1993). "Sustainable development" came into fashion as an attractive-seeming compromise mantra in the wake of the World Commission on Environment and Development's 1987 report, *Our Common Future* (Oxford: Oxford University Press, 1987). Sachs (1999: 23–41) finds it a self-undermining devil's bargain compromise: "development" will always trump sustainability. By contrast, Hajer (1995) provides a sophisticated and cautiously upbeat analysis (he prefers the rubric "ecological modernization"), as a synergy of diverse "discourse coalitions" with non-identical agendas (p. 65). On "eco-managerialism" more generally, with particular reference to academic environmental studies, see Luke (1999).
32 Symptomatic of the way we live now, ecocritically speaking, is the collaborative *Literature of Nature: An International Sourcebook*, ed. Patrick D. Murphy with Terry Gifford and Katsunori Yamazato (Chicago: Fitzroy Dearborn, 1998), a very useful but also rather balkanized collection of essays on different traditions of environmental writing around the world, in which Malta and Romania perforce talk past each other.
33 William Gibson, *Pattern Recognition* (New York: Berkeley, 2003), 79.
34 Sassen's three nominees – New York, London, and Tokyo – are three of Gibson's four central cities, Moscow being the fourth (reflecting the novel's post-Cold War thematics).
35 Derek Walcott, *Omeros* (New York: Farrar, Straus, 1990), 75–6.

36 Theodor W. Adorno, *Aesthetic Theory*, trans. Robert Hullot-Kentor, ed. Gretel Adorno and Rolf Tiedemann (Minneapolis: University of Minnesota Press, 1997), 68.

37 1988 interview with Paula Burnett, quoted in Burnett, *Derek Walcott: Politics and Poetics* (Gainesville: University Press of Florida, 2000), 39.

38 Burnett, *Derek Walcott*, p. 55. Bill Maurer, "Ungrounding Knowledges Offshore: Caribbean Studies: Disciplinarity and Critique," *Comparative American Studies*, 2 (September 2004): 334–7, presents a concrete example of the post-*Omeros* transformation of St. Lucia into "a node for Chinese capital" by making its "offshore sector" a major entry point for the diffusion of imports from China through the whole Caribbean. This certainly makes for a different image of the island nation's "center" than Walcott's oscillation between the subsistence culture of Achille and his compatriots and the tourist trade. Yet Walcott might conceivably wish to claim that the new degree of transnational modernization is merely the latest chapter in an older neocolonial story that his previous work has already anticipated.

Chapter 4 The Ethics and Politics of Environmental Criticism

1 Emerson, "Lecture on Slavery" (1855), *Emerson's Antislavery Writings*, ed. Len Gougeon and Joel Myerson (New Haven, CT: Yale University Press, 1995), 91.

2 Perhaps the two chief groups of deniers are premillennialist religious groups like the Jehovah's Witnesses who look welcomingly to the idea of environmental apocalypse as ushering in a divine remaking of the earth, and advocates for technoeconomic growth who dismiss the existence of an environmental problem. For a keen analysis of the latter's "Politics of Denial," see F. Buell (2003: 3–37).

3 See the glossary for the distinction between these two overlapping terms.

4 See Diane Osen's interview with Lopez in *The Book That Changed My Life* (New York: Modern Library, 2002), 84–96, which unfolds not so much an antithetical as a complementary story of authorial self-making.

5 Ursula K. LeGuin, *Buffalo Gals and Other Animal Presences* (New York: Penguin Books, 1990), 35–6.

6 John Clare, "The Nightingale's Nest," *"I AM": The Selected Poetry of John Clare*, ed. Jonathan Bate (New York: Farrar Straus, 2003), 171; Mary Austin, *Land of Little Rain: Stories from the Country of Lost Borders*, ed. Marjorie Pryse (New Brunswick, NJ: Rutgers University Press, 1987), 21; W. S. Merwin, "The Last Lone," *The Lice* (New York: Atheneum, 1967), 10–12; Ursula LeGuin, "Vaster than Empires and More Slow," *Buffalo Gals*, 109–54.

7   For Darwin's and/or Darwinist literary influence, see especially Beer
    (1983) and Krasner (1992) (for British literature) and Martin (1981) (for
    American).
8   Austin, *Land of Little Rain*, 17.
9   Darwin, *The Descent of Man, and Selection in Relation to Sex* (London: John
    Murray, 1871), 161–7. See Callicott (2001: 204–6) for the suggestion that
    Darwin's hypothesis stands in back of Leopold's thinking about community
    as the precondition to ethics.
10 When push comes to shove, Leopold cannot cleanly be classified as an
    ecocentric monist, any more than Darwin can. See, for example, Norton
    (1995: 341), who writes especially against Callicott's first formulations of
    Leopoldian ethics, which Callicott (e.g., Callicott 2001) has qualified.
11 Naess himself does not seem to have been much influenced by Heidegger.
    The first and most influential popularization of deep ecology, *Deep Ecology:
    Living as if Nature Mattered* (Devall and Sessions 1985) lists a potpourri of
    12 "sources of the deep ecology perspective" among which Heidegger stands
    as number eight. The first three are "the perennial philosophy" (i.e., all tra-
    ditions of thinking about selfness as relational that stand in opposition to
    the Enlightenment model of the rational isolated self), "the literary tradi-
    tion of naturalism and pastoralism in America," and "the science of ecology"
    (Devall and Sessions 1985: 79–108). As this same chapter suggests (pp.
    98–100), American philosopher Michael Zimmerman was especially influ-
    ential during the 1980s in calling attention to the resonances between deep
    ecology and Heidegger's thought, although Zimmerman has since basically
    retracted his view of Heidegger as a significant forerunner (Zimmerman
    1994: 91–149). Yet, at the turn of the twenty-first century, Heidegger
    continues to seem a key precursive figure for many environmental critics,
    though a somewhat embarrassing one (in light of his Nazism and the
    "green" face of National Socialism), whose legacy must be carefully sifted
    if ecocentrism is not to be tarred by this brush. See particularly in this
    regard Bate (2000: 243–83).
12 "There is no getting around the fact that it is by our bodies that we belong
    to the place-world," Casey (1997: 239) sums up Merleau-Ponty. Casey's
    student Abram (1996) has been additionally influential in calling attention
    to Merleau-Ponty. For the literary-critical result at its best, see for example
    Louise Westling, "Virginia Woolf and the Flesh of the World," *New Literary
    History*, 30 (autumn 1999): 855–75.
13 Mathews (1991) is the best example known to me of a contemporary eco-
    centric ethics strongly based on Spinoza. For Naess and Hinduism as well
    as Gandhi, see Jacobsen (2000: 231–52); for Naess and Buddhism (with
    reference to his admiration for Spinoza), see Curtin (2000). (Note that the

best overview of world environmental movements to date (Guha and Martínez-Alier 1997: 153–68) argues persuasively against conceiving Gandhi as ecocentric.) For some of the many helpful short accounts surveying the bearing of indigenous and Asian traditions on ecocentric thinking, see for example Whitt et al. (2001) and Peterson (2001: 77–126). No significant Anglophone writer identified with the ecocritical movement shows the full range of these influences more strikingly than does poet-critic Gary Snyder. See Snyder (1990, 1995) for critical texts, as well as his epic *Mountains and Rivers Without End* (Washington, DC: Counterpoint, 1996) and selected shorter poems, *No Nature* (New York: Pantheon, 1992).

14   Quotation from Luke (1997: 24). His critique is all the more instructive (pp. 7–27), given that he also credits deep ecology with some (small) promise.

15   See Bramwell (1985, 1989).

16   Soper (1995: 259) goes on to caution, however, against concluding that anthropocentric ethics are likely to be more coherent than ecocentric ethics.

17   Mathews' (1991) "Nature" (capital N) implies a somewhat mystical theory of the universe as a "self-realizing system" (or "the ecocosm," as she calls it), but this does not undermine her argument about modern cultures' characteristic underrepresentation of the ecosystemic imbrication of human selves.

18   The passage quoted is surrounded by a prefatory distinction between "green critics" and Marxists, feminists, and multiculturalists who "bring explicit or implicit political manifestos to the text about which they write" and a final caveat that "when it comes to practice" as distinct from ecopoetics, "we have to speak in other discourses."

19   J. Baird Callicott has been the environmental ethicist most influential in pressing Leopold's historic importance. His much-reprinted essay, "Animal Liberation: A Triangular Affair" (Callicott 1980), which declares Leopoldian environmental ethics incompatible with animal rights, created a firestorm. Callicott has since become more irenic toward alternative readings of Leopold and more receptive to the proposition that the land ethic as he framed it is not definitive.

20   *The Collected Poems of Wallace Stevens* (New York: Knopf, 1961), 9–10.

21   Tim B. Rogers, "Reinvisioning Our Views of 'Nature' Through an Examination of Aldo Leopold's *A Sand County Almanac*," *ISLE*, 10 (summer 2003): 57.

22   To be specific, Leopold ends his essay with a mini-reflection on the hazards of excessive striving after "safety" and "peace in our time," left for the reader to interpret, that must be read in the context of *Sand County*'s composition during World War II, the European stage of which broke out after British

Prime Minister Neville Chamberlain (from whom the last phrase is taken) had notoriously deceived himself into thinking he had appeased Hitler. But the relation between the military and the ecological remains somewhat murky.

23　For series and title description, see Center for the Study of World Religions, "Religions of the World and Ecology," www.hds.harvard.edu/ cswr/publications/rel_world_ecol.html.

24　Some might reasonably object that McFague's "earth as God's body" is not truly ecocentric, but rather a secularized theocentrism, as she herself elsewhere indicates. But she would also be entitled to reply that the reorientation she proposes would conduce to a *more* ecocentric spirituality than the God of Protestant Christianity, in both its "mainstream" and its evangelical forms.

25　On sentientism as against biocentrism, see especially Peter Singer (1990), a model of moral utilitarian environmentalism. On respect for nature argued along the lines of Kantian ethics, see Taylor (1986). On rights of nature, see Nash (1989).

26　Katherine Davies, "What is Ecofeminism?" *Women and Environments*, 10 (spring 1988): 4.

27　Plumwood's entire chapter on "Unity, Solidarity, and Deep Ecology" is relevant here (pp. 196–217). See also Plumwood (1993: 165–89) and Slicer (1995).

28　First, not all ecofeminists would agree with Plumwood's dismissive reading of Naess, her principal target here (cf. by contrast Spretnak 1997: 428, and Mathews 2001: 218–21). Second, Plumwood's "not identity but solidarity" formulation (which I myself find persuasive) seems to attempt to split the difference between those (like Spretnak) who find identification with the "other" credible, and nature-constructionists for whom any sort of claimed affiliation with nature might seem suspect.

29　Intelligently qualified defenses of deep ecology against some ecofeminist charges against it include Zimmerman (1994: 276–317), Sessions (1996), and Salleh (2000). Zimmerman and Sessions write from the perspective of deep ecologists attracted to (some aspects of) the ecofeminist critique; Salleh writes as an ecofeminist who sees hope for "a future symbiosis" of the two sets of persuasions around the principle and practice of "embodied materialism." Zimmerman ends with an interesting defense of deep ecology against the charge (which ecofeminism is not alone in leveling) that it amounts to a form of egoistic self-realization in disguise by arguing that its proper model is, or ought to be, rather a Zen-like emptying of the self than self-gratification.

30　On the promise of and problems with an ecofeminist ethics of care, see for example the exchange between Deane Curtin, "Toward an Ecological Ethic of Care," and Roger J. H. King, "Caring about Nature: Feminist Ethics and the Environment" (Warren 1996), as well as Sandilands (1999: 21–6 and throughout).

31 The same holds for Krista Comer's (1999) analogous redefinition of the female landscape imaginary of the "new west" so as to include urban space at the one extreme and, at the other, to reclaim the wide open spaces from "the phallocentrism of the wilderness/sexuality alliance" (p. 159).

32 In addition to Carolyn Merchant and Donna Haraway (1991: 297), both of whom Alaimo cites, see also Hayles' (1995) theory of "constrained" constructivism.

33 Opinions vary worldwide as to whether Bookchin should be thought of as "the originator of social ecology as a distinctive branch of green political theory" (Mathews 2001: 227) or as presumptuously appointing himself as "the sole guru of 'social ecology'" (Pepper 1993: 220), sympathetically summarizing a critique by G. Purchase, *Anarchist Society and Its Practical Realisation* (1990). In context, it's not clear that Warren's "a social ecology" means to refer to Bookchin specifically, although she cites him earlier (p. 21). Her rationale for characterizing ecofeminism thus is simply that it "recognizes the twin dominations of women and nature as social problems rooted" both in concrete socioeconomic historical circumstances and in institutionalized patriarchal frameworks that sanction those.

34 Janet Biehl and Murray Bookchin, "Theses on Social Ecology and Deep Ecology," August 1, 1995, www.social-ecology.org. Pepper (1993: 164–5) comments on Bookchin's utopianism in the course of a series of generally respectful but also pointedly critical appraisals (esp. pp. 220–1) of Bookchin's eco-anarchism.

35 This is by no means to say that deep ecology is unwilling or incapable of taking positions on social issues. See, for example, David Johns' (1990) reply to Guha's (1989b) well-known "third-world critique" of deep ecology.

36 The 1991 Principles are widely reprinted. See for example Merchant's (1994) very useful anthology of critical readings (pp. 371–2).

37 To take but one example: there's a good deal in common (though no precise correspondence) between the contributions of (for example) Peña (1998), focused on Chicano ecological stewardship in the upper Rio Grande Valley and animated by the poetry and narrative of Joseph Gallegos (1998), and the "mainstream" bioregionalism of (for example) Wendell Berry and McGinnis (1999).

38 See, for example, Spence (1999), Cronon (1991), and Gottleib (1993, 1997) (but also the critique of Gottleib's limitations in Pulido 1996: 192).

39 This book's title, *Environmentalism of the Poor*, is also the title of the author's article-length epitome (see Martínez-Alier 1998). It was first used in con-

nection with his work in a 1989 interview for the Peruvian journal *Cambio: "El ecologismo de los pobres."*

40 In the same symposium just discussed, the contribution by Indian scholar-activist Vandana Shiva (1999), whose critique of myopic and predatory globalization is well known to US environmental radicals (see Shiva 1988), deploys the adjective "indigenous" elastically to cover local in-country forms of environmental knowledge/practice generally, as well as that of minority or "tribal" groups specifically.

41 This cogent and fascinating case study in strategic essentialism makes clear the importance to the survival of a Chicano collective of arguing the case for grazing on public land in terms of the culture's ancient pastoral heritage – a heritage of ecological stewardship.

42 Though neither mention the nuclear contamination issue specifically, for discussion of telltale skewing and omission in these texts see (for Silko) Comer (1999: 130–7) and (for Abbey) Campbell (1998). See Adamson (2001: 31–50) for a further critique of *Desert Solitaire*'s blind spots and selective portrayal of "Abbey Country."

43 Oliver Goldsmith, *The Deserted Village* (1780–3), *The Norton Anthology of English Literature*, 7th edn., ed. M. H. Abrams and Stephen Greenblatt (New York: Norton, 2000), 1C: 2859. Note that in this poem the exact cause of emigration is not spelled out; enclosure is one possibility, but not the only one.

44 Take, for example, Carson's lyrical excursus on the western grebe, which the spraying of insecticide exterminated from California's ironically named Clear Lake: "It is a bird of spectacular appearance and beguiling haabits . . . it glides with scarcely a ripple across the lake surface, the body riding low," etc. See Carson, *Silent Spring* (Cambridge, MA: Houghton, 1962), 47. The nature writing dimension of this chapter is, strictly speaking, irrelevant to the main argument, yet it is indispensable to its dramatization.

45 Sam K. Gill, *Mother Earth: An American Story* (Chicago: University of Chicago Press, 1987). "Strategic essentialism" was coined by postcolonial theorist Gayatri Spivak to refer to the idea that essentialist categories can be justifiable, even necessary, to the accomplishment of certain strategic ends. See "Criticism, Feminism and the Institution: Interview with Elizabeth Grosz," *Thesis Eleven*, 10–11 (1984–5): 175–87. For its applicability to ecofeminist and to minority environmental struggles, see Sturgeon (1997) and Pulido (1998), respectively.

46 Statement by Paul Smith of the Oneida Nation, Wisconsin.

47 Thea Astley, "Inventing the Weather," *Vanishing Points* (New York: Putnam, 1992), 210, 187, 232.

169

Glossary

1   Jamaica Kincaid, *A Small Place* (New York: Penguin Books, 1988), 49.
2   Denis Cosgrove, "Culture," *Dictionary of Human Geography*, 4th edn., ed. R. J. Johnston et al. (Oxford: Blackwell, 2000), 143.
3   Edward Abbey, *Desert Solitaire: A Season in the Wilderness* (New York: Ballantine, 1968), 275.
4   Heather Eaton, "Ecofeminism," *Encyclopedia of World Environmental History*, ed. Shepard Krech III et al. (New York: Routledge, 2004), 1: 365.
5   Richard Kerridge, "Nature in the English Novel," *Literature of Nature: An International Sourcebook*, ed. Patrick Murphy et al. (Chicago: Fitzroy Dearborn, 1998), 150.
6   Laura Pulido, "Environmental Justice," *Dictionary of Human Geography*, 219.
7   Jim Duncan, "Landscape," *Dictionary of Human Geography*, 429.
8   Scott Slovic, "Nature Writing," *Encyclopedia of World Environmental History*, 2: 888.
9   Jim Duncan, "Place," *Dictionary of Human Geography*, 582.
10 Marina Fischer-Kowalski, "Ecology, Social," *Encyclopedia of World Environmental History*, 1: 396. However, this article seriously narrows its vision by treating social ecology as "a field of research," when in fact social ecologists see "research" (theoretically, at least) as leading to social transformation.
11 John Clark, "Introduction" to "Political Ecology," *Environmental Philosophy: From Animal Rights to Radical Ecology*, 3rd edn., ed. Michael E. Zimmerman et al. (Upper Saddle River, NJ: Prentice-Hall, 2001), 355.
12 *Poems and Prose of Gerard Manley Hopkins*, ed. W. H. Gardner (London: Penguin Books, 1953), 51.
13 Thoreau, "Walking," *The Norton Anthology of American Literature*, 6th edn., ed. Nina Baym et al. (New York: Norton, 2003): B, 2004.
14 Thoreau, *Walden*, ed. J. Lyndon Shanley (Princeton, NJ: Princeton University Press, 1971), 317.

Bibliography

This is a selected list of critical works referenced throughout the book. Primary sources and critical texts of relatively tangential importance for environmental criticism and/or bearing only on the work of a single writer are generally listed only in the notes. Works of "narrative scholarship" (see glossary) are generally included here.

Abram, David 1996. *The Spell of the Sensuous: Perception and Language in a More-than-Human World.* New York: Pantheon.

Adam, Barbara 1998. *Timescapes of Modernity: The Environment and Invisible Hazards.* London: Routledge.

Adamson, Joni 2001. *American Indian Literature, Environmental Justice, and Ecocriticism: The Middle Place.* Tucson: University of Arizona Press.

Adamson, Joni, Mei Mei Evans, and Rachel Stein (eds.) 2002. *The Environmental Justice Reader: Politics, Poetics, and Pedagogy.* Tucson: University of Arizona Press.

Agnew, John A. 1987. *Place and Politics: The Geographical Meditation of State and Society.* Boston, MA: Allen and Unwin.

——1993. "Representing Space: Space, Scale and Culture in Social Science." In *Place, Culture, Representation.* Ed. James Duncan and David Ley. London: Routledge, 251–71.

Alaimo, Stacy 2000. *Undomesticated Ground: Recasting Nature as Feminist Space.* Ithaca, NY: Cornell University Press.

Armbruster, Karla, and Kathleen R. Wallace 2001. *Beyond Nature Writing: Expanding the Boundaries of Ecocriticism.* Charlottesville: University Press of Virginia.

Augé, Marc 1995. *Non-Places: Introduction to an Anthropology of Supermodernity.* Trans. John Howe. London: Verso.

Bachelard, Gaston 1969. *The Poetics of Space.* Trans. Maria Jolas. Boston, MA: Beacon Press.

Bibliography

Bak, Hans, and Walter W. Hölbling (eds.) 2003. *"Nature's Nation" Revisited: American Concepts of Nature from Wonder to Ecological Crisis.* Amsterdam: VU University Press.

Barthes, Roland 1986. "The Reality Effect." In *The Rustle of Language.* Trans. Richard Howard. New York: Hill and Wang, 141–8.

Basso, Keith 1996. *Wisdom Sits in Places: Landscape and Language Among the Western Apache.* Albuquerque: University of New Mexico Press.

Bate, Jonathan 1991. *Romantic Ecology: Wordsworth and the Environmental Tradition.* London: Routledge.

——2000. *The Song of the Earth.* Cambridge, MA: Harvard University Press.

Bawarshi, Anis 2001. "The Ecology of Genre." In *Ecocomposition: Theoretical and Pedagogical Approaches.* Ed. Christian R. Weisser and Sidney I. Dobrin. Albany: State University of New York Press, 69–80.

Beck, Ulrich 1992. *Risk Society: Towards a New Modernity.* Trans. Mark Ritter. London: Sage.

——1995. *Ecological Politics in an Age of Risk.* Trans. Amos Weisz. Cambridge: Polity Press.

Beck, Ulrich, Anthony Giddens, and Scott Lash 1994. *Reflexive Modernization: Politics, Tradition and Aesthetics in the Modern Social Order.* Stanford, CA: Stanford University Press.

Beer, Gillian 1983. *Darwin's Plots: Evolutionary Narrative in Darwin, George Eliot, and Nineteenth-Century Fiction.* London: Routledge.

Bennett, Michael 1998. "Urban Nature: Teaching Tinker Creek by the East River," *ISLE,* 5 (winter): 49–59.

——2001. "From Wide Open Spaces to Metropolitan Places: The Urban Challenge to Ecocriticism," *ISLE,* 8 (winter): 31–52.

Bennett, Michael and David W. Teague (eds.) 1999. *The Nature of Cities: Ecocriticism and Urban Environments.* Tucson: University of Arizona Press.

Berg, Peter and Raymond Dasmann 1977. "Reinhabiting California," *Ecologist,* 7 (December): 399–401.

Berry, Thomas 1988. *The Dream of the Earth.* San Francisco: Sierra Club.

Berry, Wendell 1972. *A Continuous Harmony: Essays Cultural and Agricultural.* San Diego, CA: Harcourt.

——1977. *The Unsettling of America: Culture and Agriculture.* San Francisco: Sierra Club.

——1987. *Home Economics.* Berkeley, CA: North Point.

Bhabha, Homi 1994. *The Location of Culture.* London: Routledge.

Biehl, Janet and Peter Staudenmaier 1995. *Ecofascism: Lessons from the German Experience.* Edinburgh: AK Press.

Bookchin, Murray 1999. "The Concept of Social Ecology." In *Ecology.* Ed. Carolyn Merchant. Amherst, NY: Humanity Books, 152–62.

Bibliography

Bowman, Glenn 1993. "Tales of the Lost Land: Palestinian Identity and the Formation of Nationalist Consciousness." In *Space and Place: Theories of Identity and Location*. Ed. Erica Carter, James Donald, and Judith Squires. London: Lawrence & Wishart, 73–99.

Bramwell, Anna 1985. *Blood and Soil: Richard Walther Darré and Hitler's "Green Party."* Abbotsbrook: Kensal.

—— 1989. *Ecology in the Twentieth Century: A History.* New Haven, CT: Yale University Press.

Brown, Robert L. and Carl G. Herndl 1996. "Beyond the Realm of Reason: Understanding the Extreme Environmental Rhetoric of the John Birch Society." In *Green Culture: Environmental Rhetoric in Contemporary America*. Ed. Carl G. Herndl and Stuart C. Brown. Madison: University of Wisconsin Press, 213–35.

Buell, Frederick 2003. *From Apocalypse to Way of Life: Environmental Crisis in the American Century.* New York: Routledge.

Buell, Lawrence 1995. *The Environmental Imagination: Thoreau, Nature Writing, and the Formation of American Culture.* Cambridge, MA: Harvard University Press.

—— 1999. "The Ecocritical Insurgency," *New Literary History*, 30 (summer): 699–712.

—— 2001. *Writing for an Endangered World: Literature, Culture, and Environment in the United States and Beyond.* Cambridge, MA: Harvard University Press.

—— 2003. "Green Disputes: Nature, Culture, American(ist) Theory." In *"Nature's Nation" Revisited: American Concepts of Nature from Wonder to Ecological Crisis.* Ed. Hans Bak and Walter W. Hölbling. Amsterdam: VU University Press, 43–50.

Bullard, Robert (ed.) 1993. *Confronting Environmental Racism: Voices from the Grassroots.* Boston, MA: South End Press.

—— 1999. "Environmental Justice Challenges at Home and Abroad." In *Global Ethics and Environment*. Ed. Nicholas Low. London: Routledge, 33–46.

Bullis, Connie 1996. "Retalking Environmental Discourses from a Feminist Perspective: Radical Potential of Ecofeminism." In *The Symbolic Earth*. Ed. James G. Cantrill and Christine L. Oravec. Lexington: University Press of Kentucky, 123–48.

Callicott, J. Baird 1980. "Animal Liberation: A Triangular Affair," *Environmental Ethics*, 2 (winter): 311–38.

—— 2001. "The Land Ethic." In *A Companion to Environmental Philosophy*. Ed. Dale Jamieson. Oxford: Blackwell, 204–17.

Campbell, SueEllen 1996. "The Land and Language of Desire: Where Deep Ecology and Post-Structuralism Meet." In *The Ecocriticism Reader: Landmarks in Literary Ecology*. Ed. Cheryll Glotfelty and Harold Fromm. Athens: University of Georgia Press, 124–36.

173

Bibliography

—— 1998. "Magpie." In *Writing the Environment: Ecocriticism and Literature*. Ed. Richard Kerridge and Neil Sammells. London: Zed Books, 13–26.

Carlassare, Elizabeth 1999. "Essentialism in Ecofeminist Discourse." In *Ecology*. Ed. Carolyn Merchant. Amherst, NY: Humanity Books, 220–34.

Carroll, Joseph 1995. *Evolution and Literary Theory*. Columbia: University of Missouri Press.

Carter, Erica, James Donald, and Judith Squires (eds.) 1993. *Space and Place: Theories of Identity and Location*. London: Lawrence & Wishart.

Casey, Edward 1996. "How to Get from Space to Place in a Fairly Short Stretch of Time: Phenomenological Prolegomena." In *Senses of Place*. Ed. Steven Field and Keith Basso. Santa Fe, NM: School of American Research Press, 13–52.

—— 1997. *The Fate of Place: A Philosophical History*. Berkeley: University of California Press.

Chawla, Louise 1994. *In the First Country of Places: Nature, Poetry, and Childhood Memory*. Albany: State University of New York Press.

Clark, John 1997. "A Social Ecology," *Capitalism, Nature, Socialism: A Journal of Socialist Ecology*, 8 (September): 3–33.

Clarke, Bruce 2001. "Science, Theory, and Systems: A Response to Glen A. Love and Jonathan Levin," *ISLE*, 8 (winter): 149–65.

Claviez, Thomas 1999. "Pragmatism, Critical Theory, and the Search for Ecological Genealogies in American Culture." *Yearbook of Research in English and American Literature: REAL*, 15: 343–80.

Cobb, Edith 1977. *The Ecology of Imagination in Childhood*. New York: Columbia University Press.

Comer, Krista 1999. *Landscapes of the New West: Gender and Geography in Contemporary Women's Writing*. Chapel Hill: University of North Carolina Press.

Comfort, Susan 2002. "Struggle in Ogoniland: Ken Saro-Wiwa and the Cultural Politics of Environmental Justice." In *The Environmental Justice Reader: Politics, Poetics, and Pedagogy*. Ed. Joni Adamson, Mei Mei Adams, and Rachel Stein. Tucson: University of Arizona Press, 229–46.

Conley, Verena 1997. *Ecopolitics: The Environment in Poststructuralist Thought*. London: Routledge.

Cooperman, Matthew 2001. "A Poem is a Horizon: Notes Toward an Eco-poetics," *ISLE*, 8 (summer): 181–93.

Coupe, Laurence (ed.) 2000. *The Green Studies Reader: From Romanticism to Ecocriticism*. London: Routledge.

Cronon, William 1991. *Nature's Metropolis: Chicago and the Great West*. New York: Norton.

—— 1995a. "The Trouble with Wilderness; or, Getting Back to the Wrong Nature." In *Uncommon Ground: Toward Reinventing Nature*. Ed. William Cronon. New York: Norton, 69–90.

Bibliography

——(ed.) 1995b. *Uncommon Ground: Toward Reinventing Nature.* New York: Norton.

Curtin, Deane 2000. "A State of Mind Like Water: Ecosophy T and the Buddhist Traditions." In *Beneath the Surface: Critical Essays in the Philosophy of Deep Ecology.* Ed. Eric Katz, Andrew Light, and David Rothenberg. Cambridge, MA: MIT Press, 253–68.

Davion, Victoria 2001. "Ecofeminism." In *A Companion to Environmental Philosophy.* Ed. Dale Jamieson. Oxford: Blackwell, 233–47.

Devall, Bill and George Sessions 1985. *Deep Ecology: Living as if Nature Mattered.* Salt Lake City, UT: Gibbs Smith.

Diamond, Jared 1999. *Guns, Germs, and Steel: The Fates of Human Societies.* New York: Norton.

Di Chiro, Giovanna 1995. "Nature as Community: The Convergence of Environment and Social Justice." In *Uncommon Ground: Toward Reinventing Nature.* Ed. William Cronon. New York: Norton, 298–320.

——2000. "Bearing Witness or Taking Action?: Toxic Tourism and Environmental Justice." In *Reclaiming the Environmental Debate: The Politics of Health in a Toxic Culture.* Ed. Richard Hofricher. Cambridge, MA: MIT Press, 275–99.

Dietering, Cynthia 1996. "The Postnatural Novel: Toxic Consciousness in Fiction of the 1980s." In *The Ecocriticism Reader: Landmarks in Literary Ecology.* Ed. Cheryll Glotfelty and Harold Fromm. Athens: University of Georgia Press, 196–203.

Dixon, Terrell 1999. "Inculcating Wildness: Ecocomposition, Nature Writing, and the Regreening of the American Suburb." In *The Nature of Cities: Ecocriticism and Urban Environments.* Ed. Michael Bennett and David W. Teague. Tucson: University of Arizona Press, 77–90.

——(ed.) 2002. *City Wilds: Essays and Stories about Urban Nature.* Athens: University of Georgia Press.

Dryzek, John S. 1999. "Global Ecological Democracy." In *Global Ethics and Environment.* Ed. Nicholas Low. London: Routledge, 264–82.

Dunlap, Thomas R. 1999. *Nature and the English Diaspora: Environment and History in the United States, Canada, Australia, and New Zealand.* Cambridge: Cambridge University Press.

Eckersley, Robyn 1992. *Environmentalism and Political Theory: Toward an Ecocentric Approach.* Albany: State University of New York Press.

——2001. "Politics." In *A Companion to Environmental Philosophy.* Ed. Dale Jamieson. Oxford: Blackwell, 316–30.

Ehrenfeld, David W. 1978. *The Arrogance of Humanism.* Oxford: Oxford University Press.

Elder, John 1985. *Imagining the Earth: Poetry and the Vision of Nature.* Urbana: University of Illinois Press.

175

—— 1998. *Reading the Mountains of Home*. Cambridge, MA: Harvard University Press.

—— 1999. "The Poetry of Experience," *New Literary History*, 30 (summer): 649–59.

Elder, John and Robert Finch (eds.) 1990. *The Norton Book of Nature Writing*. New York: Norton.

Elgin, Don 1985. *The Comedy of the Fantastic: Ecological Perspectives on the Fantasy Novel*. Westport, CT: Greenwood Press.

Evernden, Neil 1985. *The Natural Alien: Humankind and Environment*. Toronto: University of Toronto Press.

—— 1992. *The Social Creation of Nature*. Baltimore, MD: Johns Hopkins University Press.

Ferry, Luc 1995. *The New Ecological Order*. Trans. Carol Volk. Chicago: University of Chicago Press.

Fischer, Frank and Maarten A. Hajer (eds.) 1999. *Living with Nature: Environmental Politics as Cultural Discourse*. Oxford: Oxford University Press.

Fisher, Philip 1988. "Democratic Social Space: Whitman, Melville, and the Promise of American Transparency," *Representations*, 24 (fall): 60–101.

Fletcher, Angus 2004. *A New Theory for American Poetry: Democracy, the Environment, and the Future of Imagination*. Cambridge, MA: Harvard University Press.

Flores, Dan 1999. "Place: Thinking about Bioregional History." In *Bioregionalism*. Ed. Michael Vincent McGinnis. London: Routledge, 43–58.

Foucault, Michel [1967] 1984. "Of Other Spaces." Trans. Jay Miskowiec. www.foucault.info/documents/heteroTopia/foucault.heteroTopia.en.html.

—— 1994. "The Birth of Biopolitics." In *Ethics: Subjectivity and Truth*. Trans. Robert Hurley et al. Ed. Paul Rabinow. New York: New Press, 73–9.

Fritzell, Peter A. 1990. *Nature Writing and America: Essays upon a Cultural Type*. Ames: Iowa State University Press.

Gadgil, Madhav and Ramachandra Guha 1995. *Ecology and Equity: The Use and Abuse of Nature in Contemporary India*. London: Routledge.

Gallegos, Joseph 1998. "The Pasture Poacher (Poem)" and "Acequia Tales: Stories from a Chicano Centennial Farm." In *Chicano Culture, Ecology, Politics: Subversive Kin*. Ed. Devon Peña. Tucson: University of Arizona Press, 234–48.

Gatta, John 2004. *Making Nature Sacred: Literature, Religion, and Environment in America from the Puritans to the Present*. New York: Oxford University Press.

Gifford, Terry 1996. "The Social Construction of Nature," *ISLE*, 3 (fall): 27–35.

—— 1999. *Pastoral*. London: Routledge.

—— 2002. "Towards a Post-Pastoral View of British Poetry." In *The Environmental Tradition in English Literature*. Ed. John Parham. Aldershot: Ashgate, 35–58.

Bibliography

Gilbert, Kevin (ed.) 1988. *Inside Black Australia: An Anthology of Aboriginal Poetry.* Ringwood, Victoria: Penguin Books.

Gilcrest, David W. 2002. *Greening the Lyre: Environmental Poetics and Ethics.* Reno: University of Nevada Press.

Glotfelty, Cheryll and Harold Fromm (eds.) 1996. *The Ecocriticism Reader: Landmarks in Literary Ecology.* Athens: University of Georgia Press.

Golley, Frank Benjamin 1993. *A History of the Ecosystem Concept in Ecology: More than the Sum of the Parts.* New Haven, CT: Yale University Press.

Gottlieb, Robert 1993. *Forcing the Spring: The Transformation of the American Environmental Movement.* Washington, DC: Island Press.

Gottlieb, Roger (ed.) 1997. *The Ecological Community: Environmental Challenges for Philosophy, Politics, and Morality.* New York: Routledge.

Gough, Noel 2002. "Democracy, Global Transitions, and Education: Using Speculative Fictions as Thought Experiments in Anticipatory Critical Inquiry." www.aare.edu.au/02pap/gou02326.htm.

Grove, Richard 1995. *Green Imperialism: Colonial Expansion, Tropical Island Edens, and the Origins of Environmentalism 1600–1860.* Cambridge: Cambridge University Press.

Guber, Deborah Lynn 2003. *The Grassroots of a Green Revolution: Polling America on the Environment.* Cambridge, MA: MIT Press.

Guha, Ramachandra 1989a. *The Unquiet Woods: Ecological Change and Peasant Resistance in the Himalaya.* Berkeley: University of California Press.

——1989b. "Radical Environmentalism and Wilderness Preservation: A Third-World Critique," *Environmental Ethics,* 11 (spring): 71–80.

Guha, Ramachandra and Joan Martínez-Alier 1997. *Varieties of Environmentalism: Essays North and South.* London: Earthscan.

Hajer, Maarten A. 1995. *The Politics of Environmental Discourse: Ecological Modernization and the Policy Process.* Oxford: Clarendon Press.

Haraway, Donna 1991. *Simians, Cyborgs, and Women: The Reinvention of Nature.* New York: Routledge.

——1992. "The Promise of Monsters: A Regenerative Politics for Inappropriate/d Others." In *Cultural Studies.* Ed. Lawrence Grossberg, Cary Nelson, and Paula Treichler. New York: Routledge, 295–337.

Harré, Rom, Jens Brockmeier, and Peter Mühlhaüsler 1999. *Greenspeak: A Study of Environmental Discourse.* Thousand Oaks, CA: Sage.

Harrison, Robert Pogue 1992. *Forests: The Shadow of Civilization.* Chicago: University of Chicago Press.

Hay, Peter 2002. *Main Currents in Western Environmental Thought.* Sydney: University of New South Wales Press.

Bibliography

Hayles, N. Katherine 1995. "Searching for Common Ground." In *Reinventing Nature? Responses to Postmodern Deconstruction*. Ed. Michael Soulé and Gary Lease. Washington, DC: Island Press, 47–64.

—— 1999. *How We Became Posthuman: Virtual Bodies in Cybernetics, Literature, and Informatics*. Chicago: University of Chicago Press.

Head, Dominic 1998a. "The (Im)possibility of Ecocriticism." In *Writing the Environment: Ecocriticism and Literature*. Ed. Richard Kerridge and Neil Sammells. London: Zed Books, 27–39.

—— 1998b. "Problems in Ecocriticism and the Novel." *Key Words: A Journal of Cultural Materialism*, 1: 60–73.

—— 2002. "Beyond 2000: Raymond Williams and the Ecocritic's Task." In *The Environmental Tradition in English Literature*. Ed. John Parham. Aldershot: Ashgate, 24–36.

Heidegger, Martin 1975. *Poetry, Language, Thought*. Trans. Alfred Hofstadter. New York: Harper.

Heise, Ursula 1997. "Science and Ecocriticism." *American Book Review*, 18 (August): 4–6.

—— 2002. "Toxins, Drugs, and Global Systems: Risk and Narrative in the Contemporary Novel." *American Literature*, 74 (December): 747–78.

Herndl, Carl G. and Stuart C. Brown (eds.) 1996. *Green Culture: Environmental Rhetoric in Contemporary America*. Madison: University of Wisconsin Press.

Hess, Scott 2004. "Postmodern Pastoral, Advertising, and the Masque of Technology," *ISLE*, 11 (winter): 71–100.

Higgs, Eric 2003. *Nature by Design: People, Natural Process, and Ecological Restoration*. Cambridge, MA: MIT Press.

Howarth, William 1996. "Some Principles of Ecocriticism." In *The Ecocriticism Reader: Landmarks in Literary Ecology*. Ed. Cheryll Glotfelty and Harold Fromm. Athens: University of Georgia Press, 69–91.

—— 1999. "Imagined Territory: The Writing of Wetlands," *New Literary History*, 30 (summer): 509–39.

Jacobsen, Knut A. 2000. "*Bhagavadgītā*, Ecosophy T, and Deep Ecology." In *Beneath the Surface: Critical Essays in the Philosophy of Deep Ecology*. Ed. Eric Katz, Andrew Light, and David Rothenberg. Cambridge, MA: MIT Press, 231–52.

Jameson, Fredric 1981. *The Political Unconscious: Narrative as a Socially Symbolic Act*. Ithaca, NY: Cornell University Press.

Jamieson, Dale (ed.) 2001. *A Companion to Environmental Philosophy*. Oxford: Blackwell.

Jasanoff, Sheila 2004. "Heaven and Earth: The Politics of Environmental Images." In *Earthly Politics: Local and Global in Environmental Governance*. Ed. Sheila Jasanoff and Marybeth Long Martello. Cambridge, MA: MIT Press, 31–54.

Bibliography

Johns, David 1990. "The Relevance of Deep Ecology to the Third World: Some Preliminary Comments." *Environmental Ethics*, 12 (fall): 233–52.

Johnson, Lawrence E. 1991. *A Morally Deep World: An Essay on Moral Significance and Environmental Ethics*. Cambridge: Cambridge University Press.

Katz, Eric 2000. "Against the Inevitability of Anthropocentrism." In *Beneath the Surface: Critical Essays in the Philosophy of Deep Ecology*. Ed. Eric Katz, Andrew Light, and David Rothenberg. Cambridge, MA: MIT Press, 17–42.

Katz, Eric, Andrew Light, and David Rothenberg 2000. *Beneath the Surface: Critical Essays in the Philosophy of Deep Ecology*. Cambridge, MA: MIT Press.

Kern, Robert 2000. "Ecocriticism – What Is It Good For?" *ISLE*, 7 (winter): 9–32.

Kerridge, Richard 2001. "Ecological Hardy." In *Beyond Nature Writing: Expanding the Boundaries of Ecocriticism*. Ed. Karla Armbruster and Kathleen R. Wallace. Charlottesville: University Press of Virginia, 126–42.

Kerridge, Richard and Neil Sammells (eds.) 1998. *Writing the Environment: Ecocriticism and Literature*. London: Zed Books.

Kiberd, Declan 1996. *Inventing Ireland*. Cambridge, MA: Harvard University Press.

Killingsworth, M. Jimmie and Jacqueline S. Palmer 1992. *Ecospeak: Rhetoric and Environmental Politics in America*. Carbondale: Southern Illinois University Press.

Klyza, Christopher McGrory 1999. "Bioregional Possibilities in Vermont." In *Bioregionalism*. Ed. Michael Vincent McGinnis. London: Routledge, 81–98.

Kolodny, Annette 1975. *The Lay of the Land: Metaphor as Experience and History in American Life and Letters*. Chapel Hill: University of North Carolina Press.

—— 1984. *The Land Before Her: Fantasy and Experience of the American Frontiers, 1630–1860*. Chapel Hill: University of North Carolina Press.

Krasner, James 1992. *The Entangled Eye: Visual Perception and the Representation of Nature in Post-Darwinian Narrative*. New York: Oxford University Press.

Krech, Shepard, III 1999. *The Ecological Indian: Myth and History*. New York: Norton.

Kroeber, Karl 1994. *Ecological Literary Criticism: Romantic Imagining and the Biology of Mind*. New York: Columbia University Press.

Latour, Bruno 1993. *We Have Never Been Modern*. Trans. Catherine Porter. Cambridge, MA: Harvard University Press.

—— 1999. *Pandora's Hope: Essays on the Reality of Science Studies*. Cambridge, MA: Harvard University Press.

Lefebvre, Henri 1991. *The Production of Space*. Trans. Donald Nicholson-Smith. Cambridge: Blackwell.

Leopold, Aldo 1949. *Sand County Almanac*. New York: Oxford University Press.

—— 1991. *The River of the Mother of God and Other Essays*. Ed. Susan I. Flader and J. Baird Callicott. Madison: University of Wisconsin Press.

179

Lewis, Nathaniel 2003. *Unsettling the Literary West: Authenticity and Authorship.* Lincoln: University of Nebraska Press.

Light, Andrew (ed.) 1998. *Social Ecology after Bookchin.* New York: Guilford Press.

Lopez, Barry 1986. *Arctic Dreams: Imagination and Desire in a Northern Landscape.* New York: Scribner's.

—— 1989. "Landscape and Narrative." In *Crossing Open Ground.* New York: Vintage, 61–72.

—— 1998. "We Are Shaped by the Sound of Wind, the Slant of Sunlight," *High Country News*, 30, 17 (September 14).

Love, Glen A. 2003. *Practical Ecocriticism: Literature, Biology, and the Environment.* Charlottesville: University Press of Virginia.

Low, Nicholas (ed.) 1999. *Global Ethics and Environment.* London: Routledge.

Luhmann, Niklas 1989. *Ecological Communication.* Trans. John Bednarz, Jr. Chicago: University of Chicago Press.

Luke, Timothy 1997. *Ecocritique: Contesting the Politics of Nature, Economy, and Culture.* Minneapolis: University of Minnesota Press.

—— 1999. "Eco-Managerialism: Environmental Studies as a Power/Knowledge Formation." In *Living with Nature: Environmental Politics as Cultural Discourse.* Ed. Frank Fischer and Maarten A. Hajer. Oxford: Oxford University Press, 103–20.

McKusick, James C. 2000. *Green Writing: Romanticism and Ecology.* New York: St. Martin's Press.

McFague, Sallie 1987. *Models of God: Theology for an Ecological, Nuclear Age.* Philadelphia, PA: Fortress Press.

McGinnis, Michael Vincent (ed.) 1999. *Bioregionalism.* London: Routledge.

McHarg, Ian 1969. *Design with Nature.* Garden City, NY: Natural History Press.

McLaughlin, Andrew 1993. *Regarding Nature: Industrialism and Deep Ecology.* Albany: State University of New York Press.

Malpas, J. E. 1999. *Place and Experience: A Philosophical Topography.* Cambridge: Cambridge University Press.

Marshall, Ian 2003. *Peak Experiences: Walking Meditations on Literature, Nature, and Need.* Charlottesville: University Press of Virginia.

Martin, Ronald E. 1981. *American Literature and the Universe of Force.* Durham, NC: Duke University Press.

Martínez-Alier, Joan 1998. " 'Environmental Justice' (Local and Global)." In *The Cultures of Globalization.* Ed. Fredric Jameson and Masao Miyoshi. Durham, NC: Duke University Press, 312–26.

—— 2002. *The Environmentalism of the Poor: A Study of Ecological Conflicts and Valuation.* Cheltenham: Elgar.

—— 2003. "Scale, Environmental Justice, and Unsustainable Cities," *Capitalism Nature Socialism*, 14 (December): 43–63.

Bibliography

Marx, Leo 1964. *The Machine in the Garden: Technology and the Pastoral Ideal in America.* New York: Oxford University Press.

——1973. "Between Two Landscapes." *RIBA Journal*, 8 (August): 422–4.

——1988. *The Pilot and the Passenger: Essays on Literature, Technology, and Culture in the United States.* New York: Oxford University Press.

——2003. "The Pandering Landscape: On American Nature as Illusion." In *"Nature's Nation" Revisited: American Concepts of Nature from Wonder to Ecological Crisis.* Ed. Hans Bak and Walter W. Hölbling. Amsterdam: VU University Press, 30–42.

Massey, Doreen 1994. *Space, Place, and Gender.* Minneapolis: University of Minnesota Press.

Mathews, Freya 1991. *The Ecological Self.* Savage, MD: Barnes and Noble.

——1999. "Ecofeminism and Deep Ecology." In *Ecology.* Ed. Carolyn Merchant. Amherst, NY: Humanity Books, 235–45.

——2001. "Deep Ecology." In *A Companion to Environmental Philosophy.* Ed. Dale Jamieson. Oxford: Blackwell, 218–32.

Mazel, David (ed.) 2001. *A Century of Early Ecocriticism.* Athens: University of Georgia Press.

Meeker, Joseph W. 1997. *The Comedy of Survival: Literary Ecology and a Play Ethic,* 3rd edn. Tucson: University of Arizona Press. Orig. edn. 1972.

Meine, Curt 1997. "Inherit the Grid." In *Placing Nature: Culture and Landscape Ecology.* Ed. Joan Iverson Nassauer. Washington, DC: Island Press, 45–62.

Merchant, Carolyn 1980. *The Death of Nature: Women, Ecology and the Scientific Revolution.* San Francisco: Harper Collins.

——1989. *Ecological Revolutions: Nature, Gender, and Science in New England.* Chapel Hill: University of North Carolina Press.

——1992. *Radical Ecology: The Search for a Livable World.* New York: Routledge.

——1999. (ed.) *Ecology.* Amherst, NY: Humanity Books.

Merleau-Ponty, Maurice 2002. *Phenomenology of Perception.* Trans. Colin Smith. London: Routledge.

Mohanty, Satya 1997. *Literary Theory and the Claims of History: Postmodernism, Objectivity, Multicultural Politics.* Ithaca, NY: Cornell University Press.

Mol, Arthur P. J. 2001. *Globalization and Environmental Reform: The Ecological Modernization of the Global Economy.* Cambridge, MA: MIT Press.

Moore, Donald S. 1996. "Marxism, Culture, and Political Ecology: Environmental Struggles in Zimbabwe's Eastern Highlands." In *Liberation Ecologies: Environment, Development, Social Movements.* Ed. Richard Peet and Michael Watts. London: Routledge, 125–47.

Moore, Jason 2003. "*The Modern World-System* as Environmental History? Ecology and the Rise of Capitalism," *Theory and Society*, 32: 307–77.

Bibliography

Moore, Kathleen Dean 2004. *The Pine Island Paradox*. Minneapolis, MN: Milkweed.

Morley, Dave and Kevin Robins 1993. "No Place like *Heimat*: Images of Home(land) in European Culture." In *Space* and *Place: Theories of Identity and Location*. Ed. Erica Carter, James Donald, and Judith Squires. London: Lawrence & Wishart, 3–31.

Morton, Timothy 1994. *Shelley and the Revolution in Taste: The Body and the Natural World*. Cambridge: Cambridge University Press.

—— 2000. *The Poetics of Spice: Romantic Consumerism and the Exotic*. Cambridge: Cambridge University Press.

Murphy, Patrick 2000. *Farther Afield in the Study of Nature-Oriented Literature*. Charlottesville: University Press of Virginia.

—— 2001. "The Non-Alibi of Alien Scapes: SF and Ecocriticism." In *Beyond Nature Writing: Expanding the Boundaries of Ecocriticism*. Ed. Karla Armbruster and Kathleen R. Wallace. Charlottesville: University Press of Virginia, 263–78.

Nabhan, Gary Paul 1985. *Gathering the Desert*. Tucson: University of Arizona Press.

—— 1994. *The Geography of Childhood: Why Children Need Wild Places*. Boston, MA: Beacon Press.

Naess, Arne 1973. "The Shallow and the Deep, Long-Range Ecology Movement: A Summary," *Inquiry*, 16 (spring): 95–100.

Nash, Roderick 1989. *The Rights of Nature: A History of Environmental Ethics*. Madison: University of Wisconsin Press.

Newman, Lance 2002. "Marxism and Ecocriticism," *ISLE*, 9 (summer): 1–25.

Nicholson-Lord, David 1987. *The Greening of the Cities*. London: Routledge.

Norton, Bryan 1995. "Why I am Not a Nonanthropocentrist: Callicott and the Failure of Monistic Inherentism," *Environmental Ethics*, 17 (winter): 341–58.

Oakes, Timothy 1997. "Place and the Paradox of Modernity," *Annals of the Association of American Geographers*, 87: 509–31.

Oerlemans, Onno 2002. *Romanticism and the Materiality of Nature*. Toronto: University of Toronto Press.

O'Grady, John P. 2003. "How Sustainable is the Idea of Sustainability?" *ISLE*, 10 (winter): 1–10.

Ortner, Sherry B. 1974. "Is Female to Male as Nature Is to Culture?" In *Woman, Culture, and Society*. Ed. Michele Zimbalist Rosaldo and Louise Lamphere. Stanford, CA: Stanford University Press, 67–87.

Parham, John (ed.) 2002. *The Environmental Tradition in English Literature*. Aldershot: Ashgate.

Park, Geoff 1995. *Ngō Uruora (The Groves of Life): Ecology and History in a New Zealand Landscape*. Wellington: Victoria University Press.

Bibliography

Peña, Devon (ed.) 1998. *Chicano Culture, Ecology, Politics: Subversive Kin.* Tucson: University of Arizona Press.

Pepper, David 1993. *Eco-Socialism: From Deep Ecology to Social Justice.* London: Routledge.

Peterson, Anna L. 2001. *Being Human: Ethics, Environment, and Our Place in the World.* Berkeley: University of California Press.

Phillips, Dana 2003. *The Truth of Ecology: Nature, Culture, and Literature in America.* New York: Oxford University Press.

Platt, Rutherford H. 1994. "From Commons to Commons: Evolving Concepts of Open Space in North American Cities." In Rutherford H. Platt, Rowan A. Rowntree, and Pamela C. Muick (eds.) *The Ecological City: Preserving and Restoring Urban Biodiversity.* Amherst: University of Massachusetts Press, 21–39.

Plumwood, Val 1993. *Feminism and the Mastery of Nature.* London: Routledge.

——2002. *Environmental Culture: The Ecological Crisis of Reason.* London: Routledge.

Portney, Kent E. 2003. *Taking Sustainable Cities Seriously.* Cambridge, MA: MIT Press.

Pred, Alan 1984. "Place as Historically Contingent Process: Structuration and the Time-Geography of Becoming Places," *Annals of the Association of American Geographers,* 74: 279–97.

Preston, Christopher J. 2003. *Grounding Knowledge: Environmental Philosophy, Epistemology, and Place.* Athens: University of Georgia Press.

Pulido, Laura 1996. *Environmentalism and Economic Justice: Two Chicano Struggles in the Southwest.* Tucson: University of Arizona Press.

——1998. "Ecological Legitimacy and Cultural Essentialism: Hispano Grazing in Northern New Mexico." In *Chicano Culture, Ecology, Politics: Subversive Kin.* Ed. Devon Peña. Tucson: University of Arizona Press, 121–40.

Reed, T. V. 2002. "Toward an Environmental Justice Ecocriticism." In *The Environmental Justice Reader: Politics, Poetics, and Pedagogy.* Ed. Joni Adamson, Mei Mei Evans, and Rachel Stein. Tucson: University of Arizona Press, 145–62.

Rees, William 1997. "Is 'Sustainable City' an Oxymoron?" *Local Environment,* 2 (3): 303–10.

Rhodes, Eduardo Lao 2003. *Environmental Justice in America: A New Paradigm.* Bloomington: Indiana University Press.

Ricoeur, Paul 1977. *The Rule of Metaphor: Multi-Disciplinary Studies of the Creation of Meaning in Language.* Trans. Robert Czerny et al. Toronto: University of Toronto Press.

Rodman, Margaret 1992. "Empowering Place: Multilocality and Multivocality," *American Anthropologist,* 94: 640–56.

Rueckert, William 1996. "Literature and Ecology: An Experiment in Ecocriticism." Rpt. from 1978. In *The Ecocriticism Reader: Landmarks in Literary Ecology.*

183

Bibliography

Ed. Cheryll Glotfelty and Harold Fromm. Athens: University of Georgia Press, 105–23.

Sachs, Wolfgang 1999. "Sustainable Development and the Crisis of Nature: On the Political Anatomy of an Oxymoron." In *Living with Nature: Environmental Politics as Cultural Discourse*. Ed. Frank Fischer and Maarten A. Hajer. Oxford: Oxford University Press, 23–41.

Sack, Robert David 1997. *Homo Geographicus: A Framework for Action, Awareness, and Moral Concern*. Baltimore, MD: Johns Hopkins University Press.

Said, Edward 1978. *Orientalism*. New York: Random House.

——1983. *The World, The Text, and the Critic*. Cambridge, MA: Harvard University Press.

——1993. *Culture and Imperialism*. New York: Knopf.

Salleh, Ariel 2000. "In Defense of Deep Ecology: An Ecofeminist Response to a Liberal Critique." In *Beneath the Surface: Critical Essays in the Philosophy of Deep Ecology*. Ed. Eric Katz, Andrew Light, and David Rothenberg. Cambridge, MA: MIT Press, 107–24.

Sandilands, Catriona 1999. *The Good-Natured Feminist: Ecofeminism and the Quest for Democracy*. Minneapolis: University of Minnesota Press.

Sassen, Saskia 1991. *The Global City: New York, London, Tokyo*. Princeton, NJ: Princeton University Press.

Satterfield, Terre and Scott Slovic (ed.) 2004. *What's Nature Worth? Narrative Expressions of Environmental Values*. Salt Lake City: University of Utah Press.

Scigaj, Leonard M. 1999. *Sustainable Poetry: Four American Ecopoets*. Lexington: University Press of Kentucky.

Seddon, George 2002. "It's Only Words." In *Words for Country: Landscape and Language in Australia*. Ed. Tim Bonyhady and Tom Griffiths. Sydney: University of New South Wales Press, 245–53.

Serres, Michel 1995. *The Natural Contract*. Trans. Elizabeth MacArthur and William Paulson. Ann Arbor: University of Michigan Press.

Sessions, Robert 1996. "Deep Ecology versus Ecofeminism: Healthy Differences or Incompatible Philosophies?" In *Ecological Feminist Philosophies*. Ed. Karen J. Warren. Bloomington: Indiana University Press, 137–54.

Shepard, Paul 1982. *Nature and Madness*. San Francisco: Sierra Club.

Shiva, Vandana 1988. *Staying Alive*. London: Zed Books.

——1999. "Ecological Balance in an Era of Globalization" (1999). In *Global Ethics and Environment*. Ed. Nicholas Low. London: Routledge, 47–69.

Shrader-Frechette, Kristin 1999. "Chernobyl, Global Environmental Injustice and Mutagenic Threats." In *Global Ethics and Environment*. Ed. Nicholas Low. London: Routledge, 70–89.

Shutkin, William and Rafael Mores 2000. "Brownfields and the Redevelopment of Communities: Linking Health, Economy, and Justice." In *Reclaiming the Envi-*

184

ronmental Debate: The Politics of Health in a Toxic Culture. Ed. Richard Hofricher. Cambridge, MA: MIT Press.

Silko, Leslie Marmon 1986. "Landscape, History, and the Pueblo Imagination," *Antaeus*, 57 (autumn): 83–94.

Singer, Peter 1990. *Animal Liberation*, revd. edn. New York: Avon.

Slicer, Deborah 1995. "Is There an Ecofeminism–Deep Ecology 'Debate'?" *Environmental Ethics*, 17 (summer): 151–69.

Slovic, Scott 1994. "Ecocriticism: Storytelling, Values, Communication, Contact." http://www.asle.umn.edu/conf/other_conf/wla/1994/slovic.html

—— 1996. "Epistemology and Politics in American Nature Writing: Embedded Rhetoric and Discrete Rhetoric." In *Green Culture: Environmental Rhetoric in Contemporary America*. Ed. Carl G. Herndl and Stuart C. Brown. Madison: University of Wisconsin Press, 82–110.

Smith, Neil 1984. *Uneven Development: Nature, Capital and the Production of Space.* Oxford: Blackwell.

Snyder, Gary 1990. *The Practice of the Wild.* San Francisco: North Point.

—— 1995. *A Place in Space: Ethics, Aesthetics, and Watersheds.* Washington, DC: Counterpoint.

—— 2004. "Ecology, Literature, and the New World Disorder," *ISLE*, 11 (winter): 1–13.

Sommer, Doris 1991. *Foundational Fictions: The National Romances of Latin America.* Berkeley: University of California Press.

Soper, Kate 1995. *What Is Nature? Culture, Politics, and the Non-Human.* Oxford: Blackwell.

Spence, Mark David 1999. *Dispossessing the Wilderness: Indian Removal and the Making of the National Parks.* New York: Oxford University Press.

Spirn, Anne Whiston 1998. *The Language of Landscape.* New Haven, CT: Yale University Press.

Spretnak, Charlene 1997. "Radical Nonduality in Ecofeminist Philosophy." In *Ecofeminism: Women, Culture, Nature.* Ed. Karen J. Warren. Bloomington: Indiana University Press, 425–36.

Steingraber, Sandra 1997. *Living Downstream: An Ecologist Looks at Cancer and the Environment.* Reading, MA: Addison-Wesley.

Sturgeon, Nöel 1997. *Ecofeminist Natures.* New York: Routledge.

Szasz, Andrew 1994. *Ecopopulism: Toxic Waste and the Movement for Environmental Justice.* Minneapolis: University of Minnesota Press.

Tallmadge, John 2000. "Toward a Natural History of Reading," *ISLE*, 7 (winter): 33–45.

Tallmadge, John and Henry Harrington (eds.) 2000. *Reading Under the "Sign of Nature": New Essays in Ecocriticism.* Salt Lake City: University of Utah Press.

Bibliography

Tarter, Jim 2002. "Some Live More Downstream than Others: Cancer, Gender, and Environmental Justice." In *The Environmental Justice Reader: Politics, Poetics, and Pedagogy.* Ed. Joni Adamson, Mei Mei Evans, and Rachel Stein. Tucson: University of Arizona Press, 213–28.

Taylor, Paul W. 1986. *Respect for Nature: A Theory of Environmental Ethics.* Princeton, NJ: Princeton University Press.

Thomashow, Mitchell 1999. "Toward a Cosmopolitan Bioregionalism." In *Bioregionalism.* Ed. Michael Vincent McGinnis. London: Routledge, 121–32.

Tsing, Anna Lowenhaupt 1993. *In the Realm of the Diamond Queen: Marginality in an Out-of-the-Way Place.* Princeton, NJ: Princeton University Press.

Tuan, Yi-Fu 1977. *Space and Place: The Perspective of Experience.* Minneapolis: University of Minnesota Press.

—— 1990. *Topophilia: A Study of Environmental Perception, Attitudes, and Values*, 2nd edn. New York: Columbia University Press.

Waddell, Craig 1996. "Saving the Great Lakes: Public Participation in Environmental Policy." In *Green Culture: Environmental Rhetoric in Contemporary America.* Ed. Carl G. Herndl and Stuart C. Brown. Madison: University of Wisconsin Press, 141–65.

Walcott, Derek 1998. *What the Twilight Says: Essays.* New York: Farrar, Straus.

Wallace, Anne D. 1993. *Walking, Literature, and English Culture: The Origins and Uses of Peripatetic in the Nineteenth Century.* Oxford: Clarendon Press.

Wallace, Mark I. 1997. "Environmental Justice, Neopreservationism, and Sustainable Spirituality." In *The Ecological Community: Environmental Challenges for Philosophy, Politics, and Morality.* Ed. Roger Gottlieb. New York: Routledge, 292–310.

Walter, Eugene Victor 1988. *Placeways: A Theory of the Human Environment.* Chapel Hill: University of North Carolina Press.

Wark, McKenzie 1994. "Third Nature," *Cultural Studies*, 8 (January): 115–32.

Warren, Karen J. (ed.) 1996. *Ecological Feminist Philosophies.* Bloomington: Indiana University Press.

Wasserman, Renata R. Mautner 1994. *Exotic Nations: Literature and Cultural Identity in the United States and Brazil, 1830–1930.* Ithaca, NY: Cornell University Press.

Welty, Eudora 1970. "Place in Fiction." In *The Eye of the Story.* New York: Random House.

Westling, Louise H. 1996. *The Green Breast of the New World: Landscape, Gender, and American Fiction.* Athens: University of Georgia Press.

White, Lynn, Jr. 1967. "The Historical Roots of Our Ecologic Crisis," *Science*, 155 (March 10): 1203–7.

White, Richard 1995. *The Organic Machine: The Remaking of the Columbia River.* New York: Hill and Wang.

Bibliography

Whitt, Laurie Anne, Mere Roberts, Waerete Norman, and Vicki Grieves 2001. "Indigenous Perspectives." In *A Companion to Environmental Philosophy.* Ed. Dale Jamieson. Oxford: Blackwell, 3–20.

Williams, Colin and Anthony D. Smith 1983. "The National Construction of Social Space," *Human Geography*, 7: 502–18.

Williams, Raymond 1973. *The Country and the City.* New York: Oxford University Press.

—— 1977. *Marxism and Literature.* New York: Oxford University Press.

—— 1983. *Keywords: A Vocabulary of Culture and Society*, revd. edn. New York: Oxford University Press.

—— 1986. "Hesitations before Socialism," *New Socialist*, 41 (September): 34–6.

—— 1989. "Socialism and Ecology." In *Resources of Hope: Culture, Democracy, Socialism.* Ed. Robin Gable. London: Verso, 210–26.

Willms, Johannes 2004. *Conversations with Ulrich Beck.* Trans. Michael Pollak. Cambridge: Polity Press.

Wilson, Edward O. and Stephen R. Kellert (eds.) 1993. *The Biophilia Hypothesis.* Washington, DC: Island Press.

World Commission on Environment and Development 1987. *Our Common Future.* Oxford: Oxford University Press.

Worster, Donald 1977. *Nature's Economy: A History of Ecological Ideas.* Cambridge: Cambridge University Press.

—— 1999. "Fear and Redemption in the Environment Movement." In *Ideas, Ideologies and Social Movements: The United States Experiments Since 1800.* Ed. Peter A. Colanis and Stuart Bruckey. Columbia: University of South Carolina Press.

Wright, Judith 1992. *Going on Talking.* Springwood, NSW: Butterfly Books.

Zimmerman, Michael E. 1994. *Contesting Earth's Future: Radical Ecology and Postmodernity.* Berkeley: University of California Press.

—— 1997. "Ecofascism: A Threat to American Environmentalism?" In *The Ecological Community: Environmental Challenges for Philosophy, Politics, and Morality.* Ed. Roger Gottlieb. New York: Routledge, 229–54.

Index

Glossary entries are indicated in **bold**.

Index

bioregion, bioregionalism, 77–89, **135**
    sustainability and, 162n25
biotic community (A. Leopold), 8,
    21, 100; *see also* Leopold
Bloom, Harold, 51
Bookchin, Murray, 141, 146
Bowman, Glenn, 64
Brontë, Charlotte, 34, 38
brownfields, 88, **135**
Buddhism and environmental
    philosophy, 101, 166n13, 167n29
Bullard, Robert, 117
Bullis, Connie, 109, 111
Burroughs, John, 31–2, 41
Butler, Octavia, 91–2
Buell, Lawrence, 15, 22, 25, 44, 72,
    100, 142, 144–5

Callicott, J. Baird, 166n19
Campbell, SueEllen, 10, 169n42
Canada, Geoffrey, 29
canon, environmental, 25–6, 44–61,
    112–13, 119–26
Carlassare, Elizabeth, 139
Carlyle, Thomas, 158n1
Carpentier, Alejo, 33, 55
Carrighar, Sally, 67
Carroll, Joseph, 18
Carson, Rachel, vii, 5, 27, 41, 78,
    119
    The Sea Around Us, 4
    A Sense of Wonder, vii
    Silent Spring, vii, 4, 25, 122
    Under the Sea Wind, 25
Casey, Edward, 63, 65–6, 73, 94, 101,
    165n12
Castillo, Ana, 113
Cather, Willa, 121
Chawla, Louise, 75
Cisneros, Sandra, 87–8
Clare, John, 14, 51

Claviez, Thomas, 81–2
Cobb, Edith, 75
Cobbett, William, 41
Coetzee, J. M., 55
Comer, Krista, 22, 168n31,
    169n42
Comfort, Susan, 116
Conley, Verena, 10
Cronon, William, 66–7, 159n2
culture
    (agri)cultivation and, 2, 135
    cultural constructionism as issue for
    ecotheory, 19–20, 110–11, and
    passim
    defined, **135–6**
    dominant, residual, emergent
    (R. Williams), 1, 126,
    151n3
    see also environment
cyborg, 59, 91, **136**

Darwin, Charles; Darwinism, 43, 100,
    101–2, 157n26
Davion, Victoria, 139
Davis, Rebecca Harding, 120
deep ecology, 101–4, 108, 126–7,
    137, 141
Defoe, Daniel, 51, 73
Derrida, Jacques, 10, 39
Devall, Bill, 9, 102–3, 153n23
Devi, Mahasweta, 78–9, 120
DiChiro, Giovanna, 118, 154n3
Dickens, Charles, 83, 120
Dillard, Annie, 41, 153n31
Dixon, Terrell, 144
Dreiser, Theodore, 55, 101,
    120

Eckersley, Robyn, 107–8, 137, 147
ecocentrism, 98–108, **137–8**
ecocomposition, 44

189

Index